Katherine Mansfield and the (Post)colonial

KATHERINE MANSFIELD STUDIES

Katherine Mansfield Studies is the peer-reviewed, annual publication of the Katherine Mansfield Society. It offers opportunities for collaborations between researchers with interests in postcolonial studies and in modernism in literature and the arts. Because Mansfield is a writer who has inspired successors from Elizabeth Bowen to Ali Smith, as well as numerous artists in other media, *Katherine Mansfield Studies* encourages interdisciplinary scholarship and allows for a proportion of creative submissions.

Katherine Mansfield Studies

Volume 5

Katherine Mansfield and the (Post)colonial

Edited by

Janet Wilson, Gerri Kimber and Delia da Sousa Correa

Liaison Editor, Todd Martin
Editorial Assistant, Louise Edensor

EDINBURGH
University Press

© editorial matter and organisation Janet Wilson, Gerri Kimber and Delia da Sousa Correa, 2013
© the chapters their several authors, 2013

Edinburgh University Press Ltd
22 George Square, Edinburgh EH8 9LF

www.euppublishing.com

Typeset in 10.5/12.5 New Baskerville by
Servis Filmsetting Ltd, Stockport, Cheshire,
and printed and bound in Great Britain by
CPI Group (UK) Ltd, Croydon CR0 4YY

A CIP record for this book is available from the British Library

ISBN 978 0 7486 6909 7 (hardback)
ISBN 978 0 7486 6910 3 (paperback)
ISBN 978 0 7486 6911 0 (webready PDF)
ISBN 978 0 7486 6912 7 (epub)

Contents

Contents

Illustrations

Acknowledgements

The editors would like to thank the academics with expertise in postcolonial studies who judged this year's Katherine Mansfield Society essay prize with Professor Janet Wilson, the guest editor for this volume: Professor Elleke Boehmer and Dr Simone Oettli. The prize-winning essay by Aimee Gasston is published in this volume.

The editors would also like to thank Penelope Jackson and the artist Nigel Brown for generously allowing us to reproduce the *Names Painting: Katherine Mansfield* on the front cover of this volume. We would also like to thank the Alexander Turnbull Library and especially David Colquhoun and Fiona Oliver, for so generously providing access to the new Murry archive for scholars attending a conference on Mansfield at Victoria University of Wellington in February 2013. Thanks also go to the following for permission to reproduce images or documents: King's College London Archives, Pollinger Limited and the Estate of Frieda Lawrence Ravagli.

Also available in the series:

Katherine Mansfield and Continental Europe
Edited by Delia da Sousa Correa and Gerri Kimber
Katherine Mansfield Studies, Volume 1
Hbk 978 0 7486 8470 0

Katherine Mansfield and Modernism
Edited by Delia da Sousa Correa, Gerri Kimber and Susan Reid
Katherine Mansfield Studies, Volume 2
Hbk 978 0 7486 8471 7

Katherine Mansfield and the Arts
Edited by Delia da Sousa Correa, Gerri Kimber and Susan Reid
Katherine Mansfield Studies, Volume 3
Hbk 978 0 7486 8472 4

Katherine Mansfield and the Fantastic
Edited by Delia da Sousa Correa, Gerri Kimber, Susan Reid and
Gina Wisker
Katherine Mansfield Studies, Volume 4
Hbk 978 0 7486 8473 1

Figure 1. Katherine Mansfield with parasol. Image courtesy of King's College London Archives, *Adam International Review* Collection.

Introduction: Katherine Mansfield and the (Post)colonial

Janet Wilson

The articles in this volume of *Katherine Mansfield Studies* explore Mansfield's identity as a (post)colonial writer in relation to her foremost reputation as a European modernist. In seeking new possibilities for alignments with, and resolutions to, the contradictory agendas implied by these terms, they address the clashing perspectives between her life in Europe, where her troubled self-designation as the 'little colonial' became a fertile source of her distinctive brand of literary modernism, and her ongoing, complex relationship with her New Zealand homeland.[1] As Elleke Boehmer notes, Mansfield's dualistic personae 'of modernist artist as outsider and of colonial outsider as modernist' mean that, like other modernist writers such as Jean Rhys, C. L. R. James, and Mulk Raj Anand, she can be positioned in ways that challenge and re-centre commonplace hierarchies: of the metropolitan centre over the underdeveloped periphery,[2] of male modernists like Joyce, Eliot, and Yeats, over women writers, of modernist genres of novel and poetry over that of the short story.[3] Yet this special volume goes beyond generic boundaries and historical periodisation implied by terms like 'modernist' and 'colonial'. Collectively the essays here explore Mansfield as a (post)colonial modernist writer whose anticipatory discourse demonstrates a consciousness about resistance that precedes the founding of the postcolonial state; that is, an already known postcolonial vision.[4] *Katherine Mansfield and the (Post)colonial,* marks the emergence of a current of Mansfield criticism that has previously lain dormant under the pressure of other theories and approaches: feminist, generic, biographical and social or historical. In reinvigorating this approach, with a synthesis of (post)colonial and modernist readings they increase the momentum in Mansfield studies and will advance possibilities for future scholarship.

1

The opening up of modernism to alternative inscriptions to those of the Anglo-American canon by exploring the relationship between modernism and colonialism has been the subject of several studies which postulate modernism's emergence within the broader history of nineteenth- and twentieth-century colonialism, especially that of the British Empire. Modernism, through formal innovation in art, loosens its ties to empire as a response to the disruption of cultural and social certainties after World War One, and to the cultural contact between unfamiliar cultures and the impact of the exilic, migrant writers who travelled into the imperial centre. Modernism's anxiety over colonialism can be aligned to the postcolonial challenge to the imperial mission, as studies of postcolonialism and modernism show.[5] Peter Childs, for example, comments that modernism's engagement with postcolonial perspectives from the periphery of empire, 'fashions a distinctive discourse characterized by ambivalence', because modernism is a literature concerned with 'worlding', and the challenge to European identities that it posed was both a provincial and global phenomenon.[6]

Recent essay collections, *Modernism and Empire*, edited by Howard J. Booth and Nigel Rigby (2000), and *Modernism and Colonialism*, edited by Richard Begam and Michael Valdez Moses (2007), have sought to relativise the towering influence of Anglo-American modernism by considering other indigenous cultures, although this reframing is limited by the strong representation of traditional canonical writers.[7] Begam and Moses' aim to counter the view that traditional modernists colluded with the project of empire is also at some remove from the critiques of empire and colonialism offered by a more peripheral writer like Mansfield.[8] Nevertheless, they examine the power relations involved in modernism's dynamic in a questioning of attitudes to the 'other' and to colonialism. Among these essays which emphasise heterogeneous indigenous traditions, literary modes and the attitudes of international modernism, at least one paradigm for reading Mansfield appears: James Joyce's migrant challenge to established norms of Irish nationalism, his interpretation of British imperialism and the project of Euro-modernism. Joyce works at an oblique angle in introducing a 'vernacular modernism',[9] comprising the linguistic terms and indigenous traditions of the Celtic twilight that exist in tension with the discourse of international modernism.[10] Mansfield similarly introduces idioms and phrases associated with Maoriland writing, the dominant literary discourse from about 1888 to 1914, before a New Zealand literary national culture was developed, and uses Māori legend and mythology for irony, contrast and local realism.[11] Both Anne Brown-Berens and Emmanouil Aretoulakis comment in their essays on her choice of indigenous terms such as 'whare' and 'karaka'.[12] Alongside Australian idioms from the popular frontier fiction of writers like Henry Lawson such as 'boncer' [bonzer] and 'sundowner', they evidence the multi-lingual, generically mixed utterances and diverse lexical strands of Mansfield's modernist renovation by which she created a transformed verbal environment that can only be described as colonial New Zealand modernist.[13]

The familiar framework of postcolonial binaries – empire and colony, centre and periphery – which Homi Bhabha deconstructs by emphasising the unfixing of cultural symbols, the rehistoricising of signs and reading anew, does more than situate Mansfield ambivalently as a white settler writer with contradictory allegiances and affiliations;[14] it also helps to show her modernism being refined in response to the pressure of imperial violence on colonial society, and the impact of the repressed 'other' on the subjectivity of the colonial subject. The critical exploration of overtly discordant cultural contacts between self and others is also manifested in Mansfield's aesthetics of disruption and use of discrepant positions, an important reflex of her mastery of craft and control of form, whereby she brings modernism and postcolonialism into artistic alignment. Such an aesthetics enables narrative performativity of the shock caused by the interruption of that control, and the disruption of narrative continuity caused by shadowy others, manifested as doubles, uncanny apparitions, and other intimations of disturbance of place. Such an angle takes account of postcolonialism's referencing of the occluded realms of the colonial past, its containment and exposure of the repressed other, the colonised.[15] It can be linked to Mansfield's ambivalences as a white settler subject and 'this secret disruption' that she perceived in herself.[16]

The eight essays in this collection develop previous assessments of Mansfield's ambivalent identity as a (post)colonial modernist,[17] to investigate the nature of her (post)colonial status (for example, Aretoulakis, Mari, Martin) and to reconceptualise her bifurcated emplacement as a colonial, metropolitan modernist. They focus on her liminal positioning between empire and colony, and colonial, anti-colonial, and decolonised perspectives; and the shift in status when she sought to transcend self-alienation, and her fragmented and disoriented consciousness. Essays by Aretoulakis, Wilson, Brown-Berens, Mari, Gasston, in repositioning Mansfield in relation to her colonial origins, revise the prevailing view of her as a restless, displaced and estranged modernist. They point to the alternative colonial sources, influences and communicative modes that she turned to in her aim to transform self-objectification through rupture, movement and division into a spiritual realisation (and reconciliation) of self and other. In contrast, the essays by Emily Ridge and Stefanie Rudig, by comparing Mansfield with the novelists Edith Wharton and Robert Louis Stevenson, offer new international critical and literary contexts for her (post)colonial modernism. Collectively, these essays offer insights into her diverse cultural and literary contexts by suggesting other provincial and international stylistic models for her modernism, identifying her ideological critique of society, her wish for psychological and literary re-emplacement as she grew increasingly ill, and her more radicalised postcolonial ambivalence, the new spatial positions and affiliations developed through cultural practices and psychic resources as she renewed her engagement with her New Zealand past. In different ways they pick up on and trace the continuities of cultural alignments that Mark Williams has noted with reference to Mansfield's early departure from New Zealand, as marked in her revitalised psychological, emotional attachment to her native homeland.[18] Finally they suggest, given the impossibility of making a physical return, that she recovered a paradoxically distant yet intimate sense of belonging, one that is intersected by alternative positions, for as Emmanouil Aretoulakis comments, in finding her own identity she first had to lose herself 'in a maze of far more extreme positions of otherness'.

The three opening essays focus on the way that crucial motifs, practices and orientations in Mansfield's life and work traverse numerous social and cultural boundaries and divisions; these are traceable to her ambivalence about colonisation and later determination to find ways of transcending disruption, loss and death. Aimee Gasston's prize-winning essay, 'Katherine Mansfield, Cannibal', provides a typology of those tropes and images of cannibalism, ingestion, and the gustatory, which Mansfield uses to unsettle the coloniser-colonised binary. Referring to ideas of savagery and primitive force as presented in the Brazilian Oswalde de Andrade's the 'Cannibalist Manifesto', and the modernist manifestos in *Rhythm*, Gasston analyses how Mansfield's sharp-eyed, anti-colonial critique of Bloomsbury as barbarian in the satirical story 'Sunday Lunch' destabilises cultural and class privilege. Arguing that incorporation is a key to Mansfield's personal aesthetics, she stresses that a metaphysical and transcendental endo-cannibalism (the Freudian vision of eating one's kin) appears as she acknowledges the power of death. The eucharistic symbolism of 'To L. H. B.', Mansfield's elegy to her brother, demarcates an 'anthropophagy of incorporation' and revivification through writing, as she 'returns' to New Zealand through combining spiritual and material transubstantiation, so transcending displacement. Emmanouil Aretoulakis also argues, from a different angle, that Mansfield's (post)colonialism emerges as a form of excessive identity in her oscillation between colonial, anti-colonial and postco-

lonial positions; this also appears in the hybridisation of pure identity structures, such as beauty and ugliness, purity and impurity. The
metaphysical and spiritual reconfiguration that determined Mansfield's
reorientation towards what became her life's project – to write a new
version of her childhood – is marked by the incorporation of death as
an integral part of life and source of spiritual richness. This interpenetration of oppositions to show the elided other, death, as the determin-
ing force of life, parallels her occupation of the liminal spaces between
colonial, anticolonial and postcolonial in ways that might be described
as radically postcolonial. My own essay on Mansfield's rewriting of 'the
contract with death' also explores the implications for her late work
of her vow to commemorate in prose the life of her brother, Leslie
Heron Beauchamp, and so restore him metaphorically to life. Drawing
on recent studies of late Victorian and early twentieth-century cultural
practices of the occult, telepathy and mediumship through seances,
especially after World War One, I suggest that Mansfield turned to
alternative cultural and communicative transmission channels:[19] self-
induced vision, hallucinations, telepathic communication, automatism
and occult concepts such as ghosts and visions enabled her to access
her earliest memories, return to the family and develop her vision of
possibility even while illness was diminishing her grasp on life. In the
interweaving of death with life in her later New Zealand stories, she
re-accents the (post)colonial modernism of her earlier stories, through
focusing anew on place and space as haunted, susceptible to irruption
from strange uncanny forces, while exposing the precarious boundary
between civilised and demonic, occulted domains; and locating sensa-
tions of conflict and 'difference within'.

These three essays show Mansfield's preoccupation with metaphorical re-emplacement in her homeland, combined with a metaphysic of
transcendence through art in her reckoning with mortality as the defining endeavour of her last years. They go some way to suggest a new
image: a Mansfield whose restlessness and wandering become part of a
search for a new pattern which would offer hope for the future and a
possibility of unity or wholeness, even while she continued to negotiate
a presence within the interstices of colony and empire, and they present
sharp critiques of colonial patriarchy, domination and possession, as in
the classic story, 'The Daughters of the Late Colonel'.

Other essays examine the New Zealand cultural contexts, potential
sources of stylistic influence, and Mansfield's social critique, including
self-critique of her ambivalence as colonial outsider. Mansfield's early
experimental, New Zealand regional stories – 'Millie', 'Ole Underwood',
'The Woman at the Store' – and sketches like 'Old Tar', 'Tui and Kezia',

and 'Summer Idylle', and the planned novel, *Maata*, show a preoccupation with the racially mixed society of colonial New Zealand, its uneven processes of colonisation, and imperial English underpinnings, demanding new understandings of the self in relation to a cultural other. This underpins her critique of provincialism, alongside her stylistic synthesis of its diverse literary modes with metropolitan symbolism and Wildean *fin de siècle* aesthetics. Anne Brown-Berens challenges perceptions of Mansfield's colonial outsider status by showing her as potentially linked to a local community of writers and their hybridised provincial-Victorian literary response to colonial conditions. Mansfield's New Zealand writing is located alongside novels by English and Scottish diasporic writers of the late nineteenth century, such as Dugald Ferguson, Clara Cheeseman, Charlotte Evans and Alexander Bathgate, whose cultural and natural symbols demarcate an imagery of settler displacement in the disjunctions between the gendered frontier of the masculine outdoors (a form of landscape primitivism), and the feminised genteel interior (a morally civilising presence). These are compared to Mansfield's exhibition of fake genteel interiors and imported artefacts in stories about the primitive frontier environment like 'Millie' and 'The Woman at the Store', of urban displacement in 'Ole Underwood' and of working-class life in 'The Garden Party'. Brown-Berens shows Mansfield moving beyond her predecessors by using impressionist effects to intensify her psychological realism, while her cultural symbolism disrupts their cultural assumptions and provides alternative versions of the colonial world.

Likewise, opening up new territory, Lorenzo Mari considers how Mansfield expanded the national imaginary through transgressive constructions of home and belonging in her fable, 'How Pearl Button was Kidnapped'. Mari explores the implications of this story's ethnic point of view for New Zealand nationalism in his gendered reading of it as a version of the Freudian family romance, a feminised treatment of the oedipal scheme through focusing on a female child, and a reconfiguration of the *Künstlerroman*. Drawing on Jameson's theories of third-world allegory, which claim that the individual destiny can be metonymic of that of the entire society, he argues that Mansfield locates herself obliquely to the white settler in ideological terms, in order to expose society's fissures and fractures, in this (post)colonial national allegory. The kidnapping of Pearl Button constitutes an interruption of the colonial patriarchal discourse that would present New Zealand as a utopian arcadia linked to the masculinised sphere of empire; yet patriarchy is reasserted in the story's conclusion when Pearl Button is 'rescued' by the men in blue. Mari reads the story as a momentary disruption of the national order that briefly opens up space for the indigenous view-point. He concludes that subsequent interventions in the allegory of the nation by Māori writers like Witi Ihimaera and Patricia Grace have built on the model of violent imposition, brutal interruption, contradiction and ambiguity between the family and colonial nation that Mansfield provides through her national allegory.

Mansfield's range and confidence as a writer in opening up to modernist exploration mean that her (post)colonial mask is just one of several when her entire oeuvre is considered. A story like 'The Tiredness of Rosabel', written before she left New Zealand, reveals a highly self-reflexive, layered metropolitan awareness and anticipates future stories about *la seule femme* like 'The Little Governess', 'Dark Hollows', 'The Swing of the Pendulum' and 'A Cup of Tea'. Nevertheless in early stories using a first person narrator her complex position is nuanced through self-concealing masks and silences that betray insecurity about her place, identity and social standing. Todd Martin in his essay engages with the colonial underpinnings of Mansfield's fractured identity and uncertain loyalties upon her arrival in Europe, as discernible in her apparently indefinable national status while living in Wörishofen in Germany in 1909. Stories written at that time and published as *In a German Pension* show deference to British or imperial anti-German feeling in this pre-World War One era, while also implying cultural differences in New Zealand's national attitude to Germany at that time. Focusing on Mansfield's self-perception as alienated stranger in the midst of Germans, and her obscurity in national terms – as to whether she is English or American, as several stories record – Martin suggests that these doubled identity structures and contradictory affiliations emerge through the complex prism of her narrative technique: Mansfield 'performs' a metropolitan satirical critique through the implied author, while in the voice of the first-person colonial narrator, she identifies with the German characters, sharing their excitements and sympathising with them, because, in Martin's terms, she is still seeking a way to belong. Martin points to the complexity of Mansfield's (post)colonial status in writing that, on the one hand, beneath the satiric overtones is dependent on recognisable, hegemonic and national, imperial modes, and on the other, the subversive impulses that might undermine them.

Mansfield's somewhat ambiguous position in the modernist canon means that her attitudes to the writing of others that might reflect her paradoxical determination to distance herself from her colonial nation and past, yet reclaim them as new, have not always been read in the light of this dualism within her literary modernism. Yet the strength of her commitment to a (post)colonial aesthetic or understanding of art appears through comparisons with other writers. Emily Ridge in her essay refers to Mansfield's critical review of Wharton's seminal novel, *The Age of Innocence*, written in 1920. Mansfield invokes her earlier fascination with the primitive and savage in her reaction to the Anglo-American emphasis on manners, polished speech and politeness, pointing out that the characters are 'like portraits in a gallery [...] arranged for exhibition purposes'. Ridge demonstrates that Mansfield is indirectly appraising the ambivalent quality of her own modernism by challenging the cultivated metropolitan urbanity of Wharton's prose and advocating her preference for the wild and 'a dark place or two in the soul'. Similarly illuminating is the comparison of her work with that of Robert Louis Stevenson. Stefanie Rudig, in her unexpected pairing of two writers in exile, whose independent migrations from their homelands were in diametrically opposed directions, emphasises their shared spatial constructions of South Pacific locales, and the instability of their concepts of home, as a diasporic place which combines alienation with belonging. But the contrasts are palpable: Stevenson's novella, 'The Beach at Falesa', transforms European representation with a hybridisation of discrepant styles, forms and cultures in his rewriting and entails a reinscription of European-based stereotypes of a cross-cultural romance; whereas Mansfield introduces fluid concepts of identity and home in her novella 'Prelude'.

These comparisons of Mansfield with other European writers go some way to further rehabilitate her reputation in the canons of modernism, in their demonstration of significant literary intersections as well as the light they shed on Mansfield's artistic values and literary preferences, as reflecting her insider/outsider dualism. Mansfield's rising status is evidenced in recent essays published in the *Cambridge Companion to Modernist Women Writers* (2010), the second edition of *The Cambridge Companion to Modernism* (2011), and Claire Drewery's study of modernist women writers (2011).[20]

This volume also features some of the most significant reports yet published in *Katherine Mansfield Studies*, namely on the important acquisition of Murry/Mansfield papers by the Alexander Turnbull Library and the discovery of papers relating to Katherine Mansfield in the archive of Miron Grindea, the editor of *ADAM International Review*, held in the King's College London Archives, both in 2012. In his report, Chris Mourant, a PhD student, describes the five previously unknown Mansfield stories and collection of Wildean aphorisms that he came across in the *ADAM* archive. Most significant for Mansfield scholars is 'A little Episode', a story which belongs to a painful moment in her life in 1909 after Mansfield had been abandoned by her lover, the musician

Garnet Trowell by whom she had become pregnant, and briefly married the music teacher, George Bowden. This vivid, emotionally charged vignette illuminates a period in Mansfield's life of which little other record now exists. Fiona Oliver reports on the acquisition of the Murry/Mansfield archive by the Alexander Turnbull Library after two years of negotiation with the Murry family. Her reference to earlier purchases from Murry is a story of an emerging national resource, but also, as she points out, of the resuscitation of Mansfield's spirit. The latest purchase is the largest acquired by the ATL since the 1950s. As well as Murry's papers, there are documents relating to D. H. and Frieda Lawrence, photographs, Hogarth Press first editions, locks of Mansfield's hair, her cloak and typewriter, and a Māori head carved from gum. An important discovery in this collection was made by Gerri Kimber, 'Sumurun: An Impression of Leopoldine Konstantin' (1911), a previously unknown creative impression of a play that Mansfield saw in London in January 1911. Andrew Harrison reports on the famous postcard sent by D. H. Lawrence to Mansfield from Wellington on 15 April 1922, on which the word 'Ricordi' is inscribed. Part of the recent Murry acquisition by the ATL, the postcard actually includes Frieda Lawrence's greeting as well, and the two inscriptions demolish the view that Lawrence was reminding Mansfield of her Wellington roots: 'Ricordi' is now read as his and Frieda's thoughts of her. Gaining the entire text of the postcard sheds new light on the Murry-Lawrence estranged relationship and anticipates the partial reconciliation between them after Mansfield's death. Gerri Kimber provides a report on two French books once owned by Mansfield which have recently come to light (now in a private collection): *La Femme de Trente Ans* (*A Woman of Thirty*) by Honoré de Balzac and *La Jeune Fille Bien Élevée* (*The Well-Bred Young Girl*) by René Boylesve, offering a tantalising glimpse into Mansfield's life at a specific moment in 1916. In another report, Penelope Jackson tells of her purchase of the Nigel Brown portrait of Mansfield, which adorns the cover of this volume. The painting belongs to Brown's *Names* series, which celebrates Mansfield along with other famous New Zealanders, and Jackson explains the iconographic and pictorial clues to the portrait, taken from Mansfield's early years in Wellington, the photograph from which Brown worked and the portrait's inscription of *Matthew 3.3* (found in a letter by Mansfield).

Finally, this volume showcases new creative writing, some of which was inspired by the two European conferences on Mansfield held in 2012. The short story by Witi Ihimaera, 'Waiting for La Petite Anglaise', was commissioned by Gerri Kimber on the occasion of his participation in the 'Footsteps of Katherine Mansfield' conference held at Montana, in Switzerland in September 2012. Ihimaera is well known for his attraction to Mansfield as a hybrid European/New Zealand precursor, as found in the bicultural, intertextual stories in *Dear Miss Mansfield,* and this is a very welcome addition to an already famous repertoire. A poem by C. K. Stead, 'Names and Places', reflects on his travel to the Katherine Mansfield Society conference held at Ruzomberok, Slovakia in June 2012 and his meeting with the organiser, Janka Kaskacova; while Kathleen Jones, the most recent biographer of Mansfield and Murry, offers three poems, including 'Excavating the Bones', her musings about the archaeological work of scholarly excavation on Katherine Mansfield that took place at the same conference, and which she dedicates to Gerri Kimber, and another poem, 'Nightmare', a reflection on a Mansfield comment that she had died in a dream. The three poems by Gladys Cole are also occasional; the first recreates a visit to Mansfield's Chalet Des Sapins home in Montana-sur-Sierre; the second, to the lake at Fontainebleau and Mansfield's grave with its Shakespearean inscription, while the third poem is dedicated to Mansfield's sister Jeanne Renshaw at her home in Gloucestershire, while also recalling the family home in Wellington.

This fifth volume of *Katherine Mansfield Studies,* now in a longer 'year-book' format, reflects the importance of the subject of Mansfield as (post)colonial modernist, a cross-disciplinary area which has been somewhat under-researched, and until recently has attracted little attention from scholars outside New Zealand. The efflorescence of new Mansfield research is evident, for example, in three international conferences held in three different countries in the last eight months, and the discoveries of previously unknown papers relating to Mansfield, including new stories, in two important archives. All this bodes well for the future of Mansfield studies and the continuing rise of her reputation.

Notes

1. Mark Williams, 'Mansfield in Maoriland: biculturalism, agency and misreading', in Howard J. Booth and Nigel Rigby, eds, *Modernism and Empire* (Manchester and New York: Manchester University Press, 2000), pp. 249–74 (p. 257); Margaret Scott, ed., *The Katherine Mansfield Notebooks,* 2 vols (Minneapolis: University of Minnesota Press, 2002), Vol. 2, p. 166.
2. Elleke Boehmer, *Colonial and Postcolonial Literature: Migrant Metaphors* (Oxford and New York: Oxford University Press, 1995), p. 133.
3. Dick Hebdige, 'Postmodernism and "the other side"', in David Morley and Kuan-Hsing Chen, eds, *Stuart Hall : Critical Dialogues in Cultural Studies* (London: Routledge 1996), pp. 177–8; Gerri Kimber and Janet Wilson, 'Introduction', in Gerri Kimber and Janet Wilson, eds, *Celebrating Katherine Mansfield: A Centenary Volume of Essays* (London: Palgrave, 2010), p. 2.

4. Laura Doyle, 'Geomodernism postcoloniality and women's writing', in Maren Tova Linett, ed., *The Cambridge Companion to Modernist Women Writers* (Cambridge: Cambridge University Press, 2010), pp. 129–44.

5. See, for example, Bill Ashcroft, Gareth Griffiths, and Helen Tiffin, *The Empire Writes Back* (London: Routledge, 1989), pp. 156–60.

6. Peter Childs, *Modernism and the Post-Colonial: Literature and Empire 1885–1930* (London: Continuum, 2007), pp. 1–2, citing Robert Crawford, *Devolving English Literature* (Oxford: Clarendon Press, 1992), p. 270.

7. Booth and Rigby, eds, *Modernism and Empire*; Richard Begum and Michael Valdez Moses, eds, *Modernism and Colonialism: British and Irish Literature, 1899–1939* (Durham and London: Duke University Press, 2007).

8. Begum and Moses, 'Introduction', Begum and Moses, eds, p. 7.

9. The term comes from Begum and Moses, 'Introduction', Begum and Moses, p. 6.

10. Declan Kiberd writes on Joyce in 'Postcolonial Modernism?', Begum and Moses, pp. 269–87.

11. On the parallel with Joyce see Williams, 'Mansfield in Maoriland', in Booth and Rigby, p. 260.

12. A tree cultivated by the Māori for its fruit.

13. See also boncer [bonzer] in 'Prelude' cited by Rudige, an Australian borrowing – like sundowner in 'The Woman at the Store'

14. Homi Bhabha, *The Location of Culture* (London: Routledge, 2004), p. 37.

15. See Alison Rudd's reading of 'The Woman at the Store' in *Postcolonial Gothic Fictions from the Caribbean, Canada, Australia and New Zealand* (Cardiff: University of Wales Press, 2010), p. 145.

16. Vincent O'Sullivan and Margaret Scott, eds, *The Collected Letters of Katherine Mansfield*, 5 vols (Oxford: Clarendon Press, 1984–2008), Vol. 5, p. 304.

17. See, for example, Bridget Orr, 'Reading with the Taint of the Pioneer; Katherine Mansfield and Settler Criticism'; Linda Hardy, 'The Ghost of Katherine Mansfield', in Rhoda B. Nathan, ed., *Critical Essays on Katherine Mansfield* (New York: G. K. Hall & Co, 1993), pp. 489–60 and 75–92; Lydia Wevers, 'The Sod Under my Feet: Katherine Mansfield', in Mark Williams and Michelle Leggott, eds, *Opening the Book: New Essays on New Zealand Writing* (Auckland: Auckland University Press, 1995), pp. 31–48; Janet Wilson, '"Where is Katherine?": Longing and (Un)belonging in the works of Katherine Mansfield'; Elleke Boehmer, 'Mansfield as Colonial Modernist: Difference Within' in Kimber and Wilson, pp. 57–71 and 175–88.

18. Jane Stafford and Mark Williams, *Maoriland: New Zealand Literature 1872–1914* (Wellington: Victoria University Press, 2006), p. 152.

19. Pamela Thurschwell, *Literature, Technology and Magical Thinking 1880–1920* (Cambridge: Cambridge University Press, 2001), pp. 1–8.

20. See, for example, Maren Tova Linett, ed., *The Cambridge Companion to Modernist Women Writers*, Michael Levenson, ed., *The Cambridge Companion to Modernism*, 2nd edn (Cambridge: Cambridge University Press, 2011); Claire Drewery, *Modernist Short Fiction by Women: The Liminal in Katherine Mansfield, Dorothy Richardson, May Sinclair and Virginia Woolf* (London: Ashgate, 2011).

CRITICISM

Katherine Mansfield, Cannibal

Aimee Gasston

Engaging with concepts of barbarism throughout her career, Katherine Mansfield displayed a fascination with cannibalism[1] that held both political and aesthetic significance for her 'de-centered, female, colonial, proto-postcolonial' voice.[2] Moving through a typology of cannibalisms, Mansfield used anthropophagic tropes to explore settler ambivalence and unsettle categorisations of coloniser and colonised, shifting from a negative cannibalism of revenge towards a tender anthropophagy which allowed her return to New Zealand through fiction. The self-description Mansfield sent to the editor of the *Native Companion* – that she was 'just eighteen years of age – with a rapacious appetite for everything and principles as light as [her] purse' – casts a mould for Mansfield the adult, an insatiable literary cannibal to whom taboos meant nothing.[3] The draw of cannibalism was felt by modernists more widely, as demonstrated by Conrad's *Heart of Darkness* (1902), Francis Picabia's *Manifeste Cannibale* (1920) and the Parisian Dada review *Cannibale* (1920s), as well as Oswalde de Andrade's *Manifesto Antropófago* (1928), Waugh's *Black Mischief* (1932) and Eliot's *Sweeney Agonistes* (1932). Where Sweeney sought to achieve spiritual purity by quitting London for a cannibal island, the young Mansfield would thrill at exporting her own brand of savagery to Europe. She revelled at being dubbed the 'little savage from New Zealand' by her principal at Queen's College, London, and as an adult would develop a commitment to brutalism by consistently refusing to represent a falsely civilised world view in her fiction.[4] Her Uwerera notebook comment, 'Give me the Maori and the tourist but nothing in between', reveals a preference for polarisation over equivocation, perhaps in disavowal of her own diasporic ambivalence.[5] Stories such as 'In the Botanical Gardens' (1907) and 'Old Tar' (1913) articulate a palpable colonial guilt and displacement which may bear resonance with

Mansfield's decision to leave her native country to play the tourist in Europe while enacting the 'savage spirit' of New Zealand in her fiction.[6] Eventually, cannibalism would allow Mansfield a means of negotiating between these two extremes.

The etymology of the word 'cannibal' dates from the mid-sixteenth century: from Spanish *Canibales* (plural), a variant of *Caribes*, a West Indian people reputed to eat humans.[7] While in his 1979 study, *The Man-Eating Myth: Anthropology and Anthropophagy*, William Arens claimed cannibalism as a colonial fabrication, more recent genetic research has proven that it was likely practised by early humans all over the world.[8] In spite of this, cannibalism is perpetually conceived of as something remote and emphatically other. The application of this term to denote the savage or other is therefore freighted with ambivalence. Anthropophagy is far closer to all of us than we might have first thought.

Mansfield wanted to eat the world before she wrote it. As early as 1907, she was articulating her need for a corporeal literature which closely matched that called for by Murry in the early editions of *Rhythm*. Sketching in her notebook, she depicts the butcher and the writer sitting logically together: 'And a man enters the carriage, very fair & full-blooded – he reads a book of Meat Inspection, I the poems of Dante Gabriel Rossetti – the Fleshly School of Poetry.'[9] Fittingly, Mansfield's fiction is saturated with human affairs in which one either eats or is eaten – as Claire Tomalin observes 'couples are like cannibals' – and relationships are constantly figured in gustatory terms.[10] Mansfield would despair of women who infantilise men in order to better cannibalise them, observing that 'such women fill themselves with their men – gorge themselves to a state of absolute heartlessness'.[11] In 'Bliss', the gender paradigm is reversed, when Bertha's husband talks about his 'shameless passion for the flesh of the lobster' and 'the green of pistachio ices – green and cold like the eyelids of Egyptian dancers' in expression of his desire to consume Pearl Fulton.[12] In 'Je Ne Parle Pas Français', Raoul Duquette observes passers-by at a train station and comments with anthropophagic glee: 'Into the trap they walked and were snatched and taken off to be devoured. Where was my prey?'[13] Elsewhere – as in 'Pictures' where the stout man who bears Ada Moss away is described as having fingers like sausages – human resemblance to food prefigures the sexual act and often typifies a sense of things awry, expressing disgust towards unsuited components in cannibal conjunction. While in these textual examples cannibalism is figured in terms of opposition and destruction, Mansfield herself would finally participate in a type of creative cannibalism that would enable incorporation and polyphony as well as a path to her strongest work.

Primitivist Polemics

Oswalde de Andrade's 'Cannibalist Manifesto' (*Manifesto Antropófago*) was published in Brazil five years after Mansfield's death, yet it well articulates some of the tensions which permeate and enliven her work, the best of which was indubitably modern yet, to quote her own phrase, 'old with the age of centuries, strong with the strength of savagery'.[14] In his modernist polemic, de Andrade ironically exploits ideas of savagery and Western representations of primitivism in order to forge a vision of a Brazilian cultural identity that is both original and fierce, which goes beyond a straightforward cannibalisation, or wholesale transplantation, of the culture of its European colonists – if the 'sacred enemy' is 'absorbed', it is only to 'transform him into a totem' – and resoundingly rejects all notions of the civilising effects of 'culture'.[15] The young Mansfield would consider her countrymen in equally dramatic carnal terms, declaring to Vera Beauchamp that the 'firm fat framework of their brains must be demolished before they can begin to learn'.[16] The precocious Mansfield's 'manifesto' is less considered than de Andrade's, prescribing the 'purifying influence' of European cultural icons as medicine to New Zealand's ills. There is no construction of Europe as potential enemy; it is cast quite firmly as sacred. Where Mansfield suggests a way forward based on a process of demolition and importation, de Andrade's more holistic cannibalism would allow one culture to ingest another in order to affect a more meaningful transformation. This is a view that the mature Mansfield would come to share.

The central question of the 'Cannibalist Manifesto'– 'Tupi or not tupi?' – cannibalises Shakespeare through punning, recycling and reappropriating the *Hamlet* quotation, while simultaneously probing the acumen of doing so.[17] The Brazilian Tupi people comprised several tribes who myth attests were in a constant state of battle with one another, with combat often ending in cannibal ritual. Only the greatest warriors would be consumed by Tupi tribes, in order that their strengths could endure in those who ingested them.[18] As Freud would put it in another text cannibalised by the manifesto, *Totem and Taboo*: 'by incorporating parts of a person's body through the act of eating, one at the same time acquires the qualities possessed by him'.[19] It is appropriate that Shakespeare, to whom Mansfield would also refer in similarly appreciative gustatory terminology, should be considered as potential literary fodder. In a letter to Murry of 27 February 1918, Mansfield concludes that she has been spoilt by too much Shakespeare, drawing sharp relief between the 'rich' language of English, and that of French, which she finds 'hard to stomach'.[20] De Andrade asks: should I be a cannibal, and should I be eating Shakespeare? A further question is also embedded in this rhetoric: is it ethical to import food from so far abroad? By altering Shakespeare's text as he refers to it, de Andrade answers his own question: cannibalise without limits, through it transform yourself and put *that* on the page.

For the young Mansfield, aside from Shakespeare, cannibal fodder included Oscar Wilde and Walter Pater, as well as Dickens, Byron and Bronte.[21] C. L. R. James, who made connections with the Bloomsbury set after Mansfield's death, reflected on his voracious reading habits while growing up in Trinidad to conclude: 'Intellectually I lived abroad, chiefly in England.'[22] The same was true of Mansfield. Growing up on a rich but staple diet of English literature (the brains of the dead), a question analogous to 'Tupi or not tupi?' would hang over her literary direction. This would need to sever itself from a borrowed ancestry if it was to forge its own identity while drawing authentically on its own cultural roots, howsoever experienced (as de Andrade would put it, evoking what is now a commonplace postcolonial homonym, 'Routes, routes, routes . . .').[23] Ingestion, rather than demolition, would be crucial.

The dictum, 'Before art can be human, it must learn to be brutal', could easily be mistaken for a citation from the 'Cannibalist Manifesto' but is actually drawn from the first edition of *Rhythm* (summer 1911), in a piece in which Murry set out the publication's aims and ideals.[24] The phrase is an unacknowledged quotation, originating from the poet J. M. Synge's introduction to the Cuala Press edition of his *Poems and Translations* (1909), although the word 'verse' expands to 'art' in Murry's version.[25] Synge had died in 1909, and so this reincorporation of his work is very literally Tupi in essence, simultaneously revivifying Synge and invigorating the magazine. The piece ends with an equally strident declaration: 'What is exalted and tender in art is not made of feeble blood.'[26] Another direct cannibalisation of Synge from the same text, the statement is sanguinary in both subject and form, with Synge's ideas used to inject lifeblood into the *Rhythm* enterprise, de Andrade's 'cannibalistic vaccine'.[27]

The publication thus set out aims very different to the 'mad wave of pre-Raphaelitism, of super-aestheticism' that the twenty-year-old Mansfield recommended to her native country.[28] Taking up Synge's argument where he left off, *Rhythm* declared aestheticism extinct, its focus too narrow to encompass the 'surge of the life that lay beyond its sphere'; it urged its audience to 'see that the present is pregnant for the future' and to express a preference for the raw over the cooked.[29] A pugnacious commitment to a more faithful representation of the material world was called for, and described in a currency that is extensively corporeal. The vibrant, impolite simplicity of the magazine's artwork, as well as Michael Sadler's championing article 'Fauvism and a Fauve', reinforced Murry's call to arms. *Rhythm*'s manifesto came from a different place to the *Manifesto Antropófago*, but it spoke using the same register. Both acknowledged that European culture had become too cultivated, lacked vivacity, and needed to rediscover its own barbarism to be rewarded with fecundity. It was not incidental that the first story Mansfield would publish in *Rhythm* was 'The Woman at the Store', a stark piece revolving around violence and sex, and her first pronounced portrayal of her homeland, in which 'the savage spirit of the country walked abroad and sneered at what it saw'.[30]

Colonial Revolt: The Assault on Metropolitan Elitism

In the satire 'Sunday Lunch', published in the ninth edition of *Rhythm* in October 1912 under the sobriquet 'The Tiger', it was Mansfield's turn to walk abroad and sneer at what she saw. Recoding the trope of cannibalism, Mansfield deflects it back onto the colonisers, focusing on an artistic barbarism gone awry where urbanity signifies depravity. Effectively exploring the logical consequences of misinterpreting Murry's dictum, 'Sunday Lunch' launches a caustic attack on a burgeoning intelligentsia, opening with the lines: 'Sunday lunch is the last of the cannibal feasts. It is the wild, tremendous orgy of the upper classes, the hunting, killing, eating ground of all the George-the-Fifth-and-Mary English artists'.[31] Having established this phenomenon culturally and historically as something specifically English, Mansfield narrows her geographical locus further to the privileged realm of London's most expensive quarters, evidencing the adult Mansfield's disenchantment with the city she had once apotheosised. 'The Society for the Cultivation of Cannibalism waxes most fat and kicks hardest (strictly under the table) in Chelsea, in St John's Wood, in certain select squares, and (God help them) gardens.'[32] This Society considers only 'artists' as human; servants are classified as 'marionettes' and rescued from both attention and consumption. Mansfield's ironic depiction of the automaton servants and the garden as a too rugged environment for her 'savages' to inhabit emphasises the plastic artifice of the intellectuals. They pick over the bones of each other's creations after gratuitous backstabbing: 'This obvious slaughter of the absentees is only a preliminary to a finer, more keen and difficult doing to death of each other.'[33] Invidious and insecure, the cannibals' artistic criticisms are founded on personal hierarchies of snobbism, one disparaging the audience at another's show with the words: 'People absolutely ignorant – you know the kind. Not able to distinguish a cabbage from a baby.'[34] And what cannibal could fail to recognise a cabbage from a baby?

The piece ends by admitting the hollowness of its central metaphor as well as its protagonists: 'But the horrible tragedy of the Sunday lunch is this: However often the Society kills and eats itself, it is never real enough to die, it is never real enough to consider itself well eaten.'[35] Unable either to destroy or create, the intelligentsia are ultimately ineffective cannibals, absorbed in the superficial and too alienated from their bodies to allow for incorporation, digestion or satisfaction. Their savagery cannot extend beyond the domain of dinner party gossip. Mansfield perhaps invokes the cannibal trope to revivify a link with the 'savage spirit' of her homeland, but her application of it does more to reveal her disappointment with an artistic milieu that too closely resembled the provincial, colonial society she had sought to escape. Mansfield's use of the cannibal trope shows that she means to offend the values of her targets, and consequently her perception of them as shockable, bourgeois and parochial.

As the practice of cannibalism can be dated in New Zealand to as early as its first human habitation and as late as the 1870s, it was a concept which would perhaps have felt less remote to Mansfield than her London colleagues.[36] History books allege that 'Maoris found cannibalism both socially acceptable and necessary, and they also seemed to enjoy it'.[37] In fiction, Mansfield used savagery and specifically cannibalism in order to satirise the societies most familiar to her; the comfortable colonial or European worlds where self-satisfaction could combine with sightlessness. Where Virginia Woolf would, in 1926, compare a cinema audience to a group of savages, Mansfield's depiction of the cultural elite as barbarian is far more radical.[38] It seeks to destabilise established anatomies of privilege and disrupt dominant metropolitan practices. In choosing the metaphorical modes that it does, it is also palpably anti-colonial.

Cannibalism itself has strong links with the mode of parody employed by Mansfield in 'Sunday Lunch'. While the 'Cannibalist Manifesto' enjoyed toying with European legends about Brazilian savagery, New Zealand Māori learned the art of parody by exaggerating their mythical status. Obseyesekere has observed that

> Maori mimeses of cannibalism from Cook to de Surville to Marion constitute[d] a tradition of Maori cannibalism imagined by the European. The Maori began to give a version of their cannibalism to the white visitors to terrify them, and they enjoyed the terror written on their faces.[39]

There is an apparently natural link between cannibalism and satire that reaches back to Jonathan Swift's 'A Modest Proposal'.[40] Both Mansfield's pseudonym 'The Tiger' and the biting parody of the piece serve to create an exaggeratedly intimidating version of its author, albeit an author who is not brave enough to be named.[41] Mansfield's pseudonym is appropriated like the bestial masks that were sometimes worn during cannibal rituals.[42] By privately celebrating and emphasising her perceived difference while attacking cultural imperialism, Mansfield reveals a desire to unsettle the assumed relationship between coloniser and colonised.

Jenny McDonnell posits 'Sunday Lunch' as evidence that 'Mansfield had begun to question Murry's ideals of a literary community and, by extension, coterie publication'.[43] This attack on the literati can therefore be read as a rejection of the readership for which *Rhythm* was intended, a cannibalist biting of the hand that might feed her. McDonnell also points out that 'Sunday Lunch' employs the same metaphoric modes used by Mansfield later when she expresses worries about how the intelligentsia would consume the Hogarth Press-published 'Prelude', indicating that self-defence was an additional motivation, and that 'Sunday Lunch' was a pre-emptive strike catalysed by an awareness that one must eat or be eaten oneself.[44]

Yet within the piece, Mansfield hypocritically proves herself a most effective cannibal, turning on what are (in at least one sense, as artists) her own kind with vicious effect. She also plays the coloniser by casting her protagonists as subjects, her own marionettes regarded with an acute downward inflection. Further, the caricature's reliance on a negative interpretation of the cannibal trope means that Mansfield appropriates a colonial formulation of savagery (although it is one inverted by its unusual application). While satire is used as a distancing mechanism, it is undermined by the fact that within the piece Mansfield enacts the same savagery she seeks to deride, thus embroiling herself irrevocably with her own satire.

'Sunday Lunch' therefore enacts a type of revenge cannibalism, but also self-sacrifice or auto-cannibalism as it exposes the tourist Mansfield as occupying uncomfortable territory. There is also a sense in which Mansfield apparently hopes to expiate past and present sins by drawing attention to them. The ambivalent attack of 'Sunday Lunch' recalls the sharks referred to in 'The Scholarship', which when 'attacked [. . .] switch around and eat their own entrails – Sickening!'[45] In the *New Age* the previous year, Mansfield and Beatrice Hastings had acerbically and publically lampooned contemporary writers such as H. G. Wells and Arnold Bennett, participating in exactly the same shade of cannibalism 'Sunday Lunch' repudiates and revealing the ferocious capabilities to which Mansfield's pseudonym alludes.[46] The material context of the piece also contributes to an atmosphere of unease, sitting in hypo-critical proximity to a visual caricature of Mansfield by George Banks which emphatically encourages the very cult of the artist disparaged in 'Sunday Lunch', which is in turn ensconced within a coterie publica-tion. In some ways, Mansfield does more to reveal her own similarity to her 'cannibals' than refute it.

What would further reduce the distance between Mansfield and the victims of her satire is the fact that only four months earlier she had co-authored 'The Meaning of Rhythm' with Murry. This piece was a disturbingly elitist and anti-democratic statement that laid bare those more insidious undertows of the Modernist movement that have been explored in seminal works by Raymond Williams and John Carey.[47] The penultimate paragraph reads:

> Individuality in the work of art is the creation of reality by freedom. It is the triumphant weapon of aristocracy [. . .] Only by realising the unity and the strength of the individual in the work of art is the mob brought to the knowledge of its own infinite weakness, and it loathes and is terrified by it.[48]

In this short essay, 'democracy' is set against the 'aristocracy' with inflex-ible sociological terminology used to separate an entitled cultural elite from the hopelessly barbarian masses. Comically, the piece defines 'intuition' as the quality that distinguishes the aristocratic artist, the 'power of divining individuality in other persons and other things', while revealing this as a faculty absent from its authors who concur-rently refer to the faceless conglomerate of the 'mob'.[49] Subjectivity here is palpably linked to subjectification of the culturally bereft other as inferior. Journalists are even referred to as slaves. 'The Meaning of Rhythm' is essentially an imperialist discourse; a muddled, naïve piece of political posturing.

It seems likely that 'The Meaning of Rhythm' was guided at least partly by Mansfield and Murry's own anxieties about their status and subsequent need to position themselves as heirs to the literary canon. Stafford and Williams observe that 'Uncertain of her place in language (as owner or borrower), [Mansfield] employs style always in a highly self-conscious fashion' and there is a sense in which, despite Murry's nationality, a shared disquiet was laid bare here.[50] Conscious of their outré status, Murry, the ex-scholarship student and son of a low-ranking civil servant, and Mansfield, colonial daughter of a banker and member of a family of 'bridge and golf people', perhaps felt it necessary to con-solidate their feelings of entitlement by reclaiming membership of an elite.[51] Not part of an inherited elite, they felt it necessary to cannibalise a point of entry.[52] Along with the 'Cannibalist Manifesto', they would declare: 'I am only concerned with what is not mine.'[53]

Towards a Kin(d) Cannibalism

It would be neither a Eurocentric revenge cannibalism nor colonial posturing that would allow Mansfield to carve a route to her best work. Instead, this would be founded on an ethics of incorporation, a tender cannibalism where what is loved is ingested, a Freudian vision of the cannibal as one who 'only devours people of whom he is fond'.[54] This is alluded to in a diary entry of 1915, which records Mansfield's relish at witnessing Beatrice Campbell's daughter consume Murry's letter to her:

> I read and reread the letter until it was all crumpled. Bridget half ate it in her mouth. I loved her for that. She is the only person who has come anywhere near us just like that. I sat on the sofa & watched her little hands crunching the letter and felt she understood all about us and found us delicious![55]

Here cannibalism is equated with the gathering of knowledge; it is only through literal ingestion of the couple that true comprehension is enabled, as well as intimacy and solicitude. Mansfield's strongest fiction was facilitated through similar kindly cannibalism which would allow her to bring her dead brother to life as well as conjure with the country they grew up in. As Maggie Kilgour has observed: 'cannibalism can become an image for an intense and ambivalent hunger for liberation from a discrete individual identity through reabsorption into a greater corporate identity'.[56] When Mansfield reabsorbed herself into New Zealand, its expression would be polyphonic.

Lorna Sage has noted that 'Mansfield's fiction speaks about what is irretrievably lost, material, mortal'.[57] The prandial act (and cannibalism in particular) was such an acute metaphor for Mansfield because, while it involves creation and incorporation, it is also inextricable from death. As Korsmeyer postulates, there is 'death in the act of eating – both the destruction of that which is eaten and the impermanent pleasures that foreshadow the ultimate death of the diner'.[58] Mansfield's refusal to ignore death is what lends an uncomfortably bittersweet edge to her most accomplished fiction, and is what is notably absent from the brittle satire (or revenge cannibalism) of some of her early work, as evidenced by much of the collection *In A German Pension* and the protagonists of 'Sunday Lunch' who are not real enough either to eat or die.

It is appropriate then that a path to Mansfield's best work is heralded by a poem that mourns the death of her younger brother, and suggests a ritual of reunion through endocannibalism (eating one's kin). The piece, simply entitled 'To LHB (1894–1915)' ends with the lines:

> Where – where is the path of my dream for my eager feet?
> By the remembered stream my brother stands
> Waiting for me with berries in his hands . . .
> 'These are my body. Sister, take and eat.'[59]

Appropriating eucharistic imagery, Mansfield embraces a creative construction of cannibalism to forge a link between herself, her dead brother and New Zealand. When placed against the context of wider material from the journal, it is clear that the poem articulates Mansfield's desire to revivify her brother, through ingestion, to create a particular type of fiction, a 'kind of special prose'.[60] This commitment not only envisions a need to conjure with what is lost and mortal but also constructs a material base for Mansfield's fiction, one born of flesh ('You have me,' Mansfield wrote to her brother in her notebook, 'you're in my flesh as well as in my soul.').[61] It was perversely only through appropriation of a European version of cannibalism, the eucharist, that Mansfield found her route back to New Zealand, their 'undiscovered country', by way of a pledge: 'I want for one moment to make our undiscovered country leap into the eyes of the old world. It must be mysterious, as though floating.'[62] Through a holistic cannibalism that subsumed life, warts and all, Mansfield could show us that she 'knew how to transpose mystery and death with the help of a few grammatical forms'.[63] Stories such as 'Prelude' and 'At the Bay' portray a seductive tranquility that is persistently ruptured by the ornery inelegance of material life: ducks that refuse to die quietly and grandmas who will not promise to live forever. These stories rely on hybridity, heterogeneity and ambivalence, and do not seek to suppress it.

This transubstantiation simultaneously affected in Mansfield an invigorated commitment to the modern short story. At the same time she makes her pact to produce a 'kind of special prose', Mansfield resolves 'No novels, no problem stories, nothing that is not simple, open.'[64] In doing so, she rejects the lumbering tradition of the canon, false cleverness (or etiquette) and teleology, to embrace the short fiction mode to which she had previously harboured an internal resistance. Clare Hanson has observed that short fiction is

> a vehicle for different kinds of knowledge, knowledge which may be in some way at odds with the 'story' of dominant culture. The formal properties of the short story – disjunction, inconclusiveness, obliquity– connect with its ideological marginality and with the fact that the form may be used to express something suppressed/repressed in mainstream literature.[65]

Marginality is intrinsic to the short story form, and Mansfield's modernist abandonment of the traditional plot meant that, beyond the canonical boundary, its borders could become even more capacious and labile, able to pick up and encompass marginal subjects with plethoric range. It was the anthropophagist's choice. What Deleuze and Guattari would describe as 'deterritorialization' is implicit to the modernist short fiction that Mansfield developed; it manages persistently to evade dominant social codes in retaining plurality of voice (with its roaming, nomadic subjectivity) and subject (children, the countryside, animals, objects, all reverently brought 'into the light . . . put up higher').[66] Mansfield's short story was a stomach that could pick up what might be indigestible to other genres, and which participated in a type of engagement and incorporation that did not baulk at the unpalatable.

Mansfield described her aesthetic approach in writing 'The Stranger' in terms of a serial shape-shifting: 'Ive *been* this man *been* this woman. Ive stood for hours on the Auckland Wharf. Ive been [. . .] a hotel porter whistling through his teeth.'[67] She describes her technique in similar terms in a significant letter to Dorothy Brett of 1917: 'I just don't see how art is going to make that divine *spring* into the bounding outlines of things if it hasn't passed through the process of trying to *become* these things before recreating them.'[68] Mansfield would take this ethic to its logical limits, consuming her subjects to become them, finding her own voice through the speech of others. Patricia Moran observes that in 'Bliss' 'talking, eating, and writing collapse into one another [. . .] to eat is to be able to speak'.[69] It is Mansfield's insatiable human appetite that underpins her polyphonic eloquence.

Derrida spoke of the ability of the spirit to 'incorporate history by assimilating, by remembering its own past. This assimilation acts as a kind of sublimated eating – [the] spirit eats everything that is external and foreign, and thereby transforms it into something internal, something that is its own'.[70] Through cannibalism, Mansfield was able to combine the spiritual with the material not only to locate but to reproduce her own history, incorporating displacement without denying it. By revolutionising a form that facilitated this assimilation, Mansfield articulated a transnational modernism that diversified and destabilised the colonial canon. By putting herself so directly on the page, she would also make cannibals of us.

Notes
1. I would like to thank Dr Kate McLoughlin, my supervisor at Birkbeck, for her invaluable support and for introducing me to de Andrade's 'Cannibalist Manifesto'.
2. Katherine Murphy Dickson, *Katherine Mansfield's New Zealand Stories* (Lanham, New York, Oxford: University Press of America, 1998), p. vii.

3. Vincent O'Sullivan and Margaret Scott, eds, *The Collected Letters of Katherine Mansfield*, 5 vols (Oxford: Clarendon Press, 1984–2008), Vol. 1, p. 26. Hereafter referred to as *Letters*, followed by volume and page number.
4. Margaret Scott, ed., *The Katherine Mansfield Notebooks*, 2 vols (Minneapolis: University of Minnesota Press, 2002), Vol. 2, p. 31. Hereafter referred to as *Notebooks*, followed by volume and page number.
5. *Notebooks* 1, p. 140.
6. Gerri Kimber and Vincent O'Sullivan, eds, *The Collected Fiction of Katherine Mansfield*, 2 vols (Edinburgh: Edinburgh University Press, 2012), Vol. 1, p. 271. Hereafter referred to as *Fiction*, followed by volume and page number.
7. *Oxford English Dictionary*. See also Richard B. Moore, 'Carib "Cannibalism": A Study in Anthropological Stereotyping', *Caribbean Studies*, 13: 3 (Oct. 1973), pp. 117–35.
8. M. Alpers, J. A. Beck, T. Campbell, J. Collinge, E. M. Fisher, D. Goldstein, S. Mead, M. Poulter, M. P. Stumpf, J. B. Upfill, J. Whitfield, 'Balancing selection at the prion protein gene consistent with prehistoric kurulike epidemics', *Science*, 300 (April 2003), pp. 640–3. This study found a genetic signature present almost worldwide which would have protected people from infection by prions. In Papua New Guinea's Fore tribe, disease was linked with their practice of eating the brains of their dead.
9. *Notebooks* 1, p. 162.
10. Claire Tomalin, *Katherine Mansfield – A Secret Life* (London: Penguin, 1987), p. 6.
11. *Notebooks* 1, p. 275.
12. *Fiction* 2, p. 148.
13. *Fiction* 2, p. 124.
14. 'In the Botanical Gardens', *Notebooks* 1, p. 178.
15. Oswald de Andrade, trans. Leslie Bary, 'Cannibalist Manifesto', *Latin American Literary Review*, 19: 38 (July–December 1991), pp. 38–47. Hereafter referred to as 'Cannibalist Manifesto'.
16. From a letter to Vera Beauchamp, dated April–May 1908. *Letters* 1, p. 44.
17. Shakespeare also used cannibalism as a literary device, which facilitated the dénouement of *Titus Andronicus*, and referred to anthropophagy in plays such as *Othello*.
18. Kenneth David Jackson, 'A View on Brazilian Literature: Eating the "Revista de Antropofagia"', *Latin American Literary Review*, 7: 13 (Fall–Winter 1978), pp. 1–9.
19. Sigmund Freud, trans. James Strachey, *Totem and Taboo* (London: Routledge, 2001), p. 97.
20. *Letters* 1, p. 96.
21. The older Mansfield's diet would expand to include her modernist contemporaries and non-European writers such as Chekhov, all of which would feed into her literary development. In 1922, she would conclude of *Aaron's Rod*: 'All the time I read this book I felt it was feeding me.' Katherine Mansfield, *Novels and Novelists,* ed. John Middleton Murry (New York: Alfred A. Knopf, 1930), p. 321.
22. C. L. R. James, *Beyond a Boundary* (London: Random House, 2005), p. 87.
23. 'Cannibalist Manifesto'.
24. *Rhythm*, 1: 1 (Summer 1911), p. 36.
25. Robin Skelton, ed., *Poems*, Vol. 1 of J. M. Synge, *Collected Works*, 4 vols (Gerrards Cross: Colin Smythe, 1982), p. xxxvi.
26. *Rhythm*, 1: 1 (Summer 1911), p. 36.
27. 'Cannibalist Manifesto'.
28. *Letters* 1, p. 44.
29. *Rhythm*, 1:1 (Summer 1911), p. 36.

30. *Fiction* 1, p. 271.
31. *Rhythm*, 2: 9 (October 1912), p. 223.
32. *Rhythm*, 2: 9 (October 1912), p. 223.
33. *Rhythm*, 2: 9 (October 1912), p. 225.
34. *Rhythm*, 2: 9 (October 1912), p. 225.
35. *Rhythm*, 2: 9 (October 1912), p. 225.
36. See Jeffrey Meyers, *Katherine Mansfield: A Darker View* (New York: Cooper Square Press, 2002), p. 32. See also Paul Moon, *This Horrid Practice: The Myth and Reality of Traditional Maori Cannibalism* (Auckland: Penguin, 2008) and Gananath Obeyesekere, *Cannibal Talk: The Man-Eating Myth and Human Sacrifice in the South Seas* (Berkeley, Los Angeles, London: University of California Press, 2005).
37. Nathan Constantine, *A History of Cannibalism* (London: Arcturus), p. 8
38. Virginia Woolf, 'The Cinema', *Woolf Online:* www.woolfonline.com/?q=essays/cinema/full [accessed 27/10/2012].
39. Obeyesekere, p. 70.
40. Mansfield would have been aware of Swift's outrageous propaganda, which recommended the poor of Ireland counter famine by selling their babies to the rich as food, listing Swift as one of the writers she knew well when assessing her knowledge of English literature in her notebook (*Notebooks* 2, p. 31). There are parallels between 'A Modest Proposal' and Mansfield's 'Perambulations' (*Athenaeum*, April 1919), in which a female writer 'dreamed she took her darling to a publisher, and, having placed it upon the altar, she made obeisance and waited to hear if it should be found worthy in his sight for a sacrifice'. The editor determines that both the author and her style are too old: 'We've no use for anything in the creative line that's not brought to market in the green ear [. . .] The greener the ear, the sweeter the meat!' *Scrapbook*, pp. 117–18.
41. By 1920, Mansfield had realised that this type of disguised and monological attack was not in accordance with cannibalist ethics, advising Murry that 'To sign reviews, to put them in the 1st person stimulates curiosity, *makes for correspondence*, gives it (to be 19-eleventyish) GUTS.' *Letters* 4, p. 135.
42. For examples of cannibal bird masks, see 'The Cannibal Woman Society Masks': www.chaz.org/CWS/Masks/Cannibal_Society_Masks.html [accessed 27/10/12].
43. Jenny McDonnell, *Katherine Mansfield and the Modernist Marketplace: At the Mercy of the Public* (Basingstoke: Palgrave Macmillan, 2010), p. 74.
44. McDonnell, p. 70. Mansfield would write to Dorothy Brett in 1917, 'I threw my darling to the wolves.' *Letters* 1, p. 330.
45. *The Scrapbook of Katherine Mansfield*, ed. J.M. Murry (London: Constable, 1954), pp. 117–18.
46. *Letters* 1, pp. 103–7.
47. See John Carey, *The Intellectuals and the Masses* (London: Faber, 1992) and Raymond Williams, *Politics of Modernism: Against the New Conformists* (London: Verso, 2007).
48. *Rhythm*, 2: 5 (June 1912), pp. 18–20.
49. *Rhythm*, 2: 5 (June 1912), pp. 18–20.
50. Jane Stafford and Mark Williams, *Maoriland: New Zealand Literature 1872–1914* (Wellington: Victoria University Press, 2006), p. 163.
51. Meyers, p. 22 (quote from Edith Bendall).
52. T. S. Eliot (an alien like Mansfield, born American) also wrote and thought about English literature using ancestral terminology, see T. S. Eliot, *What Is A Classic?* (London: Faber, 1944), p. 14: 'In literature [. . .] the poet is aware of his predeces-

sors, and [. . .] we are aware of the predecessors behind his work, as we may be aware of ancestral traits in a person who is at the same time individual and unique [. . .] he preserves essential family characteristics, and [. . .] his difference in behaviour is a difference in the circumstances of another age.'

53. 'Cannibalist Manifesto'.
54. Sigmund Freud, trans. James Strachey, *Civilization, Society and Religion* (London: Penguin, 1991), p. 134.
55. *Notebooks* 2, pp. 7–8.
56. F. Barker, P. Hulme, M. Iversen, eds, *Cannibalism and the colonial world* (Cambridge: Cambridge University Press, 1998), p. 246.
57. Lorna Sage, *Moments of Truth – Twelve Twentieth Century Women Writers* (London: Fourth Estate, 2002), p. 81.
58. Carolyn Korsmeyer, *Making Sense of Taste – Food and Philosophy* (Ithaca and London: Cornell University Press, 2002), p. 188.
59. *Notebooks* 2, p. 29.
60. *Notebooks* 2, p. 33.
61. *Notebooks* 2, p. 16.
62. *Notebooks* 2, p. 32.
63. 'Cannibalist Manifesto'.
64. *Notebooks* 2, p. 33.
65. Clare Hanson, ed., *Re-Reading the Short Story* (London: Macmillan, 1989), p. 6.
66. Gilles Deleuze and Félix Guattari, *Anti-Oedipus* (1972); *Notebooks* 2, p. 267.
67. *Letters* 4, p. 97.
68. *Letters* 1, p. 330.
69. Patricia Moran, *Word of mouth: Body language in Katherine Mansfield and Virginia Woolf* (Charlottesville, London: University Press of Virginia, 1996), p. 59.
70. Daniel Birnbaum and Anders Olsson, 'An Interview with Jacques Derrida on the Limits of Digestion', e-flux:www.e-flux.com/journal/an-interview-with-jacques-derrida-on-the-limits-of-digestion/#_edn1 [accessed 27/10/2012].

Mansfield as (Post)colonial-Modernist: Rewriting the Contract with Death

Janet Wilson

Mansfield's (Post)colonial-Modernism

Mansfield's dualistic positioning, which crosses international modern-ism with (post)colonial critique, stems from her habitation of multiple, layered states of being, magnified by her various allegiances to, and estrangements from, her New Zealand white settler and English migrant identities. This pluralism enables her great New Zealand stories like 'At the Bay', 'The Garden Party', and 'The Dolls' House', as well as the last stories written from late 1921 to July 1922 (the date of her final story 'The Canary'), to be located within a (post)colonial-modernist framework. Mansfield represents various images of childhood from her bifurcated positioning through a world view dominated by death and mortality, and a consciousness that goes beyond the invocations of savagery and the spirit of the place in early stories and sketches of New Zealand: for exam-ple, 'Old Tar', in which hauntings by the dispossessed 'other' create atmospheric destabilisation and undermine the settler's ostensible own-ership of land; 'In the Botanical Gardens', where a hostile emanation in the native bush implies the sense of guilt at white settler intrusion; or in 'The Woman at the Store' where the savage spirit of the land roams unchecked at sundown.[1] The white settler point of view is undermined in an aesthetics of narrative fracture in these earlier stories – ellipses, omissions, paradox – whereby ghostly emanations from the past and phantasmagoric presences are constituent of the divided and ruptured condition of colonialism. In invoking such experiences of displacement in her later stories, however, Mansfield, possibly now haunted by the past of her earlier stories, recreates her own colonial childhood. She suggests a vision of possibility, now bounded and framed by mortality, formu-lating her understanding of colonial otherness through her study of family relations and the presence of the uncanny as a form of 'difference within'.[2] These stories in particular have been associated with her elusive form of nationalism, and her reputation as a 'ghostly presence' in the national literary consciousness, 'a phantasmic and sometimes troubling sign of displacement'.[3] Yet the more psychical underpinnings of the late stories, as she worked at the limits of consciousness, creating intuitive enlightenment and visionary perspectives unmediated by language, and piling up moments or glimpses through images and epiphany, also reaffirm her literary modernism.[4]

Mansfield's propensity for psychic experiences and paranormal perceptions is evident from her journals and letters, but there has been little research on the impact of these channels of communication especially in enabling her to access, with memory, her family and early life. Only towards the end of her life, when she needed to reconnect to her childhood and aimed to incorporate the shadowy, ubiquitous presence of death, did they apparently become a catalyst for composition. The greater spirituality of her later work appears in allusions to the Bible, Shakespeare and Chaucer, marking her search for something, a religion or belief system on which she could build a faith, as her options in life diminished, and construct a barrier to physical disintegration as experienced in the premonitory dream of her own death of December 1919.

> [. . .] I went to sleep. And suddenly I felt my whole body <u>breaking up</u> – it broke up with a violent shock – an earthquake, & it broke like glass. A long terrible shiver, you understand, & the spinal cord & the bones, and every bit & particle quaking. It sounded in my ears – a low, confused din, and there was a sense of flashing greenish brilliance, like broken glass. When I woke I thought there had been a violent earthquake. But all was still. It slowly dawned upon me –the conviction that in that dream I died.[5]

From 1919–20 when she was living in Menton, she was thinking through the relationship between the body and mind, searching for a way to cure her soul so that her writing might also be improved, thus preparing a spiritual path that would take her to Fontainebleau and Gurdjieff in October 1922.[6] In October 1920, for example, she wrote to Murry in ways which suggests that salvation, linked to a pantheistic force, borders on the mystical:

> Does your soul trouble you? Mine does. I feel that only now [. . .] I realise what salvation means and I long for it. Of course I am not speaking as a Christian or about a personal God. But the feeling is . . . I believe [. . .] Help thou my unbelief. But its to myself I cry – to the spirit, the essence in me – that which lives in Beauty. [. . .] And I long for goodness – to live by what is permanent in the soul.[7]

Increasingly incapacitated by her illness, she drew upon her emotional and psychic resources to access the past, inducing pre-sleep, hypnogogic visions and images by adopting a semi-conscious state:

> It often happens to me now that when I lie down for sleep [. . .] I feel wakeful and lying here in bed I begin to <u>live</u> over little scenes from life or imaginary scenes. Its not too much to say they are almost hallucinations: they are marvellously vivid. I lie on my right side & put my left hand up to my forehead as though I were praying. This seems to <u>induce</u> the state. Then for instance its 10.30 p.m. on a liner in mid ocean . . . [. . .] All these things are far realer, more in detail, <u>richer</u> than Life. And I believe I could go on until . . . there's <u>no end</u> to it. I can do this about anything.[8]

These static, silent scenes whose pictorial detail resembles snapshot images, in presenting in outline a more vivid world than real life, can be compared to Mansfield's response to nature's mystical power as 'glimpses' of a timeless moment in which 'the whole life of the soul is contained'. Her comment on these semi-hallucinatory states, 'Only there are no personalities. Neither am I there personally. People are only part of the silence, not of the <u>pattern</u> – vastly different to that – part of the <u>scheme</u>', suggests that they brought her close to the condition of impersonality. Described as 'that moment of direct feeling when we are most ourselves and least personal',[9] this state was one she increasingly sought in her last years, finally entering Gurdjieff's Institute for the Harmonious Development of Man in the hope of achieving an organic unity and 'harmony of mind and spirit'.[10] It is comparable to, but different from, Virginia Woolf's moments of being and the images of self-dissolution in her work which include liberation from the limits of personal identity and immersion in the 'unfeeling universe'.[11]

Mansfield, Leslie Heron Beauchamp and the 'contract with death'

The telepathic gift to conjure up past events and people through entering trance-like states can be traced to what is commonly agreed to be the turning point of Mansfield's art, the tragic death of her brother, Leslie Heron Beauchamp, in a hand-grenade accident in Flanders in October 1915.[12] Her intense grief, leading to her vow to commemorate his life by discovering a new prose for the purposes of elegy, included the desire to join him in death through writing, and so transcend the boundaries between death and life. This crucial intersection between art, life and death would dominate her future.[13] In her diary entry of 29 October 1915, her fluid osmotic identification develops into a desire for reunification through death: 'I welcome the idea of death. I believe in immortality because he is not here, and I long to join him.' This is mediated by writing: 'I know you are there and I live with you – and I will write for you'; while in the poem 'To LHB', her ghostly brother's invitation to her to join him in death is imaginatively formulated through the poisoned berries he offers her, in an inversion of the Eucharist:

> By the remembered stream my brother stands
> Waiting for me with berries in his hands
> 'These are my body. Sister, take and eat.'[14]

From now on, Mansfield's earlier feelings of intimacy with Leslie intensified, for as Freud writing on melancholia says, the lost object which cannot be relinquished returns as an aspect of oneself, the ghost of the loved becomes inseparable from the self, part of one's interior being.[15] In her diaries, she mythologises the close relationship she had with Leslie as that of a twinned consciousness: 'we were almost like one child. I always see us walking about together, looking at things together with the same eyes'.[16] This intense, even dangerous intimacy, to the point of being unable to disassociate from each other, is the source of imagery of doubling and mirroring between male and female siblings in stories like 'When the Wind Blows', 'Son and Moon' and 'His Sister's Keeper'. Such symbiosis is most pointedly articulated at the conclusion of 'The Garden Party' in Laura's brother Laurie's echo of her words, after she has seen death for the first time in viewing the young carter laid out on the bed, seemingly asleep:

> 'But, Laurie' – She stopped . . . 'Isn't life,' she stammered, 'isn't life –' But what life was she couldn't explain. No matter. He quite understood.
> '*Isn't* it, darling?' said Laurie.[17]

Her meetings with her brother when he was in London in early 1915 (at a time when Mansfield was estranged from some family members), and their reminiscences about the past, reinforcing the feeling of oneness as children united against their parents, meant that Leslie became transformed into a symbolic touchstone, or 'ghostly mentor' after his death.[18] Their shared memories inspired her to compose the first draft of her seminal 'family romance', 'The Aloe', in March 1915, while Leslie's birth and childhood as the much longed-for and only son, are celebrated in 'Prelude' (a revision of 'The Aloe'), and in the later story 'At the Bay'.[19]

Leslie's symbolic importance is manifested not just in Mansfield's outpouring of grief after his death, the yearning for reunion and the resolve to commemorate his life in writing, but in his haunting of Mansfield, through ghost-like reappearances. Leslie replaces John

Middleton Murry in her affections as she records his spiritual supercession and the need for continued intimacy: 'You know I can never be Jack's lover again, You have me, you're in my flesh as well as my soul. I give Jack my "surplus" love but to you I hold and to you I give my deepest love.'[20] The uncanny apparition of Leslie displaces Mansfield's husband in the marital bed: 'I wanted J. [John] to embrace me. But as I turned [. . .] to kiss him I saw my brother lying fast asleep – and I got cold. That happens nearly always'.[21] In this 'phantasmatic space'[22] of half-waking, half-sleeping, rendering the self permeable and suggestible to body transmission, the ghost of the prone Leslie lying next to her is both consolation for loss and a silent reminder of her vow: 'I feel I have a duty to perform to the lovely time when we were both alive.'[23] Although these hallucinatory states are seemingly triggered by Mansfield's craving for reunion, they are represented as Leslie's yearnings for her. In the slippage between self and other, waking and sleeping, sexual desire and spiritual awakening, the real moment and desiring imagination, it is the neglect of writing that mobilises his spectral presence: 'When I am not writing I feel my brother calling me & he is not happy. Only when I write or am in a state of writing – a state of "inspiration" – do I feel that he is calm.'[24] Mansfield overturned the boundaries of physical death through these imagined reunions from the time she wrote herself into Leslie's death by including her name in his final words, 'Lift my head, Katy, I can't breathe', anticipating the relationship's transition into the sacred and paranormal.[25] The search for integration and catharsis, as well as the act of writing, distinguishes the haunting, uncanny elements of her work from the Gothic, which seeks to obscure rather than to penetrate to the essence of things as she came to want to do.

The manifestations of the ghostly, spiritual, and spectral in Mansfield's late stories underpin her aim to be inclusive in her writing: '"One must tell everything – everything". That is more and more real to me each day. It is after all [. . .] – our little grain of truth.'[26] Her spiritual connection to the past included the hidden reality signified by the occult which is, as Alex Owen points out, the occluded spiritual realm that can only be accessed by the psychic or medium.[27] Mansfield identified such a realm with the undiscovered country of her New Zealand childhood in imagery of mist and (un)veiling, as when she notes: 'I tried to lift that mist from my people, and let them be seen and then to hide them again.'[28] In 'At the Bay', as Angela Smith notes, the mist 'symboliz[ing] the processes of the human mind at work' may be a narrative method comparable to Woolf's use of mist to veil then reveal a person or consciousness in *Mrs Dalloway*.[29] As tuberculosis ravaged her body and depleted her physical strength after 1917, seemingly fulfilling the prophecy of the poem 'To

LHB', Mansfield turned to scenes of family life from a remembered world that she reconnected with through psychic means. This 'spectral condition' is associated with self effacement, a state of impersonality through being possessed by the dead, envisaged as though alive, and it entails the collapse of distinctions between active and passive subject positions, subject and object, witnessing and writing.[30] She comments in a letter to Dorothy Brett about writing 'At the Bay':

> It is so strange to bring the dead to life again. Theres my grandmother with her pink knitting, there stalks my uncle over the grass. I feel as I write 'you are not dead, my darlings. All is remembered. I bow down to you. I efface myself so that you may live again through me in your richness and beauty.' And one feels *possessed*.[31]

The subtle interplay between the ghostly and supernatural in bringing the family back to life in her art distinguishes Mansfield's work from the alienating spectrality of the Gothic. She personalises death as friendly and intimate, making her family live again for her just as she wishes to continue to live again in and through her art.

Mansfield and Occult Practices of the Early Twentieth Century

There is no evidence that Mansfield saw herself as a clairvoyant or a medium or in any way associated with the heightened occult practices of late Victorian and Edwardian England. Yet her attitude towards the mystical seems to vary according to whom she was close to at the time. William Orton, in his autobiographical account of his relationship with Mansfield in 1910–11, referring to what they called 'the Buddha room', stresses that 'to Catherine [. . .] the problem of achieving a firm spiritual peace, in the midst of a life that insisted on being vivid and restless, was becoming urgent'.[32] But writing in *Rhythm* in 1912, only a year later, she suggests that belief in the supernatural and mystical is inimical to true art:

> Mysticism is perverted sensuality; it is 'passionate admiration' for that which has no reality at all. It leads to the annihilation of any true artistic effort. It is a paraphernalia of clichés. It is a mask through which the true expression of the poet can never be discerned.[33]

This attitude probably reflects Murry's influence on her thinking then, for his abhorrence of the occult was well known; it was a point of contention between them that caused them to separate in June 1922. In Murry's words: 'Her mind was now moving fast towards the expectation of the other miracle – the attainment of such psychic control as would enable her to ignore her bodily condition. Into this realm I could not enter at all.'[34] By 1921 Mansfield was manifesting a more pronounced interest in otherworldly phenomena and Eastern or occult systems of thought, as evidenced in her reading of the arcane text, *Cosmic Anatomy and the Structure of the Ego*, sent to Murry by A. R. Orage in autumn of that year, Arthur Waley's translations of poems from the Chinese, and then in 1922, through the introduction of Orage, who had been a theosophist, the theories of Gurdjieff and Ouspensky. In this last year of her life, her spiritualist leanings were directed not just to communication with the deceased Leslie, as if through a medium, but to her search for a cure for her illness in the belief that its cause was non-physical, 'But something else & and that if this were found and cured all the rest would heal.'[35]

Nevertheless Mansfield's capacity to communicate telepathically with family members in her art is analogous to the practice of calling up the dead that had a following in Victorian England and became more pronounced after World War One when bereaved parents attempted to get in touch with their dead sons. Recent research on telepathy, spiritualism, the supernatural, and other cultural practices of late Victorian and early twentieth-century England delineate the range of practices and the corresponding aspirations.[36] Women predominated in functioning as both spiritual and hypnotic channels in developing the new forms of interpersonal connection, according to Jill Galvan, due to their perceived 'sensitivity or sympathy, often imagined as the product of women's delicate nervous systems; and an easy reversion to automatism or a state of unconsciousness'.[37] Mansfield's highly nervous, febrile state, heightened by her illness, gave her an increased capacity to enter trance-like states. She comments, 'its only since I was really ill that this shall we call it "consolation prize" has been given me. My God, its a marvellous thing!'[38] In particular her evidence of nocturnal visitations by ghost-like apparitions of Leslie suggests that hers was a spectral personality, predisposed towards the supernatural, in keeping with Shane McCorristine's modern conception of the ghost as reflecting the haunted nature of the self. Ghosts, phantasms and spirits, for her were not just objective phenomena, but suggest, in the words of McCorristine, that she was 'haunted by death, the past, a fixed idea, hard wired to apparitions of the dead'.[39] Such a categorisation implies that the world of Mansfield's experience, the 'everything' that she wished to tell of, existed both in material and immaterial or ghostly forms. In this sense, then, of moving between different realms as a medium or conductor, she is comparable to the occultists whose practice was to make connections with the spirits of the dead in order to offer comfort and reassurances for the bereaved.

At the same time, Mansfield's spirituality suggests that, as with spiritual mediums and the practice of seances, the permeability of these realms reflected a tightening of the grasp between them, a refusal to let go of the dead and a belief that 'there is no death'.[40]

Certainly her intense belief in the subliminal self and her capacity to recall the dead in lifelike detail, as appears in these and other passages of her non-fictional writings, can be compared to the hope of those who belonged to The Society of Psychical Research (founded in 1882), with its focus on the spiritual, mesmerism and the paranormal, that a spiritual plane of human existence was discoverable.[41] That these 'recovered' memories reappear in the stories, animating the characters, furthermore suggests a practice not far removed from automatic writing, as inaugurated by a subliminal self that is potentially separate from the body. 'At the Bay' introduces Mansfield's recovered memories as recorded in her letter to Dorothy Brett: 'Theres my grandmother with her pink knitting, there stalks my uncle over the grass.'[42] Kezia's grandmother, Mrs Fairfield, 'sat in a rocker at the window, with a long piece of pink knitting in her lap'; while in the encounter between Kezia's uncle, Jonathan Trout and his sister-in-law, Kezia's mother Linda Burnell in the garden, the memories are transposed; Linda 'stalks over the grass' viewed by 'my uncle': 'He had meant to be there before, but in the front garden he had come upon Linda walking up and down the grass.'[43]

The Family: 'At the Bay' and 'Six Years After'

Clare Hanson points out that home for Mansfield was *unheimlich* from the beginning, due to her doubled identity structures, caught between the imperial centre and the colonial periphery, and that her colonial background was a copy without an original.[44] Such ambivalences about self and place help determine the ghostly quality of her nationalism; they are reinforced by her construction of the colonial space of childhood through a nexus of personal interactions, and the obliteration of any sense of temporal sequentiality.[45] The occult and spiritual forces by which Mansfield, like other mediums in the early twentieth century, was able to locate life alongside death, and that insisted on 'the commensurability between disparate people and things',[46] can be linked to a spatio-temporal model which critic Laura Doyle describes as the geomodernism of Mansfield's modernist contemporaries. For example, Virginia Woolf, notably in *Mrs Dalloway*, introduces disparate world views from 'over there' in 'continual horizon reversals', that project a 'strange global circuitry', so presenting 'under the pressure of this post/colonial

world, discrepant subjectivities' and contradictory and conflicting cultural perceptions, as the white characters 'absorb the violence of imperialism'.[47] Similar disjunctures dominate *A Passage to India*, culminating
in the experience in the Malabar caves. Mansfield's New Zealand stories
anchor character and event to a local domain rather than introducing
explicit horizon reversals that the more expansive novel form made
possible, yet the apparently safe domestic realm is threatened by the
sudden irruption of the unfamiliar and uncanny. Her stories register
disturbances within the white settler class which undermine its occupation of space and are suggestive of the pressure of colonialism and
its disruptive legacy: for example, awareness of the proximity of wild,
irrational forces to the ordered, civilised world, underpins the violence
of the duck's beheading in 'Prelude'.

Like Mansfield herself, her characters are prone to sudden visitations as the uncanny appears in the midst of the everyday, a tangible
reminder of Homi Bhabha's point that the colonial presence is 'always
ambivalent', and 'partial'.[48] Beryl, in 'At the Bay', for example, is one of
Mansfield's divided and disrupted characters who, like Raoul Duquette
in 'Je ne parle pas français', evade the present moment and construct
a false self.[49] Tropes of hauntology and the uncanny appear in Beryl's
interweaving of fantasy with reality as lovers materialise in her room,
and she reprises the very compliment – 'what a little beauty you are!' –
that the odious Mrs Harry Kember had paid her earlier. 'But, in spite
of herself, Beryl saw so plainly two people standing in the middle of
her room. Her arms were around his neck; he held her. And now he
whispered, "My beauty, my little beauty".'[50] As Nicholas Royle states,
the uncanny conveys 'a sense of ghostliness, of strangeness, given to
dissolving all assurances about the identity of a self'; its performative
dimension appears in Beryl's self-appellation, a calling into selfhood, as
she names herself to the imagined other:[51]

> [. . .] it's as though, in the silence, somebody called your name, and you
> heard your name for the first time. 'Beryl!'
> 'Yes, I'm here. I'm Beryl. Who wants me?'
> 'Beryl!'
> 'Let me come.'[52]

The blurring of boundaries between inner and outer worlds and the
apparent inseparability between the inner voice that calls out, and the
juxtaposed response to that call, registers the structure of the uncanny
where identity is haunted from within.[53] Beryl's real-life suitor appears
like a ghostly shadow as if summoned up from the dead: enigmatic, manifested only as a voice, then tantalisingly within reach, he is a nameless

apparition and so all the more sinister and threatening: '"Good evening, Miss Beryl," said the voice softly.'[54]

Mansfield's most overtly haunted story, 'Six Years After', composed in early November 1921, six years after Leslie's death, imagines her parents' reaction to their loss.[55] But through the question – 'Can one do nothing for the dead?'[56] – Mansfield also projects the sense of widespread suffering at needless death in the years after the Great War, the contemporary concern about the souls of the dead, evident, for example, in the advertising of lectures intended to instruct on how to make contact with the departed that Freud noted.[57] The story stresses how the needs of the dead continue to intrude upon and interrupt the lives of the living. Its apparently normal opening, introducing a couple travelling on a steamer, is destabilised to reflect the mother's grief and intense identification with her son. Relationships are skewed, as Mansfield herself experienced when the phantom Leslie returned to haunt her. Cognitive mistakes occur as in the wife's address to her husband as 'Father' or 'Daddy' (reminiscent of Mansfield's address to her brother in her journals as though either a lover or a child), suggesting the presence of the ghost-like child who appropriates and ventriloquises the mother's voice.[58] As the ferry throbs along, the wife 'gazed through the rust-spotted railing along which big drops trembled, until suddenly she shut her lids. It was as if a warning voice inside her had said, 'Don't look!' The appearance of the irrational disturbs and distorts natural phenomena, 'Lonely birds, water lifting, white pale sky – how were they changed?' Her reverie turns into a hallucination that he is calling to her, creating a phantasmatic space, similar to what Mansfield herself experienced in her paranormal reunions with Leslie:

> And it seemed to her there was a presence far out there, between the sky and the water; something very desolate and longing watched them pass and cried as if to stop them – but cried to her alone.
> 'Mother!'
> 'Don't leave me,' sounded in the cry. 'Don't forget me! You are forgetting me, you know you are!' And it was as though from her own breast there came the sound of childish weeping.[59]

The dead's haunting of the living appears through the symbiotic mother-child relationship – his apparent weeping at being lost coming from her own breast at losing him. The story's setting on a steamer that crosses over from one place to another, symbolically from life to death, reinforces the hallucinatory, dreamlike state and the transitions between different time frames that suggest their permeability. The conclusion reprises an earlier sentence – 'And the little steamer pressed on' – which occurs before the mother's hallucinatory vision of her dead son, and anthropomorphises the steamer, an animistic trope that is also associated with the uncanny and the spectral: 'And the little steamer, growing determined, throbbed on, pressed on, as if at the end of the journey there waited . . .'[60] The ellipses which break off the throbbing, suggestive of a heart beat, hint at a darker ending, the encroachment of death.[61]

Antony Alpers notes that all but three of Mansfield's last stories share the subject of death or bereavement;[62] but it would seem that her encounter with the dead as living figments is inseparable from her desire to reimagine the family circle which has been broken by death, separation, distance – of reassembling it in a new configuration. Just as haunting and haunted as 'Six Years After' is 'The Dolls' House'. According to Mary Burgan, 'our Else' wearing 'a long white dress, rather like a nightgown', whose 'cropped hair and enormous solemn eyes' made her look like 'a little white owl',[63] is a spectral figure of Mansfield's baby sister, Gwen, who died when only three months old and Mansfield was less than two years; her guilt at not being able to share the dolls' house with her sister makes this story an act of symbolic restitution, Burgan claims, a completion in art when 'our Else' sees the little lamp, of what real life had denied.[64] A similar need to complete the family circle by recalling the members who have been lost or excluded by death, is the symbolic 'rebirthing' of Leslie through writing, of making recompense to the dead, in the fragments called 'The New Baby'.[65] These reprise the hints of Leslie's birth at the end of 'The Aloe' and 'Prelude', and of Linda's encounter with the new baby in 'At the Bay'. Four versions of this fragment exist, consisting of different parents (one of the mother and grandmother and three of the father) so comprising a full picture of the adults' response. Like the ellipses which signal the conclusion of stories deemed formally incomplete – 'Six Years After' and the missing sections of another late story written in September 1921, 'Weak Heart' – these ghostly textual fragments, which survive Mansfield's destruction of much else that was fragmentary, suggest the desire to construct a larger picture of a revitalised sense of family and of future possibility.

Conclusion: Mansfield's Haunted Imagination

Mansfield's attraction towards the ghostly and spectral to access an occluded realm and for creative renewal, can be deduced from comments in her critical writing such as that 'childhood must have a haunting light upon it if it is to satisfy our longing as well as our memory'.[66] In her last months the process of dying became imbued with the desire for self-reform, spiritual repair, and the shedding of false selves; as James Moore writes, 'Katherine bent her will to the ideal of spiritual regeneration.'[67] Her dissatisfaction with her old stories, according to Orage's report of conversations they had at Fontainebleau, was because 'The old details now make another pattern; and this perception of a new pattern is what I call a creative attitude to life.'[68] This comment can be read alongside Mansfield's account of her psychic recall of past events in her journal entry of December 1919, where the term 'pattern' refers to art, and the term 'scheme' to life: 'People are only part of the silence, not of the pattern – vastly different to that – part of the scheme.'[69] Yet 'a series of patterns' made by the grandmother in 'Prelude', also resonate with homeliness, defining a place where one can reside.[70] Her mediumship provides access to phantom-like, silent characters in order to animate them, and the silent world becomes a source of joy, as she wrote to Murry: 'What is this something that waits – that beckons?'[71] During her time at Fontainebleau (when she rejects her earlier satires as malicious and a little deceiving), she implies that this shaping process requires a particular attitude and that artistic merit should be linked to moral value:

> The artist communicates not his vision of the world, but the attitude that results in his vision; not his dream, but the dream state; and as his attitude is passive, negative, or indifferent, so he reinforces in his readers the corresponding state of mind.[72]

Mansfield's use of modern modes of communication, such as telepathy, mediumship or automatism, as well as other space-and time-collapsing technologies of the early twentieth century like the camera and the telegraph, which obliterated temporal linearity in reconstructing the past, is an overlooked dimension of her literary modernism. It has never been linked to her problematic status as a colonial writer in Europe, which as Alpers points out made her insecure because she did not know her audience.[73] Yet her command of these communicative conduits enabled her to reconnect with her imagined colonial audience from her doubled outsider/insider position, extend her project of family reconnection and overcome the twin abysses of distance and death. Significantly the female characters of the late stories – the mother in 'Six Years After', the heroine of another late story, 'Taking the Veil' – are also granted spectral glimpses of the invisible world of the beyond that interrupt and overlap with their material, mundane world, through fleeting phantasmagoric appearances or perceptions which are only partially discerned or apprehended. Mansfield's telepathic reconnections to family members and to her childhood self, as she imaginatively re-emplaces herself in her homeland through a network of domestic links, allow her to shape (post)colonial space as disturbed and newly disordered. In the sense that her writing is 'time frozen' (by contrast to the animation of space), it is comparable to that of contemporary diasporic writers who can only access their homeland through limited points and references to particular moments in time: as in the case of Indian born, Canadian-based writer Rohinton Mistry who, in novels like *Family Matters* and *A Fine Balance*, recreates Mumbai society and its history from a distance.[74] But the difference is that Mansfield's late stories, written when a physical return to New Zealand was impossible, access a world of doubled forms, ghostly appearances and phantom-like spirits, as responses of the haunted imagination to the urgent need to overcome distance and loss and to outmanoeuvre impending death, by repossessing and recreating the vanished world of childhood, and arresting and redefining her life in new forms of her art.

Notes

The phrase 'Rewriting the contract with death' is Roger Luckhurst's. See Shane McCorristine, '"Magical Thinking": a Symposium', University of London, 11–12 May 2007, *Journal of Religion and Popular Culture*, 17 (Fall 2007); http://www.usask.ca/re/lst/jrpc/report17 magicalthinking-print.html (accessed 14/08/12).

1. Janet Wilson, '"Where is Katherine?": Longing and (Un)belonging in the Works of Katherine Mansfield', in Gerri Kimber and Janet Wilson, eds, *Celebrating Katherine Mansfield: A Centenary Volume of Essays* (London: Palgrave, 2010), pp. 175–88.
2. The term comes from Homi Bhabha, *The Location of Culture* (London: Routledge, 1994), pp. 109–10, and cited by Elleke Boehmer in her essay 'Mansfield as Colonial Modernist: Difference Within', in Kimber and Wilson, eds, pp. 57–71 (p. 58).
3. See C. K. Stead, 'Meetings with "the Great Ghost"', in Kimber and Wilson, eds, pp. 214–28; Linda Hardy 'The Ghost of Katherine Mansfield', in Rhoda B. Nathan, ed., *Critical Essays on Katherine Mansfield* (New York and Toronto: G.K. Hall & Co and Maxwell Macmillan Canada, 1993), pp. 75–92 (p. 78).
4. Roger Luckhurst, *The Invention of Telepathy 1870–1901* (Oxford: Oxford University Press, 2002), p. 62.
5. Margaret Scott, ed., *The Katherine Mansfield Notebooks*, 2 vols (Minneapolis: University of Minnesota Press, 2002), Vol. 2, p. 180. Hereafter referred to as *Notebooks* followed by volume and page number.
6. Antony Alpers, *The Life of Katherine Mansfield* (New York: Viking Press, 1980), pp. 311–12, records how she contemplated Catholicism after her cousin, Connie Beauchamp, and her friend, with whom she stayed in Menton, tried to convert her.
7. Vincent O'Sullivan and Margaret Scott, eds, *The Collected Letters of Katherine Mansfield*, 5 vols (Oxford: Clarendon Press, 1984–2008), Vol. 4, pp. 82–3. Hereafter referred to as *Letters*, followed by volume and page number. This passage is cited by Maurizio Ascari, 'Katherine Mansfield and the Gardens of the Soul', *Katherine Mansfield Studies*, 2 (2010), pp. 39–55 (pp. 52, 55) (n. 65) with reference to 'In the Botanical Gardens'.
8. *Notebooks* 2, p. 181.
9. *Notebooks* 2, pp. 181, 204.
10. Angela Smith, *Katherine Mansfield: A Literary Life* (London: Palgrave, 2000), p. 142.

11. Makiko Minow-Pinkney, *Virginia Woolf and the Problem of the Subject: Feminine Writing in the Major Novels* (Edinburgh: Edinburgh University Press, [1987] 2010), p. 185.

12. See, for example, Ian Gordon, ed., *Undiscovered Country: The New Zealand Stories of Katherine Mansfield* (London: Longman, 1974), 'Introduction', p. xv.

13. On this crisis see the essays by Gasston and Aretoulakis in this volume.

14. *Notebooks* 2, pp. 15, 16, 29.

15. Freud 'Mourning and Melancholia', trans. J. Strachey, Pelican Freud Library 14 (Harmondsworth: Penguin), pp. 237–58. Cited by Nicola Bown, Carolyn Burdett and Pamela Thurschwell, eds, *The Victorian Supernatural* (Cambridge: Cambridge University Press, 2004), pp. 10–11.

16. *Notebooks* 2, p. 15.

17. *The Edinburgh Edition of the Collected Works of Katherine Mansfield*, Gerri Kimber and Vincent O'Sullivan, eds, 2 vols (Edinburgh: Edinburgh University Press, 2012), Vol. 2, *The Collection Fiction of Katherine Mansfield 1916–1922*, p. 413. Hereafter referred to as *Collected Fiction* 2. See Emmanouil Aretoulakis's reading of this story in his essay in this volume pp. 45–62.

18. Andrew Gurr, *Writers in Exile: The Literary Identity of Home in Modern Literature* (Brighton, Sussex: Harvester Press, 1981), p. 46.

19. On Mansfield's relationship with Leslie and her responses to his death see Mary Burgan, *Illness, Gender and Writing: The Case of Katherine Mansfield* (Baltimore and London: The Johns Hopkins University Press, 1994), pp. 101–5.

20. *Notebooks* 2, p. 16.

21. *Notebooks* 2, p. 58.

22. Pamela Thurschwell, *Literature, Technology and Magical Thinking: 1880–1920* (Cambridge: Cambridge University Press, 2001), p. 2. Mansfield illustrates her claim that such spaces of bodily transmission 'redefine intimate, sexual, familial, national ties between people against the usual patriarchal models of inheritance and community via marriage and the nuclear family', in 'Six Years After'.

23. *Notebooks* 2, p. 16.

24. *Notebooks* 2, p. 58.

25. See J. Lawrence Mitchell, 'Katie and Chummie: Death in the Family', in Kimber and Wilson, eds, pp. 28–41 (pp. 35–6).

26. *Letters* 4, p. 57.

27. Alex Owen, *The Place of Enchantment: British Occultism and the Culture of the Modern* (Chicago: University of Chicago Press, 2004), p. 19.

28. *Letters* 1, p. 174.

29. Angela Smith, *Katherine Mansfield & Virginia Woolf: A Public of Two* (Oxford: Clarendon Press, 1999), p. 167.

30. H. D.'s theory of impersonality, consisting of 'dialectical tensions that continuously dissolve and subsequently reinscribe categories of identity such as gender', is comparable to the transitions in these moments of recall; see Rochelle Rives, *Modernist Impersonalities, Affect, Authority and the Subject* (London: Palgrave, 2012), pp. 17, 53. See also F. W. H. Myers, *Human Personality and its Survival of Bodily Death* (Charlottesville, VA: Hampton Roads, 2001), p. 47.

31. *Letters* 4, p. 278. This seems to have been an ongoing preoccupation; see the journal entry of April 1915: 'You cannot think what pleasure my invisible, imaginary companion gave me. [. . .] but – it's a game I like to play – to walk and to talk with the dead who smile and are silent – and <u>free</u> quite finally free' (*Notebooks* 2, p. 13).

32. William Orton, *The Last Romantic* (London: Cassell, 1937), p. 277.

33. Mansfield, Review of Victor B. Neuberg's *The Triumph of Pan* (Thomas Burleigh, 155 Victoria St., S.W.), in *Rhythm*, 6 (July 1912), p. 70.

34. Alpers, p. 362. In Alma de Groen's play about Mansfield's final days in Fontainebleau, the differences of opinion over her belief in the occult bring about her separation from Murry. See *The Rivers of China* (Paddington: Currency Press, Pty Ltd, 1988), Act 1, Sc. 3, p. 9. I should like to thank Dr Anna Smith for this reference and for her comments and suggestions made on a draft of this essay.

35. 20 January 1922, *Notebooks* 2, p. 319.

36. See, for example, Luckhurst, *The Invention of Telepathy 1870–1901*; Nicola Bown, Carolyn Burdett, and Pamela Thurschwell, eds, *The Victorian Supernatural*; Tatiana Kontou and Sarah Willburn, eds, *The Ashgate Research Companion to Spiritualism and the Occult* (London: Ashgate, 2012); Nicholas Royle, *Telepathy and Literature* : *Essays on the Reading Mind* (Oxford: Basil Blackwell, 1991); Tatiana Kontou, *Spiritualism and Women's Writing from the Fin de Siècle to the Neo-Victorian* (London: Palgrave, 2009).

37. Jill Galvan, *The Sympathetic Medium: Feminine Channelling, the Occult, and Communication Technologies, 1859–1919* (Ithaca and London: Cornell University Press, 2010), p. 12. She adds, 'Women were exemplary go-betweens because they combined the right kind of presence with the right kind of absence.'

38. *Notebooks* 2, p. 181.

39. Shane McCorristine, *Spectres of the Self: Thinking about Ghosts and Ghost-Seeing in England 1750–1920* (Cambridge: Cambridge University Press, 2010), p. 19.

40. Tatiana Kontou and Sarah Wilburn, 'Introduction', in Kontou and Willburn, eds, p. 4.

41. Galvan, *The Sympathetic Medium*, p. 4.

42. *Letters* 4, p. 278.

43. *Collected Fiction*, pp. 357, 364.

44. Clare Hanson, 'Katherine Mansfield's Uncanniness', in Kimber and Wilson, eds, pp. 115–30 (p. 119).

45. Doreen Massey, *For Space* (London: Sage, 2005), p. 9.

46. Kontou and Wilburn, 'Introduction', in Kontou and Willburn, eds, p. 1.

47. Laura Doyle, 'Geomodernism, postcoloniality and women's writing', in Maren Tova Linett, ed., *The Cambridge Companion to Modernist Women Writers* (Cambridge: Cambridge University Press, 2010), pp. 129–45 (pp. 139–40).

48. *The Location of Culture* (London: Routledge, 1994), pp. 107, 86.

49. Sarah Sandley, 'The Middle of the Note: Katherine Mansfield's "Glimpses"', in Roger Robinson, ed., *Katherine Mansfield: In From the Margin* (Baton Rouge and London: Louisanna State University Press, 1994), p. 85.

50. *Collected Fiction* 2, p. 368.

51. Nicholas Royle, *The Uncanny* (Manchester: Manchester University Press, 2003), p. 16.

52. *Collected Fiction* 2, p. 369.

53. Julian Wolfreys, *Victorian Hauntings: Spectrality, Gothic, the Uncanny and Literature* (London: Palgrave, 2002), p. 124.

54. *Collected Fiction* 2, p. 370.

55. This is close to what Claire Drewery calls an 'uncanny story', about the haunting of a psyche; see her *Modernist Short Fiction by Women; The Liminal in Katherine Mansfield, Dorothy Richardson, May Sinclair and Virginia Woolf* (London: Ashgate, 2011), pp. 68–9.

56. *Collected Fiction* 2, p. 424.

57. See Clare Hanson, 'Katherine Mansfield's Uncanniness', p. 116, citing S. Freud's *The Uncanny*, trans. D. McLintock (London: Penguin, 2003 [1919]), pp. 148–9.

58. *Collected Fiction* 2, pp. 421, 424.
59. *Collected Fiction* 2, p. 423.
60. *Collected Fiction* 2, pp. 423, 424.
61. Antony Alpers in his edition of *The Stories of Katherine Mansfield* (Oxford: Oxford University Press, 1974), p. 574, notes that this is a posthumous fragment, or an abandoned story, but the ellipses may be a substitute ending.
62. 'Preface' to *The Stories of Katherine Mansfield*, p. xxvii.
63. *Collected Fiction* 2, p. 417.
64. Burgan, pp. 18–20.
65. Burgan, pp. 101, 104, comments that Mansfield's project of recapturing the past included re-establishing Leslie's 'rebirthing', i.e. his right to be reborn.
66. Katherine Mansfield, *Novels and Novelists, 1888–1923,* ed. John Middleton Murry (London: Constable, 1930), p. 288. Review of *Adam of Dublin*, by Conal O'Riordan.
67. James Moore, *Gurdjieff and Mansfield* (London: Routledge, 1980), p. 140.
68. A. R. Orage, 'Talks with Katherine Mansfield', *The New English Weekly*, 19 May 1932, p. 111; compare her comments after Leslie's death: 'Only the form that I would choose has changed utterly, I feel no longer concerned with the same appearance of things. The people who lived or who I wish to bring into my stories don't interest me any more. The plots of my stories leave me perfectly cold' (*Notebooks* 2, p. 32).
69. *Notebooks* 2, p. 181.
70. *Collected Fiction* 2, p. 69.
71. 18 October 1920; Letters 4, p. 75. Quoted by Alpers, *Life,* p. 320.
72. Orage, p. 111.
73. Alpers, *Life*, pp. 329–30. See Todd Martin's essay in this volume, pp. 76–86.
74. I am grateful for this insight to Melanie Wattenbarger, a Marie Curie doctoral student at the University of Mumbai, who is currently working on Rohinton Mistry and other migrant novelists based in Canada.

Colonialism and the Need for Impurity: Katherine Mansfield, 'The Garden Party' and Postcolonial Feeling

Emmanouil Aretoulakis

Does Katherine Mansfield's writing pertain to the sphere of what we today call 'postcolonial'? And how radical and productive a notion is the postcolonial?[1] In an important essay, Ella Shohat argues that the postcolonial is probably much less radical than is generally thought, insofar as it reproduces the colonial narrative of progress and linearity, predicated upon an ethics of chronological expansion from a 'pre' to a 'post'.[2] Even if we suppose, for the sake of the argument, that over a period of several decades we went from colonialism to anti-colonialism, and then to postcolonialism, we cannot but accept that the post-colonial, by expanding spatially, also involves micro-mechanisms of producing both colonial and anti-colonial elements.[3] In this essay, I want to argue that the postcolonial, if examined through a number of Mansfield's journals, letters and her famous short story 'The Garden Party', may be seen more broadly as a *spatial* as well as a chronological entity, or even a frame of thinking that runs counter to the mentality and practice of the colonial, without, however, precluding or eliminating the work or influence of coloniality. The postcolonial, in that sense, does not constitute an airtight category or territory but is rather infiltrated by a fusion of colonial practices and anti-colonial techniques, thus forming something resembling Homi Bhabha's insight concerning the existence of a *third* space which 'problematises the binary division of past and present, tradition and modernity, at the level of cultural representation and its authoritative address'.[4] In this light, the post-colonial, as feeling or cultural experience much more than objective situation or material condition, is constituted by a continuous oscillation from the colonial to the anti-colonial to decolonisation, and then onto an indefinable territory of in-betweenness – a hybrid ontology. Mansfield is a figure who encapsulates the postcolonial precisely as a mechanism of producing such spaces of hybrid in-betweenness. My purpose is to show how the overlap of the colonial and the postcolonial, in both her personal writing and her fiction, is exemplified in the radical interpenetration of life and death, beauty and ugliness, or 'purity' and 'impurity' within her thought processes. An ambivalently 'postcolonial' moment in Mansfield, in terms of the aforementioned production of in-betweenness, emerges when death becomes for her integral to a proper way of living; that is the point of realising that life without the possibility of death is experienced as something sterile and therefore as a kind of spiritual death.

Mansfield can already be seen as a *postcolonial* figure (in the strict sense of the term) to the extent that she moves from the colony, New Zealand, to the Western metropolitan centre, the very source of colonialism, only to discover that her own sense of identity is in excess of the conventional dichotomy 'colonising centre/colonised periphery' or 'colonial/anti-colonial'. Janet Wilson has called her a liminal, colonial modernist writer, especially in the 'ambivalent locatedness' and 'ontological state of (un)belonging' of her white settler characters.[5] Kathleen Beauchamp, as her real name was, the 'little colonial' from New Zealand, turned, at a young age, into a harsh critic of her white settler community and a lover of the sophisticated and profoundly artistic society of London, the metropolitan centre. Having already received a British education at Queen's College in London from 1903 to 1906 (she entered Queen's at fifteen), she was shocked to discover, on her first and last return to New Zealand, the provinciality and cultural illiteracy of the people as well as the 'savage' nature of her own parents:

> They are worse than I had even expected. They are prying and curious, they are watchful and they discuss only the food. [. . .] A physically revolted feeling seizes me. [. . .] *She* is constantly suspicious, constantly overbearingly tyrannous. [. . .] I shall never be able to live at home. [. . .] For more than a quarter of an hour they are quite unbearable, and so absolutely my mental inferiors.[6]

If colonial discourse is contagious, then little Kathleen contracts the virus, when as a nineteen-year-old girl she talks of her own parents as mentally 'inferior'. It would seem that by visiting 'Home', as Britain was called in colonial times, she had unconsciously appropriated the language of imperialism, which she would subsequently employ to 're-colonise' her native land, New Zealand, by arguing for, or simply showing off, her own superiority over it. As we are informed by the historian James Belich, New Zealand was at the time under the sway of a new recolonisation project initiated by Britain. More specifically, up to the

1880s New Zealand imported people and goods at 'rates that were gargantuan in proportion to the numbers already here'.[7] After the 1880s the link between Britain and the colony (or, rather, the dependence of New Zealand on Britain) was strengthened both economically and emotionally. Thus, whereas the colonial power and its metropolis, London, relied upon the colony for its own welfare, the latter (the colony) had to paradoxically derive its cultural and artistic status exclusively from the colonial power itself. Mansfield desired to return to the metropolitan centre, as her sense of 'unbelonging' in New Zealand was heightened after she came back in 1906, due to her yearning for artistic creation and individual realisation within the metropolitan ambience. 'Mansfield could not have wished', as Gerri Kimber contends, 'for a more creative home', as a young 'colonial New Zealander living in London, with a passion for the "new" and the "modern" in music, literature, and art.'[8] As a colonial subject, she could only realise her talents outside the colony and after adopting a westernised attitude:

> Here in my room, I feel as though I was in London. In London! To write
> the word makes me feel that I could burst into tears. [. . .] I do not care at
> all for men, but *London* – it is life. [. . .] I am longing to consort with my
> superiors.[9]

It is those 'superiors', however, who made her feel alienated and alone after her return to London. As Jeffrey Meyers says, 'Katherine's poverty, obscurity and solitude intensified her feeling of being an outsider in London.'[10] 'They burn with arrogance & pride. And I am the little colonial walking in the London garden patch – allowed to look, perhaps, but not to linger.'[11] At the same time that Mansfield tried to establish her own (post)colonial 'stature' within the utterly colonising metropolitan centre, the latter tended to contain her postcolonial entity by displacing her even further.

By espousing the culture of other European metropolitan centres besides London – for instance, Paris or Montana, Switzerland – without, of course, erasing the memory of her colonial experiences in New Zealand, Mansfield created unknowingly a *hybridised* individuality in terms of 'consolidating' a loose identity that was permeated by her need to be 'impure' rather than 'pure' – the latter referring to a strictly white settler community subjectivity.[12] It is no coincidence that she only began to reflect on the condition of, and her own feelings about, New Zealand *after* she settled in Europe, thus accommodating her vision of otherness associated with the fact that she wrote her celebrated New Zealand stories, such as 'The Garden Party', from the point of view of a 'westernised' intellectual eye, gazing back with semi-abhorrence at the habits and way of life of the white colonial settler community of Wellington.[13] Mansfield seems to adopt neither a purely colonial stance, nor a purely anti-colonial one insofar as she is continually oscillating between the centre and the so-called 'periphery', being simultaneously in excess of them both, thus occupying an area which is much like the 'third space' proposed by Homi Bhabha, not in the sense of her 'in-betweenness' only, but also in terms of enriching (therefore *altering*) both ends of the binary colonial–anti-colonial.[14]

Colonisation is usually seen as an act of creating 'vital space'. To colonise a land, to accommodate a number of people on 'newly-dis-covered' territory, is supposedly to generate new life cells in the body of the empire or colonising power. Edward Said suggests that 'neither imperialism nor colonialism is a simple act of accumulation and acqui-sition. Both are supported and perhaps even impelled by impressive ideological formations that include [. . .] such words and concepts as [. . .] "dependency", "*expansion*", and "authority"' [my emphasis].[15] So, according to the imperial myth, the colonial power does not need to dominate; it simply needs to survive through *expansion*. It has no inten-tion to appropriate foreign lands; it merely wants to explore 'unclaimed' territory so as to renew itself. As Said implies, the project of colonisation subscribes to the narrative of progress for a (Western) humanity that strives always forwards, aspiring to a better (and wealthier for both, the colonising power *and* the white settler community) future, which will be a future of no geographical or other limits. Simply put, colonisation flaunts the importance of living and 'expanding' for colonial settlers.[16] But this kind of life, for Mansfield, represented a sterile form of exist-ence, a kind of survival which reduced the possibility of a 'cultured' and meaningful existence. To satisfy her desire for artistic fulfillment, there-fore, she had to return 'Home' (to the European centres) to reconnect with former states of being and creating, to risk losing herself in order to find herself anew, and eventually disentangle herself from secure, senseless living by embarking upon a precarious journey. That journey would increase her chances of feeling absolutely free, as well as prepare the ground for the romantic espousal of death *precisely* in order to attain that kind of freedom.[17] It was also a journey that led to Mansfield's literal and physical incapacitation, as she contracted tuberculosis while trying to push her artistic horizons beyond their boundaries: still, it appears almost as if the sterility of life in New Zealand was not prefer-able to the death-in-life experiences that she had, especially during her last years spent in Switzerland and France as a postcolonial displaced 'other'. One possible reason bears on the question of how illness is capable of energising the imagination in so many different ways that it paradoxically redeems one's life by turning it into something 'meaning-ful' and artistically prolific.[18]

The death-in-life experiences that Mansfield had in Europe in her final years, and more broadly, the meaningful life that she sought, albeit shot through with literary risk and dark sentiment, attest to her profound need to decolonise herself by dismissing the idea of purity, as reflected in her colonial upper-middle-class family life (which was devoid of any literary development) while flirting instead with the notion and practice of an 'impure' (and, to an extent, bohemian) kind of living inextricably bound up with true, rather than affected (artificial) beauty. That 'beautiful' impurity can arguably be connected with the so-called 'postcolonial' feeling, in other words, with a feeling of subjective (or, rather, 'subject-al') de-centredness evoked by the aforementioned 'death-in-life' experience in Mansfield's later life and writings. But how exactly is what we call 'true' beauty, or the 'impure' moment, postcolo-nial? Well, it seems that Wellington, after 1906, bored Mansfield insofar as it provided her with 'empty' beauty; namely, a beauty that does not allow for the possibility of ugliness, or even, a beauty which concentrates on harmony, perfection and moderation rather than aesthetic excess, artistic eccentricity and decadence (the concept that beauty, in order to be real, has to consider also the importance of the *ugly* and of *raw* reality became dominant in her mind once she compromised it with the idea of dying).[19] She could only begin to comprehend her boredom after her first visit to Europe. The feeling of boredom is attributable to the predominance of rootless, unaccounted-for purity and beauty in white settler life, such as the natural landscape of New Zealand.

Antony Alpers refers to Mansfield's trip to the Urewera region of the North Island in 1907 and points out that 'when travelling in her native country, she wasn't sure whether she belonged there or not', adding that '[t]he Māoris had something which she recognised, and was drawn to: they reminded her of Europe, where people had roots. In her white compatriots she sensed no nutrient for her ambition, no humus of tradition'.[20] Mansfield liked English tourists and the Māori because they both had roots, a cultural background, and a complete sense of the natural trajectory of human existence, from life to death. Employing as much smugness as she can, she protests: 'I am so tired & sick of the thirdrate article. Give me the Maori and the tourist but nothing in-between.'[21] The 'in-between' here stands for the white settler community which she rejects as rootless and culturally as well as artisti-cally primitive, a pure, 'dead white' mutant species indulging in a mean-ingless and artificial utopia. Through a postcolonial lens, however, it is Mansfield herself who occupies an in-between space insofar as she is neither a tourist from the metropolis nor a Māori (although it turns out she is related to one);[22] neither psychologically integrated into the white settler society nor completely alienated from it. Alternatively though, she may represent all of the above simultaneously to the extent that she appears to belong to a different 'category' of hybridity, one that accommodates her 'unclean' or impure identity as well as her view of the validity of an unclean and impure world – a world devoid of fake purity and artificial cleanliness.

The boredom felt by Mansfield in the colonial ambience is not necessarily a symptom of her own individual peculiarity, but may characterise an entire colonial landscape. Saikat Majumdar maintains that the boredom experienced often by colonial cities is due to

> among other things, the insistent appearance of lack, and the incomplete nature of the colony that always gives the impression of having its political, economic and cultural center located in an 'elsewhere'. This 'elsewhere' was, of course, the metropolitan center of the empire that held the colony in a subordinated, fragmented, and perpetually unfulfilled relation with itself. [. . .] A major site of colonial domination was therefore the desire of the colony for the empire's center, a desire destined never to be fulfilled. The perpetuation of this desire for satisfaction leads to the pervasive sense of boredom that defines the colonised's sense of their own inadequacy.[23]

It would be inaccurate to say that Mansfield felt 'inadequate', since by 1907 she was already acquainted with the 'empire's centre' and ready to immerse herself in British and European culture. However, she did sense a kind of lack or the 'incomplete nature of the colony', precisely because New Zealand was so much *like* Britain, only it was *not* Britain. At the time, New Zealand was viewed as the 'Britain of the South',[24] which led to the assumption that 'no homesickness would be produced by their move across the planet, because New Zealand was simply Britain relocated and improved [. . .] This Arcadian vision [imagined a] less polluted version of the British Isles [. . .]'[25] It was that 'less polluted' version that Mansfield abhorred more than anything else, while the country's similarity to 'Home' served to reinforce that abhorrence. And as she bluntly admitted:

> I am ashamed of young New Zealand, but what is to be done. All the firm fat framework of their brains must be demolished before they can begin to learn. They want a purifying influence–a mad wave of pre-Raphaelitism, of super-aestheticism, should intoxicate the country. They must go to excess in the direction of culture, become almost decadent in their tendencies for a year or two and then find balance and proportion.[26]

What Mansfield means is that New Zealand needs a strong shot of '*im-purity*', a more 'polluted' vision of life as well as an excessively decadent spirit injected into its veins because it is apparently intellectually 'sober' and shallow. Colonial New Zealand could be likened to Britain, but without Britain's history and culture: an empty simulacrum of the motherland. As a simulated version of Britain the country repelled Mansfield, since it reminded her of the authentic culture and the natural, rather than artificial, beauty of the ancestral homeland. By 'natural' beauty one means the kind of beauty which is ready to befriend decadence and ugliness; or the purity that befriends the impure. New Zealand's vision of life as penetrated by the colonial project of expansion, wealth and untainted beauty leaves much to be desired. Mansfield yearned to break free from those chains of unsophisticated colonial artificiality, as well as meaningless beauty, by visiting the metropolitan centre. When she finally embarked upon her second voyage 'Home', she consciously broke away from the unnatural complacency of her colonial family and entered a far darker artistic world that involved risks such as living in poverty, ill health, and isolation. Accessing the centre, therefore, hardly solved all of her problems; on the contrary, it introduced new ones.

In 'The Garden Party', Mansfield dramatises the reconfiguration of the subject (her protagonist Laura Sheridan) as a 'postcolonial' entity, one that resides in another realm beyond and in excess of the colonial and the anti-colonial. When she wrote the story in 1921, she was staying at Montana-sur-Sierre in Switzerland. As Jeffrey Meyers informs us, 'the tranquility of Montana, the comfort of the Chalet, the company of Murry, the quiescence of her disease and the artistic example of [her second cousin] Elizabeth inspired Katherine's creative imagination and made these months the most fruitful of her entire life', despite the fact that she was simultaneously trying to fight tuberculosis.[27] Mansfield wrote 'The Garden Party' not in the face of illness but precisely *because of* it. The story, as art, does not signify for Mansfield a way out of the misery of her life as a consumptive but, rather, the way *into* the natural process of life, a process that involves also pain and death. The story, as well as many of her personal letters written during the same period, enact her personal agony of coming to terms with, 'or submitting to', the very beauty of a life which is not only about living but about dying as well; a life, that is, which points out the need for the emergence of the *impure* as purity's inevitable counterpart. Postcolonial subjectivity, as explained earlier, retains purity and impurity (or beauty and ugliness) as symbiotic realms, without, however, fusing them into oneness.

Undoubtedly the freshness of the climate in Montana would have a soothing effect upon any person in physical distress. In a letter written to Lady Ottoline Morrell on 24 July 1921, Mansfield expresses her enthusiasm over the clear atmosphere:

> Here it is simply exquisite weather. We are so high up (5,000 feet above the sea) that a cool breeze filters through from Heaven, and the forests are always airy . . . I can't imagine anything lovelier than this end of Switzerland. [. . .] Sierre [. . .] was so perfect that I felt I would like to live there. [. . .] But since we have come up the mountains it seems lovelier still. [. . .] The air feels wonderful but smells more wonderful still. I have never lived *in* a forest before. One steps out of the house and in a moment one is hidden among the trees.[28]

However, was such purity what Mansfield really needed to get better? She admittedly went to Switzerland 'because', as she says, 'I have consumption. [. . .] Consumption doesn't belong to me. It's only a horrid stray dog who has persisted in following me for four years, so I am trying to lose him among these mountains.'[29] Therefore, she moved high up to the Swiss mountains to dwarf pain, to fool pain, to outwit her disease by overcoming the physical difficulties, despite her increasing realisation that the beauty of real life dictates that one succumb to the pain and suffering accompanying it:

> *Everything has its shadow.* Is it right to resist such suffering? Do you know I feel it has been an immense privilege. [. . .] How blind we little creatures are! [. . .] We resist, we are terribly frightened. The little boat enters the dark fearful gulf and our only cry is to escape – 'put me on land again'. But it's useless. Nobody listens. The shadowy figure rows on. One ought to sit still and uncover one's eyes.[30]

By letting go, by submitting to the shadow or pain, Mansfield aspires unconsciously to demystify death by befriending it. If purity is identical to a healthy, but very ordinary, life, Mansfield calls for impurity, which is identical to *real* life, namely, one that combines living and dying, or beauty and ugliness, but without fusing these realms. Assuming that the postcolonial alludes to what Bhabha calls the *third space*, which dismantles the dichotomy 'colonial-anticolonial', it is likely that Mansfield embodies a postcolonial subjectivity in refusing to opt for either colonial purity (pure and absolute health, for instance) or anti-colonial impurity (absolute disease), favouring, instead, an oscillation between the two states. Simultaneously, she fends off consumption's 'colonising blows' by externalising (or 'un-internalising') the disease, thereby distancing herself from the colonial influence of the tubercular virus ('It's a stray dog following me'). By witnessing death, Laura Sheridan, the upper-class girl in 'The Garden Party', unconsciously abstains from the unnatural purity of her Arcadian, colonial household and bears witness to the beauty of a life that allows for and befriends death. Along similar lines, Mansfield appears to cling to impurity (translated as 'non-health' or 'death') in order to transcend her illness. In essence, she needs death in order to be able to live more fully. To recover from illness, she seems to argue, you have to erase the fear of pain and death by espousing their inevitability: 'I believe the greatest failing of all is *to be frightened*'.[31]

In 'The Garden Party', the Sheridans are preparing for their annual garden party when suddenly news arrives about the accidental death of a working-class neighbour in a street just below their house. Laura thinks it's only natural to call off the party out of respect for the deceased, but her mother does not share her feelings: 'You are being very absurd, Laura', she says. 'People like that don't expect sacrifices from us. And it's not very sympathetic to spoil everybody's enjoyment as you're doing now.'[32] On the surface, the story is about awareness of class distinctions and the many ways in which a society, at the beginning of the twentieth century, is structured around them. On a deeper level, it could be read against the backdrop of British rule over its established colonies. It is not at all inevitable that the two readings should contradict each other, especially if we take into account the fact that class consciousness is, by definition, one of the most important characteristics of turn-of-the-century Britain. This encourages speculation that the society depicted in the story is to be directly linked to the British Empire's construal of cultural forms and institutions. Although this is famously one of her 'New Zealand' stories, with its white settler community setting, Mansfield surgically removes almost all information or details particular to a typical New Zealand scene. One immediate effect that geographical non-particularity has on the story is that a more universalised aspect of the human condition is produced. On the other hand, a colonial subtext underlies it on account of the fact that, as Andrew Bennett argues, 'the ethnic, national, and cultural identifications [in 'The Garden Party'] are complicated by the way that the class and cultural assumptions of characters' thoughts and actions are overlaid by an "English" sensibility' to such an extent as to make one believe that 'a powerful dimension of New Zealand society is a simulacrum of England'.[33]

The backdrop of the story is, therefore, colonial. However, the treatment of the story gives off an air of 'postcoloniality', a certain tinge of 'in-betweenness' related to Laura's ambivalent reaction to the possibility of death. Laura, being a child and as yet uncontaminated by the traditional colonial distinctions between classes, provides early in the story a somewhat 'postcolonial' view of societal structures: 'It's all the fault [. . .] of these absurd class distinctions.'[34] It would be interesting to view Laura and the story through the lens of the conflict between colonial and postcolonial discourse, as encapsulated in the rupture between the Sheridans and the lower classes 'at the far bottom of the road'. The Sheridans have kept death outside their space as they prefer an artificial life which preserves immunity to dying, whereas the lower-class district seems to espouse the reality of death in all its natural magnificence. This kind of reality encompasses happiness as well as stoic patience in the face of life's vicissitudes: 'Women in shawls and men's tweed caps hurried by [. . .]; the children played in the doorways. A low hum came from the mean little cottages. In some of them there was a flicker of light, and a shadow, crab-like, moved across the window.'[35] This excerpt epitomises an ethical kind of living, which means experiencing life in all its intensities.

Laura's presence might be viewed as an allegory of how the postcolonial subject looks at death: not as the opposite of life but, rather, as symbiotic with it. Symbiosis does not conflate opposites; it keeps them in suspension and on parallel lines. The symbiosis of life and death dictates that you cannot possibly talk of the one without also addressing the other. Still, there is a fundamental irreconcilability or untranslatability governing this affinity. In *Orientalism*, Edward Said argues that translation serves 'to domesticate the Orient and thereby turn it into a province of European learning'.[36] Borrowing Said's terminology, we could say that Laura, in deference to the suffering of the dead carter's family, wants the party to be cancelled but has no intention to 'domesticate' the other (the lower-class family) by encountering the grieving people and thus turning them 'into a province of European learning', figuratively speaking. Such an allegorical reading identifies the Sheridans as white colonial settlers and the lower-class district as the exotic 'other', the 'indigenous' other, or even the cultured other, who would look exotic to someone like Laura or Mansfield. In *The Wretched of the Earth*, Frantz Fanon juxtaposes the elegance of the European quarters in colonial cities with the slum districts in them and shows how '[t]his world divided into compartments, this world cut in two is inhabited by two different species'.[37] Fanon's insight that in a colonial city there may reside two different species, one superior and the other inferior, a coloniser and a colonised, provides the framework for the aforementioned allegorical reading.

Any contact that the Sheridans may try to establish with the carter's family would inevitably constitute an act of 'colonisation', an opportunity to contaminate the wretched (yet proud and wise) other. Such a contact is precisely what Laura's mother unconsciously wants to make by sending her daughter off to alleviate the pain of the dead man's family and offer them colonial 'leftovers'. There is an inherent untranslatability between the two worlds and their discourses – one cannot possibly translate the one into the other, so to speak – and the postcolonial subject needs to bear witness to that. Even Mrs Sheridan, Laura's mother, unknowingly, bears witness to that when the second she is informed of the incident of the carter's death she responds with alarm: 'not in the garden?'[38] This amounts to admitting openly that contact with the undesirable is fine as long as it happens elsewhere, not in the colonial haven. Laura's mother attempts to metaphorically colonise the realm of the lower working-class by way of appropriating their grief. But Laura abhors the prospect of fusing or uniting the two worlds as that would lead to the disruption of the symbiosis between them: she can only be *made* to go to the lower district.

The Sheridan homestead is, not accidentally, located on a higher level, symbolically above and away from the harshness of real life, untouched by the pain or unhappiness that afflicts the humble lower districts. The Sheridans metaphorically dwarf pain and misery by holding pleasurable parties that leave death out of the equation, in accordance with the colonial project of familial happiness within a white settler framework. Thus Laura's idea to cancel the festivities comes as a shock to everyone since it allegedly reintroduces the possibility of human weakness and the shadow of death into their relaxed lives. Like the Sheridans, Mansfield physically moves to a higher level in going to Montana to seek refuge from weakness and disease, in a place of purity normally associated with perfect health and joyful life. Still, one discovers in Mansfield's letters her repugnance at the purity of the Swiss locale: 'The cleanliness of Switzerland! Darling, it is frightening. The chastity of my lily-white bed! The waxy-fine floors! [. . .] Every daisy in the grass below has a starched frill – the very bird droppings are dazzling.'[39] She flirts with purity only to realise that the concept and sight of purity are paradoxically disgusting. Absolute cleanliness is frightening because it is not natural. Bird droppings have to stay dirty to be real, the bed not perfectly made has to be natural and the floor somewhat unpolished has to look earthly. Just as Laura feels, in her innocence (yet, without being able to articulate it) that a life of bliss, if it is to be real, cannot possibly remain separate from the uninvited presence of death, Mansfield bristles at the unnatural and utterly unrealistic purity of the Swiss locale, which remains uninfected by impurity or imperfection. In a letter to Dorothy Brett, she cries out:

> But do you really feel all beauty is marred by ugliness and the lovely woman has bad teeth? I don't feel quite like that. For it seems to me if Beauty were Absolute it would no longer be the kind of Beauty it is. Beauty triumphs over ugliness in Life. That's what I feel. And that marvelous triumph is what I long to express. The poor man lives and the tears glitter in his beard

and that is so beautiful one could bow down. Why? Nobody can say. I sit in a waiting-room where all is ugly, where it's dirty, dull, dreadful, where sick people waiting with me to see the doctor are all marked by suffering and sorrow. And a very poor workman comes in, takes off his cap humbly, [. . .] has a look as though he believed that behind that doctor's door there shone the miracle of healing. And all is changed, all is marvelous.[40]

In this excerpt she expresses her objection to considering beauty as an absolute quality. Far from being untouched by ugliness, real beauty has to be accompanied 'symbiotically' by ugliness to have any meaning at all. Therefore, beauty is not marred by ugliness; rather, ugliness enriches beauty and turns it into a beautiful (or 'marvelous') reality. If 'beauty' evokes life and 'ugliness' evokes death, it can be inferred that life acquires its meaning from the inevitability of death, a marvellous end to an otherwise 'empty' period of meaningless breathing.

Here we can definitely discern Mansfield's agonising attempt to derive meaning from her disease by means of connecting perfect health with senseless life, and non-health with the marvel of life, which has already incorporated shadow, eclipse, the vision of death. For her, the absolutely beautiful is identical to the absolutely pure, which she resists as unnatural. Since her own life is marked by illness, absolute purity, too, has to be contaminated with elements of impurity to be regarded as real beauty. Tuberculosis constitutes the shadow that enriches her life and transforms it into something that is really beautiful *because* natural. Laura is portrayed as having inside her a built-in mechanism for responding, in her own childish way, to the simultaneity of death and life. Thus, when informed that the best place for the marquee is against the karaka-tree – probably the only sign of coloniality in the story – she is resistant to the idea:

> Against the karakas. Then the karaka-trees would be hidden. And they were so lovely, with their broad, gleaming leaves, and their clusters of yellow fruit. They were like trees you imagined growing on a desert island, proud, solitary, lifting their leaves and fruits to the sun in a kind of silent splendour. Must they be hidden by a marquee?[41]

The karaka-trees may be lovely with gleaming leaves and beautiful yellow fruit but there is a catch: their fruit contain a poisonous substance called karakin. So, on the one hand, the karaka-tree seems to be a celebration of life, while on the other, it is inextricable from death. By associating emotionally with the karaka-tree, Laura acts out that 'in-betweenness' which keeps life and death – or beauty and ugliness – separate but also symbiotic. Similarly, the lilies 'growing in her breast' may be symbolic of her closeness to death as well as life, since most lilies live for a very short period of time, though still, they are a very beautiful sight.[42] The lily and the karaka-tree are emblematic of Laura's 'cohabitation' with, and resistance to, the colonial (non)culture of the white settler community. Additionally, they prefigure the alternative path that will lead Laura as well as the reader to feel the contiguity of beauty and dying. This is very similar to how Mansfield conceptualises ill-health and pain towards the end of her life. Both Laura and Mansfield can attest to the full marvel of life as soon as they exit the 'colony', their 'upper-class house on the hill', and enter a postcolonial state of mind, familiarising them with a 'third' universe: one that simultaneously borrows from, and rejects, the colony.

In 'The Garden Party', Laura pays, very reluctantly indeed, a visit to the dead man's house only to discover that unprecedented beauty lies in the working-class life of pain and drudgery: 'There lay a young man, fast asleep – sleeping so soundly, so deeply [. . .] Oh, so remote, so peaceful. [. . .] What did garden parties [. . .] matter to him? He was far from all those things. He was wonderful, beautiful.'[43] Laura is suddenly exposed to a side of life that she only knew from the newspapers. She has been living a life without concerns, wallowing in infinite 'pure' pleasures that rule out pain or death. But now, she glimpses the beauty of life as never precluding misery. She is experiencing the element of impurity entering the domain of the absolute purity of senseless bliss, and in fact, deriving real pleasure from that moment of sincerity – Mansfield, too, as we know, took moments of sincerity to be invaluable. By being exposed to death, Laura starts to think more philosophically about life, in the same way that Mansfield yearns to sip at every drop of a life threatened by pain and disease. In a letter to William Gerhardi (11 March 1922), she concedes that the beauty of life consists of its diversity, and that was what she meant by writing 'The Garden Party':

> The diversity of life and how we try to fit in everything, Death included. That is bewildering for a person of Laura's age. She feels things ought to happen differently. First one and then another. But life isn't like that. We haven't the ordering of it. Laura says, 'But all these things must not happen at once'. And Life answers, 'Why not? How are they divided from each other?' And they do all happen, it is inevitable. And it seems to me there is beauty in that inevitability.[44]

Of course, this excerpt may be seen as exonerating the Sheridan family insofar as it appears to argue that they are fully aware of the diversity of life and the simultaneity of beauty and ugliness, or pain and well-being, and that is why they refuse to disrupt the normal flow of their leisurely routine, knowing that death is always a possibility, just not for them. Laura, according to Mansfield, is confused by the simultaneous occurrence of life and death because she does not know that within life death is not far away, just as ugliness (or impurity) is not far away from beauty (or purity). The consumptive Mansfield is, at this point, coping with a situation where pain should not be exempted from natural, real life. This is the key to unlocking her elaborate attitude towards the beauty of the inevitability of death.

In many Mansfield letters, the word 'unspoilt' recurs. For instance, she refers to the 'unspoilt' ambience of Sierre and the 'tiny mountain towns on the way to Sierre'; later she talks about the ugly but 'unspoiled' character of the Swiss.[45] Gradually, though, the unspoiled nature of things assumes a negative tinge: 'Anne, Switzerland is revoltingly clean' (from her letter to Anne Drey, 12 May 1921).[46] 'Unspoiled', here, would mean fake, artificial, while the purity of the (unspoiled) snow turns into pure evil, the devil incarnate. If Montana boasts the magnificence of the snowcapped mountains, Mansfield becomes horrified by the revolting purity of those mountains: '[P]oor lamb! To think he will not be able to scratch *through* until April. I suppose snow is beautiful. I hate it. [. . .] And then there is no movement. All is still-white-cold-deathly, eternal.'[47] It is impressive how beauty and ugliness swap places in her narrative, as she comes to redefine snow as something that prevents the natural flow of animal life. The lamb will not be able to survive owing to that eternal beauty of pure whiteness. Mansfield implies that pure beauty – sheer, eternal snow – is overrated and tries to seek out an impure version of it; one that implicates the symbiosis of all living beings that breathe under the same sky. She never attempts to transcend, in a poetic or romantic way, the barriers of her life as a consumptive. On the contrary, she attempts to submit to those barriers, to befriend her illness, which will allegedly acquaint her with the full-fledged reality of life as it should be lived, namely, as a mystical mode of existence, constantly regulated by the imponderable factors of pain and death. That mystical mode of existence is permeated by the indelible feeling that purity needs its opposite, impurity, to be established as purity. The two opposites, however, should not be fused into one entity; far from it, they should be held symbiotically along parallel lines, and that is the postcolonial identity or feeling that I have been trying to capture in this essay.[48]

As Laura Sheridan runs into her brother Laurie on rushing out of the dead man's house in the final scene of the story, she almost collapses in his arms, not out of shock or grief but, rather, out of happiness or even gratitude that she has finally seen a glimpse of what it means to *really* be alive. Far from articulately and glibly expressing her views on life, she merely stammers: 'Isn't life –'.[49] She never completes the thought, with

Mansfield leaving that question unresolved so as to goad the reader's imagination about the seriousness of the effort to trace what she, both in her life and her works, calls 'beauty' and 'purity'.

Kathleen Beauchamp, female short-story writer and a colonial from Wellington, New Zealand, already speaking from a marginal position, sought to realise herself outside her homeland as a 'deterritorialised' personality, writing from within the European metropolitan centres, as if she had known that to find one's own identity one needs first to lose oneself in a maze of far more extreme positions of otherness.[50]

Notes

1. I would like to express my gratitude to the anonymous reviewers for their very helpful comments upon this work. In addition, I want to thank Janet Wilson for offering me important feedback on several aspects of the essay.
2. Ella Shohat, 'Notes on the "post-colonial"', *Social Text*, 31/32 (1992), pp. 99–113.
3. By casting light upon spatial postcoloniality, one can by no means dismiss the chronological dimension, since, as Stuart Hall asserts, the Postcolonial is indeed related to specific historical periods of European colonialism and decolonisation. See Stuart Hall, 'When was the "postcolonial"? Thinking at the Limit', in Iain Chambers and Lidia Curti, eds, *The Post-Colonial Question: Common Skies, Divided Horizons* (London: Routledge, 1996), pp. 242–60. More recently, Laura Doyle and Laura Winkiel raised the issue of a spatio-temporal model that can be 'applied' to the question of modernity under 'postcolonial eyes'. In their *Geomodernisms: Race, Modernism, Modernity*, they insist that 'so much depends [. . .] on place, proximity, [and] position' that what is needed is a 'geomodernist' reading of modernist texts, that is, a reading that calls for privileging position and location when studying modernity and its chronological dimensions. See Laura Doyle and Laura Winkiel, eds, *Geomodernisms: Race, Modernism, Modernity* (Bloomington: Indiana University Press, 2005), pp. 1–4.
4. In *The Location of Culture*, Homi Bhabha posits that 'the pact of interpretation is never simply an act of communication between the I and the You designated in the statement. The production of meaning requires that these two places be mobilised in the passage through a "third space", which represents both the general conditions of language and the specific implication of the utterance in a performative and institutional strategy of which it cannot "in itself" be conscious' (pp. 35–6). In other words, that 'third space' does not aim at bridging the gap between the I and you, between past and present, tradition and modernity, or colonial and anti-colonial, but instead bears witness to the fact that 'the meaning and symbols of culture have no primordial unity or fixity; that even the same signs can be appropriated, translated, rehistoricised and read anew' (p. 37). Bhabha elucidates his argument about the 'third space' being neither *I* nor *You*, neither tradition nor modernity, etc., when he refers to the Algerian people's liberation struggle from French imperialist politics. As he argues, by igniting a revolution the people of Algeria become 'bearers of a hybrid identity' insofar as they disrupt the continuity and homogeneity of the nationalist tradition that underpins the politics of resistance to colonial power. The implication here is that before French colonialism Algeria was in a state to which it can never return; all nationalist anti-colonial strategies will take the country to a wholly new (third) cultural territory/space rather than bring it back to where it was

before the French oppression. That new territory represents a postcolonial, hybrid, cultural identity that is neither purely pre-colonial (national) nor anti-colonial (nationalist) but rather elusively 'inter-national' (with the focus on the 'inter' rather than 'national'). See Homi Bhabha, *The Location of Culture* (London: Routledge, 1994).

5. Janet Wilson, '"Where is Katherine?": Longing and (Un)belonging in the Works of Katherine Mansfield', in Gerri Kimber and Janet Wilson, eds, *Celebrating Katherine Mansfield: A Centenary Volume of Essays* (New York: Palgrave Macmillan, 2011), pp. 175–88 (p. 176).

6. Margaret Scott, ed., *The Katherine Mansfield Notebooks*, 2 vols (Canterbury, NZ: Lincoln University Press and Daphne Brasell Associates, 1997), Vol. 1, pp. 79–80. Hereafter referred to as *Notebooks* 1 and *Notebooks* 2.

7. James Belich, *Paradise Reforged: A History of the New Zealanders from the 1880s to the Year 2000* (Honolulu: University of Hawai'i Press, 2001), p. 30. Belich points to 'The Great Tightening' of the moral and social structure of New Zealand during that age, insofar as there was an increasing pressure on everyone to be the *same as* the other (p. 189). The puritan principle of 'sameness' was an inherently colonial one, which leads us to the idea that Mansfield, by desiring to be *different*, endorsed a 'decolonised' version both, of herself and New Zealanders. At the same time, however, no New Zealander would question the supposed cultural superiority of Britain with its metropolitan centre, London, imposing itself even more upon people's minds as the one and *only* source of art and creativity (p. 30). Mansfield was hardly an exception to that (re)colonising or imperialist 'rule', despite the fact that her will to be different rendered her more or less a decolonised figure. To be simultaneously colonial and decolonised points to the image of an intercultural figure, a figure which is 'transnational as well as national', a cultural *hybrid* to which Belich himself alludes (pp. 341, 510). But if Mansfield is a hybrid, is she any different from the other New Zealanders bearing hybrid identities too?

8. Gerri Kimber, 'Mansfield, *Rhythm*, and the Émigré Connection', in Janet Wilson, Gerri Kimber and Susan Reid, eds, *Katherine Mansfield and Literary Modernism* (London: Continuum, 2011), pp. 13–29 (p. 27).

9. *Notebooks* 1, p. 108.

10. Jeffrey Meyers, *Katherine Mansfield. A Biography* (London: Hamish Hamilton, 1978), p. 38.

11. *Notebooks* 2, p. 166.

12. See Belich and Bhabha's notion of the 'hybrid', notes 7 and 4, respectively.

13. Delia da Sousa Correa has suggested that Mansfield 'was writing [her New Zealand stories] predominantly for a European audience'. See Delia da Sousa Correa, 'The Stories of Katherine Mansfield', in Richard Danson Brown and Suman Gupta, eds, *Aestheticism and Modernism: Debating Twentieth-Century Literature 1900–1960* (Abingdon: Routledge, 2005), pp. 68–116 (p. 78).

14. See Bhabha's discussion of the Algerian anti-colonial struggle (note 4).

15. Edward W. Said, *Culture and Imperialism* (London: Chatto and Windus, 1993), p. 8.

16. Assuming that colonialism aims at enhancing the life of the colonial/imperialist power, and that anti-colonialism looks to decolonisation for reaching the ultimate goal of 'breathing fresh air anew', in other words, enhancing the life of indigenous populations as independent people, it can be inferred that the two tendencies simply make up the two sides of the same coin by arguing for utopias of a 'pure life'. Through this lens, postcolonialism, as a third space that deconstructs the colonial/

anti-colonial dichotomy, broaches the possibility of bringing death into the equation through the presentation of a realm where death and life co-exist in a beautiful but true – beautiful *because* true – symbiosis. Such a kind of symbiosis points to neither a 'progressive' nor 'regressive' spirit.

17. Before leaving for Europe for good, Mansfield was positive that it is not love but freedom that determines the life of a woman, and that happiness comes along once she realises that. See *Notebooks* 1, p. 88.

18. Such a case is made by Mary Burgan in *Illness, Gender and Writing: The Case of Katherine Mansfield* (Baltimore: Johns Hopkins University Press, 1994).

19. Mansfield's father tried to distract his daughter's attention away from the artistic as well as aesthetic 'buzz' of the metropolis (London) by sending her off on a caravan expedition through the volcanic region of the North Island in the Ureweras and Rotorua. But he didn't succeed. Albeit overwhelmed by the natural beauty of the region, Mansfield did not feel at home in those areas. All she encountered during the trip was, according to Alpers, the 'untamed beauty of her country [that] made Miss Kathleen no fonder of its white inhabitants'. The 'untamed' beauty that Alpers means is probably the 'pure' and 'empty' beauty that I have in mind; a beauty that lacks both, a cultural/artistic basis or reference and the romantic drive towards excess and extravagance. See Antony Alpers, *The Life of Katherine Mansfield* (New York: Viking Press, 1980), p. 58.

20. Alpers, pp. 58–9.

21. *Notebooks* 1, p. 140.

22. Alpers, p. 58.

23. Saikat Majumdar, 'Desiring the Metropolis: The Anti-Aesthetic and Semicolonial Modernism', *Postcolonial Text*, 3.1 (2007), pp. 1–14 (p. 5).

24. Belich, *Paradise Reforged*, pp. 298–9.

25. Alice Brittan, 'Australasia', in John McLeod, ed., *The Routledge Companion to Postcolonial Studies* (London: Routledge, 2007), pp. 72–82 (p. 76).

26. 'Letter to Vera Beauchamp' [? April–May 1908], from Vincent O' Sullivan and Margaret Scott, eds, *The Collected Letters of Katherine Mansfield*, 5 vols (Oxford: Clarendon, 1984), Vol. 1, p. 44. Hereafter cited as *Letters*, followed by volume and page number.

27. Meyers, p. 225.

28. *Letters* 4, pp. 251–2.

29. *Letters* 4, p. 324 [21 November 1921].

30. *Letters* 4, p. 75 [18 October 1920].

31. *Letters* 4, p. 75.

32. Claire Tomalin, ed., *Katherine Mansfield. Short Stories* (London: Guernsey Press, 1983), p. 254.

33. Andrew Bennett, *Katherine Mansfield* (Tavistock: Northcote House, 2004), pp. 36, 40.

34. *Short Stories*, p. 249.

35. *Short Stories*, p. 259.

36. Edward W. Said, *Orientalism* (New York: Pantheon, 1978), p. 78.

37. Frantz Fanon, *Les Damnes de la Terre* (1961), *The Wretched of the Earth*, trans. Constance Farrington (Harmondsworth: Penguin, 1967), p. 30.

38. *Short Stories*, p. 255.

39. *Letters* 4, p. 214 [7 May 1921].

40. *Letters* 5, p. 96 [9 March 1922].

41. *Short Stories*, pp. 248–9.

42. *Short Stories*, p. 250.
43. *Short Stories*, pp. 260–1.
44. *Letters* 5, p. 101.
45. *Letters* 4, p. 248 [20 June 1921].
46. *Letters* 4, p. 220.
47. *Letters* 5, p. 10 [9 January 1922].
48. A postcolonial feeling, as already in excess of binaries, demands that one abstain from, without renouncing completely, colonial or anti-colonial pretensions to such pure narratives as 'vital space' or the necessity of life without serious consideration of death.
49. *Short Stories*, p. 261.
50. Janet Wilson, 'Editorial: Rethinking the Postcolonial and Globalization', *World Literature Written in English*, 40. 1 (2002–3), pp. 3–11 (p. 3).

'How Katherine Mansfield Was Kidnapped': A (Post)colonial Family Romance

Lorenzo Mari

Introduction: 'How Pearl Button Was Kidnapped' as Künstlerroman

Mark Williams and Jane Stafford, who approach Katherine Mansfield's problematic relationship with her national background from a post-colonial interest in 'Maoriland writing',[1] have recently proposed that instead of focusing exclusively on the many turning points in Mansfield's career, readers should also consider the impressive continuities within her literary production:

> The common view that Mansfield became a major modernist writer by staging a break from the provincial colonial culture of early 1900s New Zealand rests on a series of binaries – modernity versus tradition, province versus centre, national versus cosmopolitan, Victorian versus modernist – that ignore the continuities within Mansfield's writing from 1906 to her death seventeen years later.[2]

This perspective allows Williams and Stafford to state that the departure of Mansfield from New Zealand in 1908 did not constitute the definitive catalyst of her modernism.

On the contrary, Mansfield's modernism often acknowledges its New Zealand origins through frequent references to a specific location in space and time, or to gender, as Keith Gregor notes in speaking of Mansfield's 'female modernist aesthetics'.[3] However, Williams and Stafford's concept of 'continuities' could be extended much further to refer not only to Mansfield's entire oeuvre, but also to embrace a more extensive literary and cultural debate. This might include those competing – and *completing* – notions that are implied by the labels 'New Zealand', 'Maoriland' and 'Aotearoa'. Paradoxically, as expected when dealing with a complex and contradictory literary corpus like Mansfield's, a fascinating starting point for this discussion can be found in a short prose piece, her 1910 story 'How Pearl Button Was Kidnapped'.[4] In fact, despite its brevity, this short story demonstrates two major trends identifiable in Mansfield's work: the relationship between women and creativity and, more importantly, the implied national allegory in her representations of the family.

Both issues can be approached in a simple, but effective way through the function of Mansfield's free indirect discourse, which partially assumes the perspective of the young child, Pearl Button. The story begins with Pearl swinging on the gate in front of the house in which she lives, mysteriously referred to as 'the House of Boxes', when two 'dark women' approach her and ask her: '"You coming with us, Pearl Button?"' (20). Pearl agrees to follow them, eventually ending up in their village, which is distant from her family house and close to the seaside. While she rejoices in this sight, as she has never seen the sea before, 'a crowd of little blue men' (23) – most likely to be policemen, although this is not stated – come and 'rescue' her. This apparently happens against her will, since 'Pearl had never been happy like this before' (22). The story ends with the re-establishment of the status quo, and Pearl's return to her family.

At first glance, this basic narrative pattern seems to enact a creative version of the Freudian scheme of the *Familienroman*, which was originally theorised by Freud in his 1908 essay 'Der Familienroman der Neurotiker' ('Family Romances').[5] Although Mansfield may not have been aware of Freud's work before writing her short story,[6] 'How Pearl Button Was Kidnapped' implicitly introduces a reinterpretation both of the narrative patterns of the *Familienroman*/family romance and of the oedipal scheme which is the source of the *Familienroman*. In considering how her story might be linked to the Freudian scheme of the family romance, therefore, it is worth elaborating on Freud's theorisations, before comparing his scheme with the narration presented in Mansfield's story.

Freud's essay on the *Familienroman* was originally conceived to explain the fantasies that the young male child builds about his family once he has entered the sexual stage of his life. According to Freud, these fantasies are due to unease during development of the Oedipus complex, when the male child – by oversimplifying the issues at stake – is attracted to his mother and competes with his father. This leads the child to imagine himself living in another family, which he deems to be 'superior'[7] to his biological one. Freud gestures at a relationship between these 'imaginative romances'[8] and the offspring of literary creativity. Although links between the family romance and literature are not overtly claimed in Freud's text, a subsequent corpus of academic criticism – starting with *Roman des origins et origins du roman* (1972) by Marthe Robert – has developed this hypothesis, making the Freudian family romance and the history of the western novel roughly coincide.

Robert's totalising argument was later questioned by theorists, most notably by feminist critics. Marianne Hirsch's *The Mother/Daughter Plot: Narrative, Psychoanalysis, Feminism* (1989), for instance, constitutes an important reference point, because of her reversal of the Freudian theory. By shifting away from a purely psychoanalytical reading, Hirsch interprets the family romance as 'an imaginary interrogation of origins' that 'describes the experience of familial structures as discursive'.[9] Consequently, Hirsch sets the importance of the mother-daughter relationship (or the 'mother-daughter plot', in her words) against the pivotal confrontation of both the family romance and the Oedipus complex, which is the son-father relationship. Conforming to Hirsch's thesis Katherine Mansfield, like other nineteenth- and twentieth-century women writers, eschews oedipal narratives; she avoids repetition of the oedipal scheme even when she engages with literary genres, such as the *Bildungsroman* and the *Künstlerroman*,[10] which were traditionally based on the dynamics of the father-son relationship. Mansfield decides to put women on stage: this choice, as in the work of other writers of the time, shows that the Oedipus complex does not always manage to explain the education of a person or an artist, given that the Freudian focus is limited to men and, more specifically, those men who have not completely overcome their complex.

Hirsch's position – though well established, from a theoretical point of view – is, however, based on a simplified dichotomy of the mother-daughter plot versus the son-father relationship, and so is somewhat incomplete. Firstly, resistance to the oedipal cultural scheme might be enacted simply through the appropriation and re-signification of this kind of narration from a female gendered perspective, without necessarily resorting to a different plot. Secondly, if one is to consider 'familial structures as discursive', then it is also necessary to consider the entire 'family frame' – to quote the title of a subsequent work by Hirsch herself[11] – as the context in which the *Familienroman* and other plots, such as the *Bildungsroman* and the *Künstlerroman*, develop.

Mansfield's story encompasses both operations. Pearl Button follows the same 'steps' as the male child who is caught in his Oedipus complex, but this process of rebellion is depicted through the eyes of a *female* child. In addition to this, her transgressive act has clear repercussions on the whole representation of her family. As for the 'pseudo-oedipal' narration retraceable in the story, Pearl is evidently upset by her family – they live in a symbolically constrictive 'House of Boxes' – and she openly rejoices when the two women carry her away and introduce her to the sea. As a matter of fact, Pearl's father is completely absent from the narration, whereas her mother is confined 'in the kitching, ironing-because-its-Tuesday' (20). It is only at the end of the short story that the presence of a father-like, moral authority resurfaces, when 'the crowd of little blue men' rescues Pearl.

It might fairly be argued that the two women who 'kidnap' Pearl do not constitute an alternative family for her, as this possibility is never stated in the text; nevertheless, Pearl sets up a comparison between the two familial conditions, implying that her temporary situation is in many ways better than home life: '"Haven't you got any House of Boxes?" she said. "Don't you all live in a row? Don't the men go to offices? Aren't there any nasty things?"' (22). Pearl's questions are left unanswered, revealing that they are correct, quasi-tautological questions. The village to which the two women take Pearl is far more colourful and populous than the *Pakeha* settlement – '[p]ink and red and blue washing hung over the fences, and as they came near more people came out, and five yellow dogs with long thin tails' (22) – and their house is undoubtedly less constrictive than the House of Boxes, since it gives them direct access to the seaside. Besides, in this village there is no trace of 'nasty things' at all, as Pearl repeatedly asserts that she is happy that the two women have brought her there.

Pearl is even happier when she 'discovers' the sea. At first, she is frightened but after a while, upon seeing the two women digging into the sand and collecting seashells, she becomes excited and starts to imitate them:

> Pearl forgot her fright and began digging too. She got hot and wet, and suddenly over her feet broke a little line of foam. 'Oo, oo!' she shrieked, dabbling with her feet, 'Lovely, lovely!' She paddled in the shallow water. It was warm. (22–3)

The discovery of the sea and digging in the sand for seashells can be considered as ways for a young child to refine her aesthetic sensibility – especially when considering, as Keith Gregor does, the Romantic and symbolist underpinning of Mansfield's modernism.[12] In fact, according to this cultural legacy, a liberating spiritual experience in a natural environment can trigger one's aesthetic sensibility, and this seems to be what actually happens to Pearl Button on the seashore.

This passage could be interpreted as a remarkable step forward in the definition of Mansfield's approach to the '*Künstlerroman* motif'. As a matter of fact, the development of the young female child's aesthetic consciousness might be seen as a parallel to representations that are frequently analysed as defining a relationship between women and creativity in Mansfield's oeuvre: the conflicts between mothers and daughters dominate analyses by Hirsch and Susan Gubar, while Janka Kaščáková focuses on the condition of the unmarried woman.[13] Indeed, both conflictual situations might be legitimately considered as further implementations and developments of the 'pseudo-oedipal' conflict of the young female child with her biological family. This variation is particularly evident at the end of the short story, when Pearl Button experiences the sudden interruption of her fantasies by the re-establishment of the previous order of family (the 'return', though *en masque*, of the father) and society (the rescue by the police).

In other words, the female child's difficult relationship with her biological family is part of Mansfield's unique and complex representation of the family, as is apparent from the experiences of mothers and single women in other short stories. What the 'daughter' perceives can be assessed alongside what the 'mother' perceives, or the woman who does not want to be, or cannot be, a 'mother' (thus representing the 'fear of maternity' from which Mansfield has always sought to escape, according to Hirsch's analysis).[14] Mansfield's focus on the family might be also considered as further evidence that Hirsch's focus on the 'mother/daughter plot' is not fully comprehensive without consideration of the whole 'family frame'.

Jameson's Theory of Third World National Allegories Revisited

Mansfield's permanent engagement with 'familial structures as discursive', which is also apparent in the later cycle of short stories dedicated to the Burnell family,[15] urges an investigation of thematic and ideological foundations alongside biographical and psychoanalytical ones. Biographical interpretations, in fact, are not always viable, even when they are effectively grounded in a well-known family history,[16] without a proper framing in a thematic and/or ideological perspective. From this position, a critical approach which could be fruitfully applied to Mansfield's short story – neither forgetting nor excessively emphasising the autobiographical tenor of her writing – derives from the well-known article by Fredric Jameson, 'Third-World Literature in the Era of Multinational Capitalism' (1986). As a matter of fact, family romances constitute a paradigmatic example of those narrations '*of the private individual destiny*', which, according to Jameson, should be read as allegories '*of the embattled situation of the public third-world culture and society*' (emphasis in the original).[17]

Postcolonial literature, which Jameson labels as 'third-world' (he still

uses a Cold War terminology), provides many examples of this mingling of private and public destinies: stories of couples who give birth
to a child are said to engage in the re-production of the nation; stories
recounted by children frequently show them sharing patterns of growth
with the nation; finally, family romances, as long as they are analysed
by considering the 'familial structures as discursive', can also be considered as metonymic of the nation.

Nonetheless, Jameson's essay has often been targeted by postcolonial
criticism as a reductionist and eurocentric approach to the complexity
of postcolonial cultures and literatures.[18] As a matter of fact, Jameson's
full hypothesis reads:

> All third-world texts are necessarily, I want to argue, allegorical, and in a
> very specific way: they are to be read as what I will call *national allegories,*
> even when, or perhaps I should say, particularly when their forms develop
> out of predominantly western machineries of representation, such as the
> novel. (emphasis in the original)[19]

If this can be said of many postcolonial texts, especially for those published during the era of postcolonial nationalism, it is not relevant to all
of them: Jameson's generalising statement directly leads to an absurd
conflation of all postcolonial societies and cultural systems into one
undifferentiated whole. However, Jameson's argument might be taken
out of these totalising premises and treated as a working hypothesis,
which might be confirmed or rejected on the basis of the confrontation
with the contingent textual politics.

Mansfield's 'How Pearl Button Was Kidnapped' seems to illustrate
Jameson's hypothesis, but in order to develop this reading two of the
critical patterns proposed by Jameson have to be reshaped. First of all,
his exclusive focus on 'third-world native authors' is reductive when
compared with the literary traditions of postcolonial societies, where
national allegories might be discerned in both colonial and postcolonial texts. Secondly, Mansfield's short story enacts Jameson's 'working
hypothesis' within the short story, whereas Jameson concentrates his
reading only on 'third-world' novels.[20] As mentioned earlier, Mansfield
also uses the genre to introduce the complex representation of the
'*Künstlerroman* motif', which is commonly associated only with novels.

In any case, while opening up Jameson's argument to other literary
genres like the short story is relatively unproblematic, the positioning of Mansfield's short story among postcolonial texts seems to be
highly debatable. In fact, Katherine Mansfield is undoubtedly tied to
the settler-colonial culture, but her literary production does not support its ideological discourse; rather, her work – with a special reference

to 'How Pearl Button Was Kidnapped' – exposes the fissures and fractures of settler-colonial ideology. As Homi Bhabha puts it, 'the colonial presence is always ambivalent, split between its appearance as original and authoritative and its articulation as repetition and difference'.[21] In the light of this analysis, the family romance that Mansfield sketches in her short story can be said to be '(post)colonial', as this bracketing fully states the ambivalence of Mansfield's position in the colonial/ postcolonial literary tradition of New Zealand. A closer look at 'How Pearl Button Was Kidnapped' might highlight what kind of '(post) colonial national allegory' is enacted in the text.

From the text we can infer that Pearl Button is a white female child who lives in the 'House of Boxes' with her family, probably a settler family. No other markers of space and time are given throughout the text. This lack of a specific historical and geographical location is due to Mansfield's modernist style, but it cannot be consequentially interpreted as a lack of interest in a New Zealand setting, as can be inferred from the story more generally. The two 'dark women' (20) who carry Pearl away are very likely to be Māori, for although their ethnicity is not explicitly stated, many textual elements suggest this is the case. They are fat women, walking barefoot and wearing colourful clothes – a widespread stereotype of Māori women at the time.[22] References to Māori customs and culture occur in the 'flax basket of ferns', the 'feather mats' and the 'green ornament' (20, 21, 22, respectively) that one of them wears.[23] The women bring Pearl to their village, which is close to the seaside where Pearl's discovery of the sea – as stated earlier – enriches her mind and feelings. By repeatedly asserting her happiness, Pearl indirectly affirms that these two women are symbolically 'superior' to her biological family. Pearl also experiences a kind of imaginary sorority, when 'one of them, a young one, lifted all Pearl's hair and kissed the back of her little white neck' (21).

The glimpse of a different family and, indirectly, a different society is utterly negated in the story's conclusion, when Pearl is rescued by the police and her idyllic trip is brought to an end, restoring the previous order and condemning the kidnapping. There are, indeed, only two impositions of colonial order in relation to Pearl Button: at the very beginning of the story, the title defines her escape as a kidnapping, that is, an action against the law; at the end, the police undertake to re-establish the previous 'colonial' order by rescuing her. Appearing at the story's beginning and conclusion, the white settler ideology that is implied by these references to her being 'taken', apparently comprises a conceptual frame that violently contains and controls Pearl's idyllic escapade. This tension is productive, since it creates a strong

ambivalence between the definition of 'kidnapping' and Pearl's transgression, which is in line with the ambivalence of the (post)colonial
subject. It also underlines the fact that Pearl's happy escapade and her
romantic response is not permanent and could be undercut or interrupted at any time by a father-like authority.

Following through this analysis, the 'return of the father', evinced
through the moral authority embodied by the police, shows colonial
and national implications. This can be aligned with a perceived autobiographical pattern in the story, as Katherine Mansfield always identified
her real father, Harold Beauchamp, with the strength and meanness
of settler-colonial power.[24] It could then be argued, given this attitude,
that Mansfield's construction of the family romance and progression
towards a national allegory would always be abruptly interrupted by
the intervention of patriarchal and settler-colonial institutions. This,
however, does not prevent Mansfield from endorsing Pearl Button's
escapade and giving it centrality within the text: Mansfield's allegory of
the nation is precisely that of a shattered Arcadia,[25] where the masculine
patriarchal forces of settler-colonialism manage to destroy any possibility of conviviality between different populations and cultures, such as
the settler and the indigenous inhabitants. This is a national allegory
tout court, in line with one of Jameson's most contested arguments:
many critics have criticised his seeming defence of postcolonial nationalism, but, as Ian Buchanan has brilliantly argued,[26] the construction of
a national allegory does not imply immediate and enthusiastic participation in a nationalist discourse. What Mansfield depicts in her short story
is an allegory of the nation during settler-colonialism. In fact, Mansfield
uses the allegorical prism of family relations to build a representation
of the whole of New Zealand society, as she had experienced it before
leaving for Europe. Pearl Button, daughter of settlers, romances about
another family and, through it, about convivial life with the Māori, seen
as closer to nature than the settler. In contrast to this experience, a powerful alliance between patriarchy and colonialism takes place in order
to 'rescue' Pearl; nevertheless, by introducing a Māori family into the
'family frame', Mansfield shifts away from the mono-cultural ideal of
settler-colonial society, with its narrow identification of the white settler
family and the colony/nation. Through Pearl Button's eyes, she starts to
envision a different model for individual and collective existence.

In this sense, those critics who have acknowledged the presence
of 'familial structures as discursive' in Mansfield's oeuvre have gone
beyond the minimal identification between the family – especially the
Burnell family[27] – and the nation. If Lydia Wevers notices that 'the
family becomes the sign for both sameness and difference, and in its

characteristics and daily repetitions, it suggests the larger and constantly remade space of the family as nation',[28] Richard Brock holds
a similar but partially dissenting position, by insisting on difference
and dynamism rather than on repetition. He notes that Mansfield's
constant attempt to bring together the family and the nation is a 'work
in progress':

> The children in Mansfield's stories who possess the imaginative capacity
> to move beyond the boundaries of their domestic space are, in doing
> so, reaching out beyond the narrow boundaries of a colonial society to
> their families' and societies' Others (crucially, including the Māori). [. . .]
> Mansfield's New Zealand stories offer at least the prospect that an inclu-
> sive modern nation may one day be built on affiliative ties formed outside
> the spaces of patriarchy and colonialism. The patriarchal family structures
> in these stories may be viewed as a starting point, an arena for nation-
> forming acts which are anything but conservative.[29]

However, both Wevers and Brock – basing their argument on the
'Burnell cycle', rather than on stories such as 'How Pearl Button
Was Kidnapped' – collocate the identification of family and nation
only *within* Mansfield's work, so enabling the constant overlapping of
Mansfield's biographical family and its fictional counterpart. This kind
of interpretation constantly excludes those Māori characters and elements which Mansfield had actually introduced in 'How Pearl Button
Was Kidnapped'. Besides, such a reading would hypostatise and legitimate the brutally interrupted form of national allegory which Mansfield
sets in opposition to Pearl Button's romance. This would mean kidnapping and then rescuing Katherine Mansfield herself, by reinstating her
position exclusively within the context of her family. On the contrary,
noting the continuities in her oeuvre, linking stories such as 'How Pearl
Button Was Kidnapped' with those of the 'Burnell cycle' does not give a
complete perspective unless these links are extended beyond her family
and her oeuvre. Otherwise, they would only highlight a permanent
paralysis in the process of imagining the national community.

Mansfield's Postcolonial Legacy: Patricia Grace and Witi Ihimaera

Mansfield's 'task' was taken up again, many years later, by writers of the
Māori Renaissance, such as Patricia Grace in her short story 'Letters
from Whetu' (1980),[30] and Witi Ihimaera in *The Matriarch* (1986).[31]
These texts not only constitute a postcolonial literary elaboration of a
Mansfield theme, but they also provide new alternatives by comparing
family structures and national structures for shaping and re-shaping the
image of New Zealand bicultural society.

Patricia Grace intervenes directly in the allegory of the nation established by Mansfield, by insisting on the idyllic qualities of Māori family life, especially within the whanau (the extended family). In 'Letters from Whetu', as in other stories, she portrays the serenity of communal activities such as feast preparation, gardening, or collecting mussels – so echoing Pearl Button's discovery of beauty through contact with nature. In this context, the decision of the Māori student, Whetu, to leave high school before graduating – mainly due to his unease within a Pākehā and racist institution, embodied by a sinister schoolmaster – implies the abrupt interruption of his *Bildung*; this recalls the brusque 'return of the father' which interrupts Pearl's path to enjoyment and aesthetic refinement. Therefore, seventy years after Mansfield, what is at stake in 'Letters from Whetu' is the presence of a pervasive and colonial father-like authority, which works this time through the school institution.

Ihimaera takes up the task of figuring the nation through the family in his novel *The Matriarch* (1986), published three years before his ironical though appreciative tribute to Mansfield in the short story collection, *Dear Miss Mansfield*. *The Matriarch* concerns a recovery of Māori history, which is a return *to*, and *of* the 'matriarch', conceived as both the grandmother and Aotearoa itself, according to Suzanne Romaine's interpretation of the novel.[32] From a figurative perspective, therefore, Ihimaera's 'matriarch' might be said to replace Mansfield's deceiving and intrusive 'patriarch'. However, Ihimaera does not provide a fully nativist and self-celebratory account of the nation; instead, he suggests a transnational history for New Zealand/Aotearoa, by going back through the figure of the matriarch to whakapapa (Māori genealogies), and also to the legendary migration from Polynesia, the genesis of Māori settlement in New Zealand. In addition, *The Matriarch* intertwines the Māori mythical and historical account of New Zealand/Aotearoa history with official Pākehā history, as well as with a metaphorical reference point, the history of the national foundation of Italy, that is, the Italian Risorgimento.

Once again, such a complex national, transnational, and even cross-cultural history shows that in the case of all three authors mentioned in this article there is a long-standing nexus between the family and the nation in New Zealand/Aotearoa cultural history. Some of its historical moments have also been recalled here: whakapapa was violently replaced by the genealogies of settler-colonial families; later, Māori historical and mythical accounts of the past were recovered – by Grace and Ihimaera, among other authors – in order to build a more inclusive account of New Zealand/Aotearoa history. Being inclusive and marked by the Braudelian *longue durée*,[33] such an itinerary cannot avoid a confrontation with Mansfield, since – through the staging of a (post) colonial family romance – Mansfield deliberately sought to show how violently imposed and highly debatable the relationships were between the family and the nation established within settler-colonial administration.

Though marked by sudden interruptions, manifest contradictions and persistent ambiguities, Mansfield's literary work was a landmark in the process of imagining the nation through literary allegories. However bitterly criticised, this Jamesonian task still shows some validity today, as long as it is considered not as universal and homogeneous, but as provisional and contingent; it corresponds with the process of shaping and re-shaping the New Zealand/Aotearoa nation, which is still ongoing.

Notes

1. 'Maoriland' refers to the definition of New Zealand in the first wave of cultural nationalism, between 1880 and 1915. The emphasis on the 'land of Māori' was not intended to underline the role of the Māori in the process of nation building; rather, it was introduced to distinguish New Zealand from Australia, as a necessary step in the formation of a nationalist discourse in New Zealand. The expression 'Maoriland writing' refers to literature published from the late 1860s to the early 1920s, which is relevant to that discourse of cultural nationalism.
2. Mark Williams and Jane Stafford, 'Katherine Mansfield: A Modernist in Maoriland', in Mark Williams and Jane Stafford, eds, *Maoriland: New Zealand Literature 1872–1914* (Wellington: Victoria University Press, 2006), p. 152.
3. Keith Gregor, 'Blissful Thinking: Katherine Mansfield and the Engendering of Modernist Fiction', *Cuadernos de Filología Inglesa*, 6.1 (1997), p. 74.
4. The short story was originally published in 1912 in the magazine *Rhythm*, under the pen name of Lili Heron. The edition used here is 'How Pearl Button was Kidnapped', in Katherine Mansfield, *Selected Stories*, ed. Angela Smith (Oxford: Oxford University Press, 2006), pp. 20–3. All further references to Mansfield's stories are to this edition and placed parenthetically after each quotation.
5. Freud's essay was firstly published in the anthology edited by Otto Rank, *Der Mythos von der Geburt des Helden: Versuch einer psychologischen Mythendeutung* (Wien/Leipzig: Deuticke, 1909).
6. The first English translation of the anthology edited by Rank appeared as 'The Myth of the Birth of the Hero', in the *Journal of Nervous and Mental Disease*, published in New York in 1914. The edition consulted here is Sigmund Freud, 'Family Romances', in James Strachey, ed., *The Standard Edition of the Complete Psychological Works of Sigmund Freud, Volume IX (1906–1908): Jensen's 'Gradiva' and Other Works* (London: Hogarth Press and the Institute of Psychoanalysis, 1959), pp. 235–42.
7. Freud, 'Family Romances', p. 241.
8. Freud, 'Family Romances', p. 240.
9. Marianne Hirsch, *The Mother/Daughter Plot: Narrative, Psychoanalysis, Feminism* (Bloomington: Indiana University Press, 1989), p. 9.
10. According to Susan Gubar, the most notable examples of the '*Künstlerroman* motif' in Mansfield's oeuvre are three short stories: 'The-Child-Who-Was-Tired' (1910), 'The Woman at the Store' (1912) and 'The Dolls' House' (1921). Susan Gubar, 'The Birth of the Artist as Heroine: (Re)production, the *Künstlerroman* Tradition, and the

Fiction of Katherine Mansfield', in Carolyn Heilbrun and Margaret Higonnet, eds, *The Representation of Women in Fiction* (Baltimore: The Johns Hopkins University Press, 1983), pp. 19–59.

11. Marianne Hirsch, *Family Frames: Photography, Narrative, and Postmemory* (Cambridge: Harvard University Press, 1997).

12. Keith Gregor states that 'Mansfield unfortunately never explains how private epiphanies [in 'Bliss'] can be articulated through a poetics of fiction, or how they might embody a step beyond the aesthetics of Romanticism and symbolism' (p. 65).

13. Janka Kaščáková, '"My Flowerless Ones": Representations of Unmarried Women in the Short Stories of Katherine Mansfield', *Brno Studies in English*, 35.1 (2009), pp. 137–45. For Susan Gubar, see note 10 above.

14. Hirsch, p. 97.

15. The main stories in this cycle are 'Prelude', 'At the Bay' and 'The Dolls' House'. 'Prelude' was first published as an autonomous work in 1918 by the Hogarth Press; later, it was included in the collection *Bliss and Other Stories* (London: Constable, 1920). 'At the Bay' and 'The Doll's House' were published, respectively, in *The Garden Party and Other Stories* (London: Constable, 1922) and *The Dove's Nest and Other Stories* (London: Constable, 1923).

16. Notable among the numerous publications about Mansfield's life experience and its relationship to her writing are Cherry Hankin, *Katherine Mansfield and her Confessional Stories* (London: Macmillan, 1983) and Gillian Boddy, *Katherine Mansfield: The Woman and the Writer* (Basingstoke: Penguin, 1988).

17. Fredric Jameson, 'Third-World Literature in the Era of Multi-National Capitalism', *Social Text*, 15 (Autumn, 1986), pp. 65–88 (p. 69).

18. After the first dismissal of Jameson's hypothesis in Aijaz Ahmad's article 'Jameson's Rhetoric of Otherness and the "National Allegory"' (*Social Text*, 17 (1987), pp. 3–25), which served as a blueprint for much of the following criticism, Jameson's article was eventually rehabilitated by scholars such as Imre Szeman ('Who's Afraid of National Allegory? Jameson, Literary Criticism, Globalization', *South Atlantic Quarterly*, 100.3 (2001), pp. 803–27) and Neil Lazarus ('Fredric Jameson on "Third-World Literature": a defense', in *The Postcolonial Unconscious* (Cambridge: Cambridge University Press, 2011), pp. 89–113).

19. Jameson, p. 69.

20. One of the first objections to Jameson's limited focus on novels is to be found in Aijaz Ahmad's reply, where Ahmad, before completely dismissing Jameson's thesis, defends the possibility of also creating political allegories through poetry (Ahmad, p. 4).

21. Homi Bhabha, *The Location of Culture* (London and New York: Routledge, 1994), p. 107. Bhabha's argument has been recently applied to Mansfield by Janet Wilson in her essay 'Where is Katherine?: Longing and (Un)belonging in the Works of Katherine Mansfield', in Gerri Kimber and Janet Wilson, eds, *Celebrating Katherine Mansfield. A Centenary Volume of Essays* (Basingstoke: Palgrave MacMillan, 2011), p. 178.

22. A full historical account of stereotypical representations of Māori culture can be found in Leonard Bell, *The Māori in European art: a survey of the representation of the Māori by European artists from the time of Captain Cook to the Present day* (Wellington: Reed, 1980).

23. As Angela Smith reports in the 'Explanatory Notes' at the end of her edition of Mansfield's stories, the 'flax basket of ferns' refers to the kete, 'baskets of plaited flax

which Māori use for carrying, and for storing food'; the 'feather mats' refer to the 'the tail-feathers of the huia' that 'were once worn by Māori as a badge of rank'; the 'green ornament' is 'a jade pendant that was usually part of Māori girls' dress' (p. 377).

24. Mark Williams and Jane Stafford repeatedly argue that Kathleen Mansfield Beauchamp saw her father Harold Beauchamp, who became chairman of the Bank of New Zealand, as the quintessential image of British colonialism, in 'Katherine Mansfield: A Modernist in Maoriland', in Williams and Stafford, pp. 142–70.

25. Among the unquestionable racial and cultural biases which permeate Mansfield's short story, the belief in the Rousseauian definition of *bon sauvage* – the 'good savage' who enjoys life, for its unmediated relationship with nature – is prominent in the text.

26. Ian Buchanan, 'National Allegory Today: A Return to Jameson', in *On Jameson: From Postmodernism to Globalization*, ed. Ian Buchanan and Caren Irr (Albany: SUNY Press, 2006), pp. 173–88.

27. Many textual elements – including the easy identification of Kezia Burnell with Mansfield herself, whose childhood nickname was Kass – hint at the identification of the Burnell family with the Beauchamps. See, for instance, Lydia Wevers, 'The Sod Under my Feet: Katherine Mansfield', in Mark Williams and Michelle Leggott, eds, *Opening the Book: New Essays on New Zealand Writing* (Auckland: Auckland University Press, 1995), pp. 31–48.

28. Wevers, pp. 41–2.

29. Richard Brock, 'Disapprobation, Disobedience and the Nation in Katherine Mansfield's New Zealand Stories, *Journal of New Zealand Literature*, 24.1 (2006), pp. 58–74 (p. 71).

30. Patricia Grace, 'Letters from Whetu', in *The Dream Sleepers and Other Stories* (Auckland: Longman Paul, 1980), pp. 28–42.

31. Witi Ihimaera, *The Matriarch* (Auckland: Pan Books, 1986).

32. Suzanne Romaine, 'Contested Visions of History in Aotearoa New Zealand Literature: Witi Ihimaera's *The Matriarch*', in *The Contemporary Pacific*, 16.1 (2004), p. 48.

33. The concept of *longue durée* (which could be translated in English as 'long-term') informs Braudel's masterwork *La Méditerranée et le Monde Méditerranéen à l'époque de Philippe II* (1949) and his following production. It is applied here to literary history, which, starting from the recent theorisations in the field of 'world literature' (such as David Damrosch's *What is World Literature?* (Princeton: Princeton University Press, 2003), seems to require it, especially when confronted with transnational frameworks.

'Unmasking' the First-Person Narrator of *In a German Pension*

W. Todd Martin

When James Joyce left Ireland to 'forge in the smithy of [his] soul the created conscience of [his] race',[1] he meant to escape the provincialism of the people he felt were holding him back as well as to separate the full sense of his heritage from the Empire that had brought its influence to bear on Ireland. The famous 'tundish' scene in *A Portrait of the Artist as a Young Man* reveals this interplay of influences between coloniser and the colonised. In the midst of a discussion on aesthetics with the dean – an 'English convert'[2] and 'a poor Englishman in Ireland'[3] – Stephen Dedalus reflects upon the cultural impact of language after the dean uses the word 'funnel' instead of the term, 'tundish':

> The language in which we are speaking is his before it is mine. How different are the words *home, Christ, ale, master,* on his lips and on mine! I cannot speak or write these words without unrest of spirit. His language, so familiar and so foreign, will always be for me an acquired speech. I have not made or accepted his words. My voice holds them at bay. My soul frets in the shadow of his language.[4]

Recognising the 'nets flung at [the soul] to hold it back from flight', Stephen – and by extension Joyce – attempts to escape these nets: 'nationality, language, and religion'.[5]

Similarly, Katherine Mansfield left New Zealand to escape its provincialism, and, as she matured as a person and as a writer, she determined to 'make [her] undiscovered country leap into the eyes of the old world'.[6] In essence, she forged the soul of her own race by exploring the dialectic between home and not-home, between New Zealand and England. Perhaps the most obvious contrast can be found in her story, 'Millie' (1913), in which Mansfield contrasts an English print of Windsor Castle which depicts the 'emerald lawns planted with immense

oak trees, and in their grateful shade a muddle of ladies and gentlemen and parasols and little tables' with Millie's wedding picture which
shows 'some fern trees and a waterfall, and Mount Cook in the distance,
covered with snow' behind the couple.[7] In so doing, Mansfield draws
attention not only to the contrasting scenes, but also to the pervasive
influence a country so distant geographically and geologically can have
on its colony.

However, Mansfield's earlier work – especially her first published
collection of short stories *In a German Pension* (1911) – reveals a greater
complicity with the Empire than her later works. Immature and still
unsure of herself, Mansfield seems to have accepted the notion that
England was the seat of culture, and as a colonial still trying to find
her place in the world and develop her style and purpose as a writer,
she longed to escape the provincialism of New Zealand to be a part
of the broader, dominant cultural milieu. Thus, while many 'settler
and creole writers became concerned to legitimate from their particular geographic and cultural perspective a subjectivity distinct, even
if adapted, from Europe',[8] Mansfield borrowed considerably from
the aesthetic and ideological views of England. Lee Garver indicates
that

> In the context of prewar British cultural discourse Germany was not only
> regarded as an immediate military threat to Britain, but also considered
> a nation whose dynamic birthrate and economy posed long-term ques-
> tions about the status of Britain as a great power. For many of Mansfield's
> contemporaries, Germany's military ambitions and birthrate were obverse
> sides of a single coin: if left unchallenged, they would together spell doom
> for Britain's imperial aspirations. These widely held cultural anxieties
> were of enormous concern to the milieu of Edwardian intellectual debate
> out of which Mansfield's stories emerged.[9]

Drawing on this context, Garver argues that Mansfield's early stories,
which incorporate negative portrayals of Germans, have been 'ill served
by prevailing views of her indifference to political and social contro-
versy'[10] and that they actually participate 'in the political and cultural
ferment through their prominent and forcefully negative portrayals of
German imperial culture and maternity'.[11] Unfortunately, Mansfield
destroyed the notebooks from her time in Bavaria, which might have
shed light on her personal feelings toward the Germans, but there is
no clear indication of anti-German sentiments in the letters she wrote
during her tenure at the *New Age* where many of the stories from *In a
German Pension* were originally published. As a New Zealander, though,
it is unlikely Mansfield would have harboured the same hostile senti-

ments as the English contributors to the magazine, except perhaps in a broader, pro-Empire context. Nevertheless, she appears to have capitalised on English tendencies of nationalism and anti-German sentiment, relying on stereotypes in many of her early stories to conform to the general sentiments of anxiety leading up to World War One. However, many of the stories in the collection provide a corrective, subverting the dominant cultural perspective of the English and demonstrating a more conflicted Mansfield – a colonial trying to find her place in Europe. Arguing that Mansfield should be considered a liminal writer, a 'colonial modernist', Janet Wilson explains that Mansfield's 'mixed feelings about colonial New Zealand are central to her self-positioning in metropolitan Europe'.[12] Mansfield was determined to escape what she perceived as the petit bourgeois mentality of her family and nation, but the separation from home affected her more severely than she anticipated.[13] Wilson traces Mansfield's divided self through some of the earlier New Zealand stories and sketches, demonstrating how she often distances herself from the white settlers (even though she was one), usually in favour of the indigenous Māori. In London, however, Mansfield 'saw herself as "a stranger", as "the little colonial"' which, Wilson posits, accounts for her later 're-enter[ing] the same colonial space through memories of childhood' in her stories about the Sheridan and Burnell families in Wellington.[14] Parallel with Wilson's reading of doubling in the early New Zealand stories, in which Mansfield distances herself from white colonials, I suggest that in the 'Pension Sketches' – those pieces from *In a German Pension* with a first-person narrator[15] – Mansfield undermines the dominant, anti-German sentiment of the metropolitan implied author through the colonial narrator's desire to participate in the community at the pension.

Jenny McDonnell demonstrates how Mansfield had everything to gain in her negative portrayal of Germans. 'Mansfield's sarcastic lampooning of a series of German institutions and stereotypes was granted an obvious marketability in the years leading up to World War One, and when they came to be collected as *In a German Pension* [...] it was primarily from this source that they derived their marketability.'[16] According to Diane Milburn, the *New Age* was following the political trends in Germany as early as 1907, although a prominent political writer at that time, Cecil Chesterton, made a clear distinction between the German people and the German Kaiser, Wilhelm II.[17] The *New Age* even argued that 'the enemy of England was not Germany, but rather some of the sensationalist outpourings of Fleet Street journalists, intent on stirring up anti-German feelings'.[18] By May 1910, though, around the time Mansfield was placing some of her 'Pension Sketches' in the

New Age, S. Verdad (the pen name of J. M. Kennedy) was named foreign affairs correspondent for the periodical. Milburn notes that 'his articles [were] violently anti-German in tone'.[19]

Anti-German sentiments had thus been building during the years after Mansfield returned to England in 1908, and one cannot entirely blame Mansfield, a fledgling writer at the time, for tapping into the ideological ferment of her day in order to get her work into print. As McDonnell points out, Mansfield understood 'the practicalities of the marketplace'.[20] Yet later in her career, she very consciously divorced herself from this particular collection of stories, despite the fact that some of them – for example 'Frau Brechenmacher Attends a Wedding' and 'At Lehmann's' – share thematic and stylistic qualities with some of her strongest works. John Middleton Murry recounts in his Introductory Note to *In a German Pension* that when he encouraged Mansfield to republish the stories for which she would have received a significant advance, she responded, '"I cannot have *The German Pension* reprinted under any circumstances. It is far too immature, and I don't even acknowledge it today. I mean I don't "hold" by it. [. . .] It's positively juvenile, and besides that, it's not what I mean; it's a lie. Oh no, never".'[21] And, in a letter to Eric Pinker, she writes:

> I think it would be very unwise to republish it [*In a German Pension*]. Not only because its [sic] a most inferior book (which it is) but I have, with my last book, begun to persuade the reviewers that I don't like ugliness for ugliness sake. The intelligentsia might be kind enough to forgive youthful extravagances of expression and youthful disgust. But I don't want to write for them.[22]

Significantly, Mansfield indicates that she doesn't '"hold" by it' and that 'it's not what I mean; it's a lie', and she doesn't want to convey that she likes 'ugliness for ugliness sake'. These comments suggest that Mansfield wanted not only to separate herself from these stories aesthetically, but also because of the pettiness of these often biting portrayals of her subject, because they do not – and probably never did – ring true for her.

As a New Zealander, Mansfield would have had certain sympathies with the Empire as the general sense among New Zealanders was that there was not a perceived contradiction between nation and empire in the years following the status change from colony to Dominion;[23] this would help to explain Mansfield's affinity with England when she first arrived as a schoolgirl and her later perception of it as the metropolis to which she paid homage as a young writer. However, the anti-German sentiments would have most likely been fostered once Mansfield returned to England in 1908, for being far removed from the political intrigue and social prejudices of Europe, New Zealanders would not have developed at this stage such antagonism for the Germans. In fact, in discussing New Zealand's involvement in World War One, historian James Belich claims, 'New Zealanders in 1914 did not investigate the cause of the conflict'.[24] And, while anti-German sentiments were displayed in New Zealand once it entered the war,[25] there was no precedent for such feelings until then. In fact, according to Belich, New Zealand's entry into the war was not due to any direct anti-German sentiment:

> The objective of the New Zealand war effort was to entrench and augment the special relationship with Britain [. . .] The method was to create a moral debt in British minds to New Zealand in particular by exceeding the unquestioning loyalty and eager sacrifice of the other dominions.[26]

It is my contention, then, that while Mansfield wrote stories that conformed to the negative attitudes towards Germans expressed in the pages of the *New Age*, she created a first-person narrator who – while not directly identifiable with the author – suggests a subversive response to the German stereotypes otherwise expressed in the stories. And, while it is typically fallacious to identify the narrator with the author, there is reason to believe that Mansfield associated closely with the first-person narrator of these stories. First, of course, the stories are based on Mansfield's own experiences in Bavaria, where she stayed after her mother removed her from England due to a pending social scandal following her sudden marriage to George Bowden.[27] Second, early versions suggest that Mansfield had infused herself directly into the stories. In the first version of 'Germans at Meat', for example, 'the story is narrated in the third person by the English-speaking "Kathleen" [Mansfield's given name], but this is later altered to an anonymous first-person narrator who sets herself primarily apart, observing and recording [. . .]'.[28] This use of her given name in an earlier version of the story suggests a close association with the narrator, along the lines of the autobiographical first-person narratives she later wrote for the *New Age*, namely 'The Journey to Bruges' (1911) and 'A Truthful Adventure' (1911), which recount her voyage to Bruges and her disappointment that its reality did not live up to the accounts in her guide book. These narratives, which contain aesthetic elements of Mansfield's fiction, demonstrate at the very least that Mansfield did at times inject herself into her work, and the autobiographical context of the 'Pension Sketches' would certainly have lent themselves to this narrative position.

Apart from this change in the narrator's identity in 'Germans at

Meat', the stories themselves appear to suggest that the narrator is English. Most of the pension guests for example, presume the narrator is English, and critics typically follow suit in their discussions of the collection. Yet, for the most part, the narrator neither fully affirms nor denies her nationality. The closest she comes to conceding her nationality as English occurs in 'The Advanced Lady' (1911) in which the title character asks, 'I think you are English?', to which the narrator indicates, 'I acknowledged the fact' (236). And this seems to settle the matter. However, in another story, 'The Luft Bad' (1910), the narrator begins to deny her association with the English, but finding her audience little interested in such – to them – minor distinctions, she lets the subject drop. A woman who has embarked on a simple diet of raw vegetables and nuts, identified as the Vegetable Lady, inquires:

> 'Are you an American?' said the Vegetable Lady, turning to me.
> 'No.'
> 'Then you are an Englishwoman?'
> 'Well, hardly – '
> 'You must be one of the two; you cannot help it.' (177)

The Vegetable Lady does not initially associate the narrator with the English, but perhaps noting something in her accent, or something else about her person, she first inquires if the narrator is American. When this is denied, she then presumes that she must be English, cutting short any further discussion by insisting that she must be 'one of the two'. The narrator, however, begins to correct the assumption, and the key word, 'hardly', opens up the opportunity for her to make a distinction between being English and being a colonial. It is not a full denial of her connection to England as a member of the larger Empire, but it does suggest that there is a distinction to be made. New Zealand's acquisition of Dominion status in 1907 may have helped its citizens to begin to establish a sense of their separate national identity.[29]

This exchange suggests that the narrator does not directly associate herself with the English, and as the stories are based on the author's own experience, readers could then conclude from biographical facts that she is from New Zealand. What this exchange reveals – along with its seeming contradiction with the scene from 'The Advanced Lady' – is the identity struggle of white colonials in a continental setting, one that Mansfield herself undoubtedly faced in her own experience in Bavaria. We know from Mansfield's journals and letters that she experienced the stigma of being singled out as a colonial while in England. While in Germany, though, wanting to identify herself with the metropolis, and being in a foreign country where any difference in her accent would not give her away as easily, she could take on that persona more readily. Her identity was more fluid. Thus, Mansfield, like her narrator, could have similarly identified herself with the English among the Germans.

However, to the extent that the narrator wants to claim her true nationality, she is hindered, for the Germans define her as English, attributing to her their stereotypical views of the English even as the stories reveal English stereotypes of the Germans. The exchange in 'The Luft Bad', then, reveals a different reason for the narrator's tolerance of the pension guests' presumption that she was English: it is just easier. Most English speakers were no doubt considered to be English, and attempts like this one to 'explain' her nationality would either fall on deaf ears or entail further explanations on the part of a narrator who typically keeps her distance from the other pensioners. Thus, in the situation with the Advanced Lady, she may merely confirm the connection because she has never taken the time to correct the other pensioners' assumption that she is English, so why should she make a special effort in this case? The Germans are quick to point out that she is 'other', yet that 'other' is not a true indication of her nationality.

As Wayne Booth suggests in his seminal work on narrative, 'the narrator is often radically different from the implied author who creates him',[30] and the implied author is often more likely to be closely aligned with the writer. However, Mansfield, a New Zealander who presumably would have held much less rancour toward the Germans than the English, appears to identify herself more fully with the first-person narrator of the stories than she does with the implied author who plays the role of satirist, telling the English audience what they want to hear. And this first-person narrator, so similar to Mansfield, is less critical of the Germans than the implied author. In fact, the narrator of the stories – while impatient of the often intrusive prying of the pensioners – associates herself with them, sharing some of their folly, and thus providing a buffer between the caricatures presented in the stories. In 'The Baron' (1910,) for example, the implied author 'mocks the excessive respect for titles and social status of the Germans'.[31] However, the narrator's own curiosity opens the story; she is just as meddlesome as the other guests and just as intrigued by the notion of royalty that the Baron represents. When she initially asks about the Baron, the woman to whom she raises the question treats her as an outsider, giving her a '"fancy-not-recognizing-that-at-the-first glance" expression' (172). By the end of the story, however, the narrator's direct encounter with the Baron, sharing his umbrella, raises her status among the other pensioners, including the woman who initially snubbed her. Throughout the story, however, the narrator demonstrates the same curiosity shared by the other pensioners, and their mutual admiration of the gluttonous Baron – misplaced as it may be – draws them together. When some of the ladies of the pension are gathered in the salon, the narrator specifically associates herself with them, using the plural pronoun 'we', and the topic she engages in is clearly one that she would have balked at in other contexts. During the conversation, one of the unmarried women mentions that a male friend may write to her mother asking permission to court or to marry her, and the narrator recounts that she and the others – she includes herself in the 'we' – are 'a little violently excited' (174). And when the Baron pokes his head in and gets a toothpick from a dish in the same room, she – along with the rest – 'raised a triumphant cry! It was the first time he had ever been known to enter the salon. Who could tell what the Future held?' (174). The implied author of the story certainly mocks the Baron's reasons for isolation, namely his desire to eat as much as he likes without being bothered. The narrator, though, shares in the excitement and curiosity about this celebrity who has joined them at the pension.

In the story 'The Sister of the Baroness' (1910), the narrator and the other pension guests fall for the ruse propagated by the daughter of the Baroness's dressmaker in her claim to be the sister of the Baroness. Their shared gullibility establishes a degree of unity resulting from the misunderstanding. It demonstrates that the narrator does not hold a superior position. The implied author, on the other hand, mocks the status bestowed upon this young woman when she arrives with her charge, the daughter of the Baroness. Again, the narrator is singled out as not belonging when the proprietor suggests that they transport a portrait of the Kaiser from the narrator's room into the young woman's room, because the portrait would not hold any significance to the narrator. The narrator's response is: 'I felt a little crushed. Not at the prospect of losing that vision of diamonds and blue velvet bust, but at the tone – placing me outside the pale – branding me as a foreigner' (190). This sentiment suggests that the narrator wants to fit in, and, as in 'The Baron', she gets caught up in the excitement of meeting this member of royalty. As the morning's discussions focus on the upcoming visit, the narrator again uses 'we' to identify herself with the excitement of the group: 'We positively scintillated. Anecdotes of the High Born were poured out, sweetened and sipped: we gorged on scandals of High Birth generously buttered' (190).

Jayne Marek, in her article, 'Anxious Narrations: Katherine Mansfield's *In a German Pension*', draws on 'feminist narratological analysis' in order to expose the anxieties of the implied author of the stories whom Marek (incorrectly, I believe) associates with the first-person narrator. Arguing that the narrator's 'willingness to judge those around her while reveal-ing very little about herself' demonstrates the narrator's refusal 'to take the reader entirely into her confidence',[32] Marek suggests that the narrator's 'sarcastic distancing' enables Mansfield to similarly evade – among other things – 'being judged for her sexuality'.[33] However, while I would agree that Mansfield does distance herself from the implied author and in so doing possibly reveals the anxiety Marek finds implied in the text, both the direct and indirect discourse of the first-person narrator suggest that she wants to fit in and not remain detached from the others. The narrator of 'The Baron' and 'The Sister of the Baroness' does not want to be identified as a foreigner, but rather to be a part of the gossip and the goings-on in the pension. Despite her critiques of the Germans, the narrator's desire to fit in suggests her humanity, distinguishing her from the satirical implied author. This desire to be a part of a group results from the fact that, as a colonial, Mansfield herself often felt like an outsider – even in England – and she demonstrates her longing to feel included through her narrator.

The narrator demonstrates some empathy with the Germans, and even when she criticises them her critiques have less to do with racial stereotypes and more to do with human weaknesses, ones that she shares. In this way, the narrator may be more closely aligned with the views Mansfield actually holds, for while Mansfield very likely targeted these stories to her English audience, using the implied author to deni-grate her German characters, she later rejected the 'ugliness' of the sto-ries. Perhaps not trusting her readers to pick up the subtle and nuanced interactions between the narrator and the Germans which undermined the satire of some pieces, Mansfield wanted to distance herself both from the derogatory depictions of the Germans – the targets of easy satire – and from the overly simplistic renderings of her characters. Her later work, in fact, gains its strength from its ability to expose human weakness in a much more sympathetic, if still critical, light.

As she matured as a writer, Mansfield would remove herself more completely from her stories, allowing her characters to reveal them-selves through dramatic circumstances and dialogue. But in the case of the 'Pension Sketches', Mansfield tries to convey her own experiences while accommodating the expectations of her audience, particularly their views of the Germans. The result is a tension between wanting to find her place in the context of the Empire while remaining true to herself and her experience in Bavaria. She undermines the cynical caricatures of the Germans by portraying a narrator who is capable of sharing in their humanity. Only later, in 'Prelude' and the stories that followed, would Mansfield fully realise her sense of self as a writer and come to understand her sense of self as a New Zealander determined to shift the colonial power structures and make the 'old world' discover the 'unexplored country' of her childhood home.

Notes
1. James Joyce, *A Portrait of the Artist as a Young Man* (Harmondsworth and New York: Penguin Books, 1982), p. 253.
2. Joyce, p. 188.
3. Joyce, p. 189.
4. Joyce, p. 189.
5. Joyce, p. 203.
6. Margaret Scott, ed., *The Katherine Mansfield Notebooks*, 2 vols (Canterbury, New Zealand and Wellington: Lincoln University Press and Daphne Brasell Associates, 1997), Vol. 2, p. 32.
7. Katherine Mansfield, 'Millie', in Gerri Kimber and Vincent O'Sullivan, eds, *The Collected Fiction of Katherine Mansfield*, 2 vols (Edinburgh: Edinburgh University Press, 2012), Vol. 1, p. 327. All referenced stories by Mansfield are from this edition and volume, and page numbers for all further references to the stories are placed after each quotation.
8. Elleke Boehmer, *Colonial and Postcolonial Literature: Migrant Metaphors* (Oxford and New York: Oxford University Press, 1995), p. 112.
9. Lee Garver, 'The Political Katherine Mansfield', *Modernism/Modernity*, 8.2 (2001), p. 228.
10. Garver, p. 225.
11. Garver, p. 227.
12. Janet Wilson, '"Where is Katherine?": Longing and (Un)belonging in the Works of Katherine Mansfield', in Gerri Kimber and Janet Wilson, eds, *Celebrating Katherine Mansfield: A Centenary Volume of Essays* (Basingstoke: Palgrave Macmillan, 2011), pp. 175, 176.
13. Wilson, p. 176.
14. Wilson, pp. 182–3.
15. Jenny McDonnell, *Katherine Mansfield and the Modernist Marketplace: At the Mercy of the Public* (Basingstoke: Palgrave Macmillan, 2010), pp. 30–1.
16. McDonnell, p. 34.
17. Diane Milburn, *The Deutschlandbild of A. R. Orage and the New Age Circle* (Frankfurt am Main: Peter Lang, 1996), p. 35.
18. Milburn, p. 36.
19. Milburn, p. 52.
20. McDonnell, p. 56.
21. John Middleton Murry, 'Introductory Note', *In a German Pension*, in *The Collected Stories of Katherine Mansfield* (Hertfordshire: Wordsworth Classics, 2006), pp. 578–9.
22. Vincent O'Sullivan and Margaret Scott, eds, *The Collected Letters of Katherine Mansfield*, 5 vols (Oxford: Clarendon Press, 1984–2008), Vol. 5, p. 165.
23. Philippa Mein Smith, *A Concise History of New Zealand* (Cambridge: Cambridge University Press, 2005), p. 124.
24. James Belich, *Paradise Reforged: A History of the New Zealanders from the 1880s to the Year 2000* (Honolulu: University of Hawai'i Press, 2001), p. 95.
25. Tom Brooking, *The History of New Zealand* (Westport, CT and London: Greenwood Press, 2004), p. 105.

26. Belich, p. 111.
27. Biographers differ in their opinion as to whether Mansfield's mother knew she was pregnant. See, for example, Antony Alpers's *The Life of Katherine Mansfield* (New York: Viking Press, 1980) p. 94, which suggests Mansfield was sent to Bavaria because of her 'relationships with women', while Kathleen Jones, in *Katherine Mansfield: The Story-Teller* (Edinburgh: Edinburgh University Press, 2010), p. 107, argues that it was Mansfield's pregnancy which was the main concern.
28. Jones, pp. 111–12. See also McDonnell p. 31.
29. Janet Wilson has made similar observations concerning the national identity of the first-person narrator in these stories in an unpublished paper delivered at the 'Celebrating Katherine Mansfield Symposium' held in Menton, France, September 2009.
30. Wayne C. Booth, *The Rhetoric of Fiction*, 2nd edn (Chicago and London: University of Chicago Press, 1983), p. 152.
31. Milburn, p. 61.
32. Jayne Marek, 'Anxious Narrations: Katherine Mansfield's *In a German Pension*', *Literature Interpretation Theory*, 8.3–4 (1998), p. 284.
33. Marek, p. 291.

Workmanship and Wildness: Katherine Mansfield on Edith Wharton's *The Age of Innocence*

Emily Ridge

In December 1920, Katherine Mansfield reviewed Edith Wharton's *The Age of Innocence* for *The Athenaeum* within a longer piece entitled 'Family Portraits'. The purpose of this article is to show that Mansfield's reading of Wharton's novel is also a self-reflexive account of her own approach to, and struggles with, the writing process. It conveys her conception of literary form and style, both by contrast and by comparison. It must equally be seen as a reading informed by her early colonial experience and later life of perpetual displacement, biographical details which serve, as we shall see, to bring her closer to Wharton, despite her intimations of significant differences of aesthetic conception in the review itself. For Mansfield, as for many other modernists, to cite Clare Hanson, 'there is a particularly close connection between critical and creative writing'.[1] That is to say, that Mansfield visibly works through certain textual dilemmas and explores her own literary place – or perhaps it would be more accurate to call it her placelessness – through her critical interrogations. Her journal reveals that certain ideas, with which she privately grappled in relation to her own writing, reappear in her reviews, sometimes almost word for word, as applied to the writings of others.[2] It is as if she used these reviews as an important means of thinking through her own ideas about art. The creative writer in Mansfield is always implicitly present behind the critic and placed in critical relation to those writers under scrutiny. Mansfield's response to Wharton's novel offers one particularly interesting example of this critical-creative interplay because it suggests that the novel itself mirrors, on a thematic level, the implied difference as well as a deeper affinity between Mansfield and Wharton as contrasting artists. Her reading of the novel thus forms, more broadly, I would argue, an appraisal of the ambivalent quality of her peculiar brand of modernism.

So how *does* she read the novel? While drawing considerable attention to and commending 'Mrs Wharton's skill and delicate workmanship' (308) in handling the impossible love-story between the Countess Ellen Olenska and married man Newland Archer, Mansfield nevertheless baulks at her ultimate restraint in forbidding their transgressive union: 'But what about us? What about her readers?' (307). For the ever-mobile and expatriated Mansfield, the outcome of *The Age of Innocence* is all too carefully curated and she takes issue with the culminating sense of static, if elegant, confinement: 'We are looking at portraits – are we not? These are human beings, arranged for exhibition purposes, framed, glazed, and hung in the perfect light' (308). We know from her journal that the inhibiting effect of over-sophistication, of 'perfect' arrangement, was a more general preoccupation as well as a target for her censure at this time. The 'cultivated mind doesn't really attract me' (234–4), she remarks in an entry in December 1920, the very same month as the review. This is a point she cannot help exuberantly and unrestrainedly expanding upon, thus playfully and self-reflexively positing herself on the side of the stylistically *un*cultivated:

> I admire it, I appreciate all 'les soins et les peines' that have gone to produce it – but it leaves me cold. [. . .] No, no, the mind I love must still have wild places, a tangled orchard where dark damsons drop in the heavy grass, an overgrown little wood, the chance of a snake or two (real snakes), a pool that nobody's fathomed the depth of – and paths threaded with those little flowers planted by the wind. It must also have *real* hiding places, not artificial ones – not gazebos and mazes. And I have never yet met the cultivated mind that has not had its shrubbery. I loathe and detest shrubberies. (234–5, emphasis in original)

The metaphorical opposition developed here between the conspicuously refined and the adventurously unkempt serves likewise to shape Mansfield's fictional expectations, as evidenced in her review of Wharton's novel.

This is an opposition which might well be construed in gendered terms. It is worth remarking that the figurative appeal of the garden as a means of representing the opposition between the refined and the unkempt is noticeable more generally in the work of women writers at the time, reflecting, perhaps more broadly, an unease with direct assimilation into 'man'-made cultural structures, access to which might well prove to be as constraining as enabling for the aspiring female author.[3] Wharton herself characterised the stylistic division between order and disorder explicitly in gendered terms, though her metaphor of choice is architectural. In a letter to Robert Grant in November

1907, she writes: 'I conceive my subjects like a man – that is, rather more architectonically and dramatically than most women – & then execute them like a woman.'[4] According to Mansfield's review, Wharton leans emphatically towards the architectonic in conceiving of *The Age of Innocence*, and I would maintain that, for her, it is purely a question of style despite the gender-specificity of the term 'workmanship'. I agree with Sydney Janet Kaplan that Mansfield, unlike Dorothy Richardson and Virginia Woolf, purposely refrained from elevating the feminine and refused essentialist gender divisions on the level of style.[5] In fact, her use of the term 'workmanship' is charged with a faint mocking quality as if she sensed and wished to undercut Wharton's aspiration to an architectonic supremacy commonly conceived of as 'masculine'. While she patently admires all 'les soins et les peines', the painstaking care in other words, that have been taken in producing the novel, this consummate workmanship, akin to the cultivated mind/garden, leaves her cold. It is also fittingly in 'architectonic' terms that she couches her critique: 'Does Mrs. Wharton expect us to grow warm in a gallery where the temperature is so sparklingly cool?' (307–8).

Setting questions of gender to one side, Mansfield's evocation in her journal of the adventurous appeal of the uncultivated must be considered, above all, in relation to the landscapes of her childhood in New Zealand. In positing Mansfield as a 'colonial modernist', Elleke Boehmer has drawn attention to the ways in which the alien and unfamiliar, 'in the form of death, violence, weird botany, irrupts into the orderly and apparently secure pastoral landscape of her lost homeland'.[6] The stories written by Mansfield leading up to her review of *The Age of Innocence*, and in the months directly after abound in images of the uncontrollable natural environment of her colonial youth, alluring yet also unnerving, as well as the failed attempts of colonial settlers to reign in elemental forces. From Matilda's attempt to salvage garden 'chrysanths' in the midst of a powerful and 'dreadful' wind which causes '[a]ll the trees and bushes to beat about her' in 'The Wind Blows', to Kezia's exploratory navigation of the 'spread tangled garden' of her family's new home in 'Prelude', Mansfield's obsession with the threshold between careful cultivation and unhampered wilderness is perceptible.[7] As Angela Smith and, more recently, Claire Drewery have discussed, the idea and experience of the 'liminal', as an in-between 'place of erratic and sometimes erotic habitation', is crucial to her modernist aesthetic.[8] It is Wharton's seemingly unerring respect, by contrast, for socially sanctioned boundaries and thresholds, as this respect is manifested on a stylistic and formal level, that Mansfield challenges in her review.

Wharton's restraint might well ensure a complexly coherent internal order as well as lending a smooth sheen to *The Age of Innocence* as a whole ('not a feather of dignity is ruffled' [307], we are told), but Mansfield's criticism addresses the stakes involved in maintaining such polished coherence throughout. It is the strain inherent in the act of restraint that the review purports to expose. Indeed, exposition, or lack of it, is, for Mansfield, the crux of the matter. Her review concludes:

> Is it – in this world – vulgar to ask for more? To ask that the feeling shall be greater than the cause that excites it, to beg to be allowed to share the moment of exposition (is not that the very moment that all our writing leads to?), to entreat a little wildness, a dark place or two in the soul?
>
> We appreciate fully Mrs. Wharton's skill and delicate workmanship; she has the situation in hand from the first page to the last; we realize how savage must sound our cry of protest, and yet we cannot help but make it; that after all we are not above suspicion – even the 'finest' of us! (308)

Her 1919 review of David Graham Philips's posthumously published *Susan Lenox* (1917) reveals that Mansfield had certain views, we might even say expectations of American writing, which cast the above words in a rather more interesting light: 'Now the chief concern of modern American fiction, as far as our knowledge of it goes, is sex.'[9] This blunt appraisal, on its own, cuts right through the perceived delicacy of Wharton's text. Yet Mansfield goes on to highlight an underlying and related fixation in American fiction on the inherent 'ferocity of man', however cultivated his veneer, a '*wildness* and capacity for devouring [...] more terrific than anything Europe has encountered'.[10] The American-European distinction drawn here is telling insofar as her evaluation of *The Age of Innocence* is concerned. We might say that Wharton is, by implication, seen to be all-too-European in her treatment of her subject. The 'ferocity' she denies is associated, moreover, with a colonial heritage akin to Mansfield's own and it is a ferocity that Mansfield, by contrast, pronouncedly embraces in her work.

Mansfield's own pointed preoccupation with locating a 'dark place or two in the soul' is in evidence throughout her collection, *Bliss*, also published in December 1920. 'Je ne parle pas français', 'Pictures' and 'A Little Governess', to cite three of the more prominent examples, all feature sudden glimpses of unsavoury, 'vulgar', or even 'savage' human behaviour. Yet it is her brusque, even violent revelation of adultery through the eyes of Bertha in the title story of the collection, 'Bliss' – 'And she saw . . .' (105) – which most strikingly sets her apart from Wharton where *The Age of Innocence* is specifically concerned. Tony Tanner has suggestively characterised adultery as the 'gap, or silence in the bourgeois novel that finally leads to its dissolution and displacement by postsocial fictional forms'.[11] If marriage constitutes the ideological framework within which the bourgeois novel establishes and maintains its formal coherence, it follows that the 'exposition' of adultery, the 'moment' to which Mansfield refers, would lead to formal collapse, a breach in the intricately worked surface and a disturbance of internal coherence. This is a kind of disorder that Wharton manifestly does not permit. The ejection of Ellen from the family sphere, that 'sparklingly cool' gallery that is New York society, and thus into a narrative gap or silence within the novel at one and the same time appears to serve the purpose, above all, of preservation through closure. According to Pamela Knights, when Wharton did experiment 'with offering her lovers some life together, she could not complete the story'.[12] This inability to allow for incompletion, on Wharton's part, forms the key point of distinction between Wharton and Mansfield as artists and between the notions of workmanship and wildness as propounded by Mansfield in her review. It is a distinction Wharton herself remarked upon, but, for her part, the incapacity lay entirely on the other side. She is known to have told a mutual friend, William Gerhardi, that though Mansfield clearly had the 'temperament' of a writer, her stories were 'all just *beginnings*, full of happy bits, but with all the difficulties shirked'.[13] As with Mansfield, we find here a guarded respect yet overshadowing reservation in considering the approach of the other writer.

I will return to Wharton's perception of Mansfield shortly but I would first like to probe a little further Mansfield's tacit relegation of Wharton to a binding tradition of conservative bourgeois realism, a tradition from which she herself, by contrast, had succeeded, to all intents and purposes, in escaping. Evidently, in begging to be allowed to 'entreat a little wildness' (308), Mansfield is positing her own self-consciously and unashamedly dishevelled finish against Wharton's more refined structure, but further to this she locates and dramatises this difference within and through *The Age of Innocence* itself. Mansfield, I would like to suggest, aligns herself with Ellen Olenska, described as 'dangerous, fascinating, foreign' (307), in this review while Wharton is aligned with Archer, as a 'man who belongs deeply to the family tradition, and yet at the same time finds himself wishing to rebel' (307). On the surface alone, Mansfield would have found much to identify with in the figure of Ellen, the 'prodigal' daughter (307), as her review puts it, whose return to the family sphere and scene causes the disturbance around which Wharton's novel turns. Mansfield cultivated an image of herself as just such a 'prodigal' daughter throughout her writing career, believing this to be a necessary factor in her artistic growth. Like Ellen, she was a bohemian figure, absorbed by (though never quite at home in) Europe and to no small degree exploiting her dislocated status to fascinate and to flout the expectations of those around her. She was thirty-two when she wrote her review, while Ellen, correspondingly, is depicted as being 'nearly thirty' (39) in Wharton's novel. This is an age-bracket in which allure is shown to be enhanced rather than compromised by experience, but also an age which can be seen to mark a point of crisis for the two; that is the demise of Ellen's marriage and of Mansfield's health.[14] To stretch the point, there is a troubled relationship with a member of the Polish gentry on both sides; an ill-fated marriage in Ellen's case and, on Mansfield's side, an ill-fated liaison with the translator, Floryan Sobieniowski, from whom she contracted the gonorrhoea widely held to have contributed to her later tuberculosis.[15]

Intriguing as these superficial points of comparison already are, the parallels go deeper. Ellen embodies the 'wildness' Mansfield sought to emulate in her own fiction and which cannot, literally, be accommodated in Wharton's. The self-confessed vulgarity of requesting 'more' of Wharton as a writer, pointedly invokes those accusations of vulgarity levelled at Ellen in the text itself. The latter is charged throughout *The Age of Innocence* with offences against 'Taste', characterised as 'that far-off divinity of whom "Form" was the mere visible representative and viceregent'.[16] This is not to mention the charges, in turn, of 'misplaced flippancy' (12), indelicacy (19), eccentricity (26) and 'careless words' (41). Moreover, Mansfield, in her entreaty to Wharton, was perhaps directly echoing Ellen's own appeal for a moment of exposition in the novel itself: 'Does no one want to know the truth here, Mr Archer?' (50). (Mansfield's letters from this period show that she was intensely engaged in the pursuit of a form of truthfulness in writing, expecting the same from the writers she encountered.)[17] Archer, on the other hand, is shown in the novel to be 'imprisoned in the conventional' (47), beleaguered with 'the effort to say just so much and no more' (84) and finally, in Ellen's absence, he is left 'blundering against familiar prejudices and traditional points of view as an absent minded man goes on bumping into the furniture of his own room' (159).

It is implied then that Mrs Wharton is caught with Mr Archer in a literary 'age of innocence' with no techniques to account for those unrefined dark places of the soul, with their 'real snakes' and unfathomable pools, their uncharted and cordoned-off psychological terrains; the waste lands or fragmented spaces of the mind which modernist writers found compelling and appalling in equal measure. That Mansfield was indeed playing with notions of what that phrase, 'the age of innocence', might mean in the context of a modernist textual experience becomes apparent in an oft-cited passage from her journal, written several months before she actually turned to Wharton's novel in April 1920; these musings would certainly have had a bearing on her later critical response:

> When autograph albums were the fashion [. . .] the popularity of that most sly, ambiguous, difficult piece of advice: 'To thine own self be true' was the despair of collectors. How dull it was, how boring, to have the same thing written six times over! And then, even if it was Shakespeare, that didn't prevent it – oh, *l'âge d'innocence!* – from being dreadfully obvious. Of course it followed as the night the day that if one was true to oneself . . . True to oneself! Which self? Which of my many – well really, that's what it looks like coming to – hundreds of selves? For what with complexes and repressions and reactions and vibrations and reflections, there are moments when I feel I am nothing but the small clerk of some hotel without a proprietor, who has all his work cut out to enter the names and hand the keys to the wilful guests. (205, emphasis in original)

What is most striking about this passage is the emphasis on a loss of proprietorial control as this is linked to the dissolution of firm boundaries of selfhood. Innocence is equated with a misplaced belief in permanence, fixity and authority. It is equally equated with a preceding literary age, an age in which the 'complexes and repressions and reactions and vibrations and reflections' of selfhood are neatly contained, 'framed, glazed and hung in the perfect light' (308), to re-invoke her description of the characters in *The Age of Innocence*. It is with such an age that Wharton is seemingly affiliated in the later review.

Yet, read in its entirety, this is a journal entry in which the metaphors are as mixed as the artistic and literary allegiances. The paragraph that follows acknowledges a desire for a unified essential self to be unknotted from the overgrowth of those 'hundreds of selves' (though it should be noted that the confessional nature of this latter paragraph is carefully obscured in the personal pronoun shift from 'I' to 'we', paradoxically reversing the inversion from multiple to individual selfhood being described):

> Nevertheless, there are signs that we are intent as never before on trying to puzzle out, to live by, our own particular self. *Der Mensch muss freisein* – free, disentangled, single. Is it not possible that the rage for confession, autobiography, especially for memories of earliest childhood, is explained by our persistent yet mysterious belief in a self which is continuous and permanent; which, untouched by all we acquire and all we shed, pushes a green spear through the dead leaves and through the mould, thrusts a scaled bud through years of darkness until, one day, the light discovers it and shakes the flower free and – we are alive – we are flowering for our moment upon the earth? (205, emphasis in original)

This is a passage Kaplan has used to demonstrate Mansfield's contra-dictory approach to modernist selfhood, the 'dynamic interaction' throughout her career of 'nostalgia for an essential, original self', and a 'defiant – and at times triumphant – admission of self-generation'.[18] Far from Mansfield's expressed imaginative penchant for the idea of an uncultivated wilderness of 'tangled' orchards, fathomless pools and obscure hiding-places, as earlier quoted, here instead is an image of careful cultivation. It is the hotel with its overgrowth of selves which constitutes the wilderness in Mansfield's extended vision and this wil-derness is hardly presented as an idyll of artistic freedom. Rather, the small clerk, as author, is characterised as powerless and constrained in the face of proliferating selfhoods. The vigilantly nurtured 'green spear' is projected as a symbol of artistic freedom in this instance and as a sympathetic expression of the persistent belief in permanence and continuity as set against a pervading and delimiting modernist '[h]otel-consciousness', to invoke Paul Fussell's phrase.[19]

In light of such contradictory approaches and figurative ambiva-lences, it becomes evident that the antagonistic relation between the artistic visions of Wharton and Mansfield I have outlined up to this point is a little too neat. Or is it, conversely, a little too crude? To reap-ply Mansfield's own (once more horticulturally-inclined) words in her review: 'These are what one might call the outer leaves of the story. Part them, and there is within another flower, warmer, deeper and more delicate' (307). The parted flower would point here to a more profound artistic affinity and understanding between these two writers despite their overt disagreements. Mansfield might deposit Wharton in a kind of literary age of innocence but this cannot be seen as a simple dismissal, not least because her analogies for innocence slip and slide between conceptions of sheltered refinement and unsheltered natural growth. Furthermore, she might disparage Wharton's careful workman-ship as restrictive and inhibiting but her journal recounts that such self-control was a quality she acutely felt herself to lack in practice as a writer. In 1918, she writes in her journal: 'How unbearable it would be to die – leave "scraps", "bits" . . . nothing real finished' (129). Even more revealingly, we find a telling reiteration of the mind-garden analogy in a passage written in February 1921, shortly after the *Athenaeum* review of Wharton's novel. But this time, the weeds, rather than the shrubberies, incite her disparagement:

> Oh, I must not yield! I must, this evening, after my supper, get something done. It's not so terribly hard after all. And how shall I live my *good life* if I am content to pass even one day in idleness? It won't do. *Control* – of all kinds. How easy it is to lack control in little things! And once one does lack

it, the small bad habits – tiny perhaps – spring up like weeds and choke one's will. That is what I find. (240, emphasis in original)

Indeed, Mansfield was prone to entreat a little workmanship in her own writing practice, perpetually chiding herself for her idle tendencies. Discipline was as important to her as wildness and Wharton herself intuited as much, regarding the self-consciously coarse texture of her stories with some suspicion. While early on branding those stories as 'all just *beginnings*', as I have mentioned, she later came to subtly revise this perception in her 1934 essay 'Tendencies in Modern Fiction': 'The mid-nineteenth century group selected; the new novelists profess to pour everything out of their bag. Maupassant ended his "slices" with a climax (if this appalling metaphor may be forgiven); Katherine Mansfield tore hers off when they had filled so many pages – *or so her imitators appear to believe.*'[20] Clearly, she is not entirely convinced of the sincerity of Mansfield's purported wildness. The artist in Wharton perceives the concealed artistry beneath the dishevelled surface of Mansfield's work, something mere imitators fail to discern. Similarly, Mansfield, in her review of Wharton, criticises traits she secretly also emulated and the conflict between workmanship and wildness which the review fore-grounds must thus be seen to represent less the conflicting approaches of Mansfield and Wharton and more the conflicting urges with which Mansfield, at all times, grappled in her own work.

I would suggest that such conflicting urges likewise shape Wharton's work and that the affinities between these writers, as such, go deeper than the differences.[21] Katherine Joslin has made a similar case for the relationship between Wharton and Virginia Woolf, drawing some illu-minating parallels between *The Age of Innocence* and *To the Lighthouse*. She shows that '[r]eading Wharton and Woolf together allows us to hear the dialogue between the writers, two dissonant yet overlapping voices' and I would argue that reading Wharton and Mansfield together achieves an analogous effect.[22] To begin with, Mansfield might foreground a wildness in her own work evocative of her early experiences in New Zealand, but we should not forget that she formed part of the upper echelons of colonial society in Wellington. If not quite on a level with Wharton's privileged aristocratic position as a member of a prominent old New York family with links to the most prestigious of early Dutch set-tlers, Mansfield's background was nonetheless one of significant social advantage in a newly-forming colonial society; she might be the 'little' alongside the larger colonial in her relationship to Wharton, but both writers emphatically grew up on the cultivated side of the garden fence within larger colonising communities (whether old or new), the very recognition of which must complicate our impression of fundamental disparity between the two writers, as well as the unrefined aspects of Mansfield's writing.[23] Correspondingly, the perception of Wharton as a conservative proponent of polished bourgeois realism overlooks the experimental quality of her writing within the formal boundaries she delineated for herself. A number of recent critics have represented her as a transitional figure, a key player in the 'development of art that was to lead to modernism' or, even as directly and productively engaged with it, despite her overt critical disavowals.[24] Furthermore, the conservative restraint Mansfield critiqued in *The Age of Innocence* did not altogether accord with the author's own life. As Knights observes, Wharton achieved a 'kind of autonomy she seldom allows her characters' and exhibited a restlessness to rival Mansfield's in her European travels.[25] She has likewise been compared to the figure of Ellen Olenska by virtue of her adventurous European existence.[26] Indeed, Jessica Levine has persuasively contended that Wharton's reticence in *The Age of Innocence* should not simply be read as a reflection of her inherent formal and stylistic conservatism; her decision to exclude a scene of consummation might alternatively be seen, on the one hand, as a 'concession to the marketplace', and, on the other, as a conscious writing against the 'received tropes of the French novel of adultery'.[27] As Levine wryly notes of the multifarious references to novels like Gustave Flaubert's *Madame Bovary* (1856) and Octave Feuillet's *Monsieur de Camors* (1867) among many others, the 'great paradox throughout [. . .] resides in the fact that Wharton's apparent rejection of European indecency depends upon a long list of subtle allusions to indecent works, which constitute a long, slow wink at an ideal reader who has also read them'.[28] Most importantly, Wharton's own experience of impassioned adultery, during her five-year affair with Morton Fullerton (1907–12), is inscribed in the text from the start; if she ultimately refuses her couple fulfilment in *The Age of Innocence*, this is not the refusal of a writer who flinches at the 'moment of exposition' in theory but one who is deeply familiar with the consequences in practice, just like Ellen herself.[29]

By the same token, we might add that, at the time of writing her review, Mansfield was in a position closer to that of May Welland in *The Age of Innocence*, than that of Ellen Olenksa. The love triangle described by Wharton was, in fact, replicated in Mansfield's own life, through her discovery of her husband John Middleton Murry's affair with the writer, Elizabeth Bibesco, also in December 1920. Indeed, the chain of events that follow this discovery enacts a parodic reiteration of the plot of *The Age of Innocence* – a reiteration, I would argue, either knowingly or unconsciously prompted by her reading of Wharton's novel around the same time. Just as May initially offers Archer his freedom from their engagement upon suspicion of another attachment, so Mansfield reacts, at first, to the news of Murry's infidelity with a measure of generosity. '[D]o *feel free*. I mean that', she tells him in a letter written on 3 December 1920.[30] This generous impulse, sincere or otherwise, is short-lived. In the spring, she sends Bibesco a letter which provocatively suggests that she was inspired by Wharton's fictional account of the calculated separation of Ellen and Archer by the prevailing tribal powers of Old New York, expressly articulating what remains conspicuously unarticulated in Wharton's work:

> Dear Princess Bibesco,
> I am afraid you must stop writing these little love letters to my husband while he and I live together. It is one of the things which is not done in our world.
>   You are very young. Won't you ask your husband to explain to you the impossibility of such a situation.
>   Please do not make me have to write to you again. I do not like scolding people and I simply hate having to teach them manners.
>   Yours sincerely,
>   Katherine Mansfield.[31]

Note the echoes here of the terms of Mansfield's account of Wharton's novel, her perception of the audacity of adultery within the 'remote, exclusive small *world*' (307, emphasis added) of New York high society, a world which jolts at the ruffle of even one 'feather of dignity' (307). The orchestrated parting of Ellen and Archer is described in her review as 'positively stately' (307) and it is certainly a 'stately' posture which is adopted in this letter.[32] Claire Tomalin has remarked upon the unusual register of the letter, surmising that the 'queenly tone' was intended to evoke the voice of Mansfield's mother: 'No one could possibly suspect from this letter that Katherine had once been a Bohemian and a merry adultress herself.'[33] To my mind, the letter dramatises a collision of real and fictional 'worlds'. It also provides a compelling illustration of the extension of Mansfield's performative bent as well as her performative versatility and unwillingness to confine herself to a single register or subject-position.

Yet such performative ventures aside, her review makes clear that her attention is more fully captured, both as reader and writer, by the Bohemian and merry adulteress, Ellen, rather than by May. Indeed, there is more than a hint in the above letter that it is less the adultery to which Mansfield objects than the inability of the 'young' Bibesco, in carrying out her 'little' intrigue, to fulfil, in all its delicate complexity, the role the alluring other woman in the grand manner of the Countess Olenska. And it is through the mutual identification with and regard for the figure of Ellen that the deeper artistic affinity between Wharton and Mansfield becomes most apparent. This is, in no small part, due to the fact that the opposing artistic impulses I have been exploring here are equally manifested in that character. Ellen is the paragon of rebelliousness in *The Age of Innocence,* yet it is she and not Archer who repeatedly quells the adulterous impulse to wildness arising from what Mansfield describes as her 'highly civilised appreciation of the exquisite difficulty of their position' (307). Ellen is poised between old and new worlds, established and modern fictional forms. She is pulled in both directions but is shown to hold few illusions either way. When Archer pleas for their escape to another world without enforced social categories, she responds:

> 'Oh, my dear – where is that country? [. . .] I know so many who've tried to find it; and, believe me, they all got out by mistake at wayside stations: at places like Boulogne, or Pisa, or Monte Carlo – and it wasn't at all different from the old world they'd left, but only rather smaller and dingier and more promiscuous.' (174–5)

Ellen's response here offers a useful figuration of the relationship between Wharton and Mansfield. Faced alike with the disenchantments and displacements of modernity, Wharton was, by and large, imaginatively compelled to return to the familiar forms of the 'old world', however innovative her formal renovations, while Mansfield creatively drew upon those dingy and fragmented wayside stations.[34] Both, however, can be found to hark the other way and the dingy wayside station is as implicit a backdrop in Wharton's work as the 'old world' is in Mansfield's. Reading Mansfield and Wharton together, not least as writers with a broadly comparable colonial heritage, discloses, furthermore, the quietly ambivalent and restrained quality of Mansfield's modernism beneath a brashly experimental and 'savage' surface.

Notes

1. Clare Hanson, 'Introduction', in *The Critical Writings of Katherine Mansfield,* ed. Clare Hanson (New York: St Martin's, 1987), p. 9.
2. The review of *The Age of Innocence* is no exception here. To give one example, she makes the following note in her journal in June 1919: '"The feeling roused by the cause is more important that the cause itself . . ." That is the kind of thing I like to say to myself as I get into the train'. John Middleton Murry, ed., *The Journal of Katherine Mansfield* (London: Constable, 1954), p. 169. (All further references to Mansfield's journals will come from this edition, cited parenthetically by page number.) This idea is refashioned in her *Athenaeum* review of Wharton's novel just over a year later:

'Is it – in this world – vulgar to ask for more? To ask that the feeling shall be greater than the cause that excites it . . .' (Hanson, p. 308).

3. It is a concern which surfaces throughout Dorothy Richardson's *Pilgrimage*, for instance, and Mansfield's journal passage compares interestingly with an observation of Miriam Henderson's in the eighth chapter of Richardson's work, 'The Trap', first published in 1925: 'The garden breeds a longing for the wild; the wild a homesickness for the garden. Is there no way of life where the two can meet?' To give a further example, Elizabeth Bowen uses a similar metaphor, in a 1947 radio interview, to describe a sense of confined girlhood: 'At the age of twelve I was finding the world too small: it appeared to me like a dull, trim back garden, in which only trivial games could be played.' These are sentiments which certainly inform her representations of young women on the cusp of adulthood in her early novels, such as Sydney Warren in *The Hotel* (1927) and Lois Farquar in *The Last September* (1929), and the image of the enclosed garden as site for trivial game-playing indeed figures prominently in the latter novel, as it does in Mansfield's earlier 'The Garden Party', written shortly after her review of Wharton's novel in 1921. Dorothy Richardson, *Pilgrimage,* 4 vols (London: Dent and Cresset, 1938), Vol. 3, p. 453; Elizabeth Bowen, 'She', *Afterthought: Pieces About Writing* (London: Longmans, 1962), p. 107.

4. Quoted in Katherine Joslin, 'Architectonic or Episodic? Gender and *The Fruit of the Tree*', in *A Forward Glance: New Essays on Edith Wharton*, ed. Clare Colquitt, Susan Goodman and Candace Waid (Newark: University of Delaware Press, 1999), p. 62.

5. Kaplan notes: '[T]he presence of certain features in her writing which might be coded "feminine" is not evidence of an underlying essential female nature, but the result of a writing practice that is conscious, deliberate, and "artificial".' I will draw further attention to Mansfield's stylistic performativity later in this article. Sydney Janet Kaplan, *Katherine Mansfield and the Origins of Modernist Form* (Ithaca: Cornell University Press, 1991), pp. 158–9.

6. Elleke Boehmer, 'Mansfield as Colonial Modernist: Difference Within', in *Celebrating Katherine Mansfield: A Centenary Volume of Essays*, ed. Gerri Kimber and Janet Wilson (Basingstoke: Palgrave-Macmillan, 2011), p. 62.

7. Katherine Mansfield, *Collected Stories of Katherine Mansfield* (London: Constable, 1980), pp. 106, 32. All further references to Mansfield's stories will come from this edition, cited parenthetically by page number.

8. Angela Smith, *Katherine Mansfield and Virginia Woolf: A Public of Two* (Oxford: Clarendon, 1999), p. 13; Claire Drewery, *Modernist Short Fiction by Women: The Liminal in Katherine Mansfield, Dorothy Richardson, May Sinclair and Virginia Woolf* (Farnham: Ashgate, 2011).

9. Katherine Mansfield, 'Lions and Lambs', in *Novels and Novelists*, p. 77.

10. Mansfield, 'Lions and Lambs', p. 77, emphasis added.

11. Tony Tanner, *Adultery and the Novel: Contract and Transgression* (Baltimore: Johns Hopkins University Press, 1979), pp. 13–14.

12. Pamela Knights, 'Forms of Disembodiment: The Social Subject in *The Age of Innocence*' in *The Cambridge Companion to Edith Wharton*, ed. Millicent Bell (Cambridge: Cambridge University Press, 1995), pp. 38–9.

13. Quoted in R. W. B Lewis, *Edith Wharton: A Biography* (London: Vintage-Random, 1993), p. 462, emphasis in original.

14. According to Claire Tomalin's biography, Mansfield spent the latter part of 1920 with Ida Baker at the Villa Isola Bella in Menton, the south of France, somewhat naïvely hoping that a change of scenery would be to her ultimate good. Her health,

however, became progressively worse during this period, partly aggravated, in the view of her doctor, by the intensity with which she persevered with her work. See Claire Tomalin, *Katherine Mansfield: A Secret Life* (London: Penguin, 1988), pp. 206–14.

15. This is Tomalin's claim: '[M]edical evidence given by Katherine later suggests that she was infected with gonorrhoea late in 1909. It is hard to see any other candidate for this particular honour unless we believe that she was totally promiscuous, which seems unlikely'. She goes on to make a persuasive case for a link between Mansfield's early contraction of gonorrhoea and her later development of tuberculosis. Tomalin, pp. 75, 75–8.

16. Edith Wharton, *The Age of Innocence*, ed. Candace Waid (New York: Norton, 2003), pp. 10–11. All further references will come from this edition, cited parenthetically by page number.

17. To give a few examples, see her letters to Sydney Schiff (dated 3 November 1920), John Middleton Murry (dated 6 December 1920) and to an unknown recipient (dated early 1921). Vincent O'Sullivan and Margaret Scott, eds, *The Collected Letters of Katherine Mansfield*, 5 vols (Oxford: Clarendon, 1984–2008), Vol. 4, pp. 98–9, 138–9, 170.

18. Kaplan, p. 179.

19. Paul Fussell, *Abroad: British Literary Travelling Between the Wars* (Oxford: Oxford University Press, 1980), p. 53.

20. Edith Wharton, 'Tendencies in Modern Fiction', in *The Uncollected Critical Writings: Edith Wharton*, ed. Frederick Wegener (Princeton: Princeton University Press, 1996), p. 171, emphasis added.

21. The correspondences between these two writers have not gone entirely unnoticed. Christine Butterworth-McDermott has, for example, recently drawn attention to a shared concern with subverting traditional fairy-tale fantasies in 'Lustful Fathers and False Princes: "Cinderella" and "Donkeyskin" Motifs in Wharton's *Summer* and Mansfield's Short Stories', *Katherine Mansfield Studies*, 4 (October 2012), pp. 63–78.

22. Katherine Joslin, '"Embattled Tendencies": Wharton, Woolf and the Nature of Modernism', in *Special Relationships: Anglo-American Affinities and Antagonisms 1854–1936*, ed. Janet Beer and Bridget Bennett (Manchester: Manchester University Press, 2002), p. 204.

23. For one attempt to review and problematise Mansfield's status both as a 'little colonial' and as a European modernist, see Bridget Orr, 'Reading with the Taint of the Pioneer: Katherine Mansfield and Settler Criticism', in *Critical Essays on Katherine Mansfield*, ed. Rhoda B. Nathan (New York: G. K. Hall, 1993), pp. 48–60.

24. Robin Peel, *Apart From Modernism: Edith Wharton, Politics and Fiction Before World War 1* (Madison, NJ: Fairleigh Dickinson University Press, 2005), p. 119. See also Knights, 'Forms of Disembodiment', p. 44 and, most recently, Jennifer Haytock, *Edith Wharton and the Conversations of Literary Modernism* (New York: Palgrave-Macmillan, 2008). Wharton expressed her reservations about modern literary trends which she saw as 'leading to pure anarchy' in *The Writing of Fiction*, first published in 1924, and she reasserted these views in two 1934 essays, 'Tendencies in Modern Fiction' and 'Permanent Values in Fiction'. See *The Writing of Fiction* (Octagon Books, 1966), p. 14; *The Uncollected Critical Writings of Edith Wharton*, pp. 170–9.

25. Pamela Knights, *The Cambridge Introduction to Edith Wharton* (Cambridge: Cambridge University Press, 2009), p. 44.

26. See Joslin, 'Embattled Tendencies', p. 212. Joslin also highlights the fact that Ellen's

residence is located, at the end of the novel, in Wharton's own area of Paris, close to the Rue de Varenne.

27. Jessica Levine, *Delicate Pursuit: Discretion in Henry James and Edith Wharton* (New York: Routledge, 2002), p. 149.

28. Levine, p. 151.

29. Indeed, Wharton did play with ideas for more explicit narratives at this time, even going so far as to publish a novella concerning an illegitimate pregnancy, 'The Old Maid', shortly after *The Age of Innocence* in 1921, causing quite a scandal. For a full account see Levine, pp. 39–65.

30. *Letters* 4, p. 133, emphasis in original.

31. *Letters* 4, p. 199.

32. Wharton accounts for the orchestrated separation of Ellen and Archer as follows: 'It was the old New York way of taking life "without effusion of blood": the way of people who dreaded scandal more than disease, who placed decency above courage, and who considered that nothing was more ill-bred than "scenes", except the behavior of those who gave rise to them' (201). In a sense, Mansfield's letter gives crude and parodic expression to such unspoken tribal beliefs.

33. Tomalin, p. 215.

34. The idea of renovation, over and above 'making it new', is key to Wharton's aesthetic. She herself noted that the 'initial mistake of most of the younger novelists, especially in England and America, has been the decision that the old forms were incapable of producing new ones'. Wharton, 'Tendencies in Modern Fiction', p. 170.

Home and Abroad in the South Pacific: Spaces and Places in Robert Louis Stevenson and Katherine Mansfield's Short Fiction

Stefanie Rudig

Introduction

> We children of the future, how *could* we be at home in this today? We feel disfavour for all ideals that might lead one to feel at home even in this fragile, broken time of transitions; as for 'realities,' we do not believe that they will *last.*
>
> Friedrich Nietzsche[1]

Nietzsche's rendering of *fin de siècle* angst anticipated Heidegger's famous dictum that 'Homelessness is coming to be the destiny of the world',[2] which aptly captures the modernist malaise – a malaise that characterises so much of Katherine Mansfield's writing. As a restless wanderer and permanently uprooted cosmopolitan she would most likely have agreed with Nietzsche on the instability of 'realities'; yet she seemed to yearn for more durable ones. In her penultimate letter to her husband a few weeks before her death, she exclaimed, '[I]f I were allowed one single cry to God that cry would be *I want to be REAL'*.[3] Robert Louis Stevenson, a contemporary of Nietzsche, whose writing is now commonly classified as 'proto-modernist', was similarly aware of discontinuity and rupture.[4] In his essay 'The Day After Tomorrow', Stevenson declares: 'The obscurest epoch is today; and that for a thousand reasons of inchoate tendency, conflicting report, and sheer mass and multiplicity of experience; but chiefly, perhaps, by reason of an insidious shifting of landmarks.'[5] 'Shifting landmarks' is a catchword for both Stevenson and Mansfield's experiences. This essay does not propose a psycho-biographical reading of their work. Rather, it will examine related questions of home and belonging as well as of displacement and alienation, studying how characters in selected short stories position themselves in and against the physical and cultural geography of the South Pacific.

At first glance it may appear incongruous to pair these two writers. Novels like *Treasure Island* or *Kidnapped* by Stevenson, whom Arthur Conan Doyle described as 'the father of the modern masculine novel',[6] strike one as being at odds with the persistently female voice of Mansfield's work. Beyond their distinctly gendered styles,[7] however, there are a remarkable number of parallels between Stevenson and Mansfield, as this essay will demonstrate.

As Elleke Boehmer among others has argued, modernism was informed by empire; Mansfield's modernism in particular was fundamentally shaped by her colonial background.[8] Born in 1888 in Wellington, New Zealand, Mansfield developed from early on a conflicted notion of 'home', since 'home' usually conjured up a place 12,000 miles distant in most white New Zealanders' minds. Mansfield, raised in a tradition of Anglophilia, began to pine for the metropolitan centre, while deploring the inadequacies of her own position on the colonial periphery.[9] To her, London was '*la seule chose*' – 'it is Life', she enthusiastically exclaimed in 1907.[10] However, once there, her sense of a bifurcated self was fostered further, and she saw herself as 'the little colonial walking in the London garden patch – allowed to look, perhaps, but not to linger'; in short 'a stranger – an alien'.[11] This impression of simultaneous belonging and displacement in her various 'homes' is inscribed in many of Mansfield's short stories, such as 'Prelude', where the garden often figures as a privileged space. Later in life, when her illness prevented her from returning to New Zealand, Mansfield became increasingly hostile towards London and turned to New Zealand as an inspiration for her work, reclaiming it as her lost homeland: 'I thank God I was born in New Zealand. A young country is a real heritage, though it takes one time to recognise it. But New Zealand is in my very bones', she wrote in a 1922 letter to her father.[12]

Stevenson may have had less difficulty in defining his 'home', but his situation was not wholly unambiguous; this even holds true for his apparent 'home' and birthplace, Edinburgh, since critics have shown that 'Stevenson loved yet also hated the place'.[13] Although Stevenson, according to Robert Fraser, 'inherited the cultural assurance' of the mid-Victorian age,[14] he also experienced a divided self, especially after he had settled in Samoa in the late 1880s. Here his writing became increasingly characterised by a productive tension between his imperialist and anti-imperialist drives. Transplanted to an unfamiliar context, he frequently sought to make sense of the unfamiliar by framing his understanding of island society through parallels with Scottish Highland culture. Jenni Calder moreover argues that, as a Scot and a Lowlander, Stevenson was both an 'intrusive colonial', in relation to the Highlander, and a 'victim of English cultural imperialism'.[15] In an 1893 letter Stevenson commented on his living a 'voluntary exile' in the South Pacific, thus fulfilling 'the Scots destiny', as he called it; he looked back to Scotland with his 'head filled with the blessed, beastly place all the time!'[16]

Both Stevenson and Mansfield were prompted by a wanderlust to travel widely; yet it was equally due to their being chronically ill that they spent significant parts of their lives in 'exile'.[17] Their movements were diametrically opposed: Stevenson ultimately left Britain as a result of his health, seeking out a South Pacific climate, whereas Mansfield travelled from the South Pacific to Europe in search of artistic fulfil-ment. Each migration involved feelings of unease and defamiliarisation as well as exhilaration and enthusiasm for the 'new' culture. Thus the authors' island stories not only share the South Pacific setting, but also a common concern for the relation between self and other.[18] Perhaps as a direct result of their experience of displacement, the two writers displayed a heightened awareness of selfhood. Stevenson, for example, was somewhat obsessed with clothes, sometimes combining a formal European style with native elements such as a red sash, at other times 'going native' in a traditional lava-lava and barefoot.[19] Mansfield, born 'Kathleen Mansfield Beauchamp', was likewise continually reinventing herself and noted for her chameleon-like quality, changing her physi-cal appearance to the point of unrecognisability or adopting different pseudonyms as a writer.[20] Stevenson and Mansfield testified to a hunger for life that was tragically cut short, as they both died young. One's South Pacific paradise and the other's sophisticated European haven were tainted by their illnesses; and each, nostalgically, looked back to their respective homes in Britain and New Zealand, just as they clung to the innocence of childhood.[21] As writers, furthermore, they entertained visions of major literary works that were unfulfilled. *The South Seas*, the book Stevenson intended in the form of a scientific study of the region, does not exist; neither does Mansfield's planned New Zealand novel *Karori*.

In their South Pacific short fiction Stevenson and Mansfield explore personal experience: notions of 'home' that are neither homogenous nor static, but multi-dimensional. Their stories reflect a sense of 'home' as being more than just a physical place, as the characters create, or attempt to create their own spaces even in foreign locations. Stevenson's and Mansfield's fictional landscape will be studied in two of the authors' longer stories: 'The Beach of Falesá', which Stevenson himself saw as 'the first realistic South Sea story',[22] and, what is now widely held as a modernist masterpiece, Mansfield's 'Prelude'.

Spaces and Places in 'The Beach of Falesá' and 'Prelude'

> Real or imagined, places are products of specific cultural conditions and,
> as such, not simply arenas for action but always already a part of the action
> and its meanings.[23]

Each of the novella-length stories by Stevenson and Mansfield begins
with the protagonist(s) moving to another place, thus indicating the
centrality of spatiality and the instability of 'home' in both narratives.
The opening of 'Prelude'[24] introduces the themes of belonging and
alienation which permeate all twelve sections of the story. The Burnell/
Fairfield household is about to move from town, that is, Wellington, to
their new country house, presumably in Karori. The reader is told at the
outset that there is literally no place for the children – 'There was not
an inch of room for Lottie and Kezia in the buggy' (79). In Stevenson's
cross-cultural romance a different tone pervades the opening lines,
which hint at the profoundly transcultural topography of Falesá:

> I saw that island first when it was neither night nor morning. The moon
> was to the west, setting, but still broad and bright. To the east, and right
> amidships of the dawn, which was all pink, the daystar sparkled like a
> diamond. The land breeze blew in our faces, and smelt strong of wild lime
> and vanilla: other things besides, but these were the most plain; and the
> chill of it set me sneezing. (3)

The protagonist and first-person narrator, Wiltshire, confronts a cre-
olised Pacific world that is lit up both from the West and the East. This
foreshadows the union of East and West, which reaches its most powerful and harmonious manifestation in Wiltshire's marriage to the native
woman, Uma. Ann C. Colley writes: 'This hybridic light will illuminate
Wiltshire as he moves through his account of mingling and hobnobbing
with the natives, missionaries, tradesmen, and beachcombers. Narrator
and reader must jointly enter into a double-voiced and intermingled
vision.'[25] The vision is also double-voiced in so far as there is a clear
sense of another narrative consciousness besides Wiltshire's. Stevenson
deconstructs the conventional depiction of the exotic setting, following an intensely physical and sensuous description of the island by
Wiltshire's mundane reflexive sneeze. Subsequently he also subverts the
tradition of the homosocial adventure story, to which he owed his fame.

The beginning of Stevenson's short story implies a preoccupation less
with the natural world of Falesá than its social space and its effects on
the protagonist. Even though the fictional Falesá holds all the promises
of an island, offering 'balm for the weary',[26] the protagonist is, above
all, attracted to the prospect of 'white neighbours' (4), of whom he felt

deprived during his four years on another Pacific island. Indeed, the beach of Falesá is not primarily important to him as a physical place, but as a 'contact zone', defined by Mary Louise Pratt as 'social spaces where cultures meet, clash, and grapple with each other'.[27] In fact, the beach epitomises such a contact zone; it marks not only the dividing line between land and sea, but constitutes an ambiguous place of transition that encompasses life and death, transcultural encounter, missionary activity, transmutation, and translation. The beach is the place of Wiltshire's landfall on Falesá, where he catches his first glimpse of the island's society as well as of his future wife Uma, and, of course, the place where he expects to make his fortune as a trader.

The signification of 'the beach' moves far beyond its physicality. Being the place where the whites live and trade, the beach also stands metonymically for the white population on the Pacific island. In addition, the phrase to be 'on the beach' means being destitute and suggests the figure of the beachcomber, as portrayed by the infamous trio in *The Ebb-Tide*, for example.[28] When Wiltshire is ostracised, he similarly assumes the deviant role of the beachcomber, who, according to H. E. Maude, is 'essentially integrated into, and dependent for [his] livelihood on, the indigenous communities',[29] by relying on the resources of his wife and mother-in-law to produce his own copra (that is, dried coconut meat). Wiltshire gradually forms an allegiance to the native community, as his experiences on the beach teach him about the corruption of the white population; as such, the story offers a vivid indictment of colonialism. The author wrote to his friend Colvin apropos of 'The Beach of Falesá':

> [T]his is a piece of realism *à outrance*, nothing extenuated or coloured. Looked at so, is it not, with all its tragic features, wonderfully idyllic, with great beauty of scene and circumstance? And will you please to observe that almost all that is ugly is in the whites?[30]

In the same letter Stevenson offered to apologise for the figure of Captain Randall, 'the father of the beach' (6), who embodies the archetype of the degenerate white trader. Wiltshire feels revolted by the sight of 'Papa Randall', 'squatting on the floor' in a room that is 'stifling hot and full of flies' (69, 8–9). Randall's depravity is thus reflected in the space he inhabits, as his small, dirty house stands, significantly, 'in a bad place, behind the village, in the borders of the bush' (9). This position places Randall out of the reach of a functioning island society and on the borders of civilisation.

The dichotomy between the bush or interior and the beach symbolises the division between a violent masculine space and a domestic feminine space. After Wiltshire realises that his livelihood is not threatened by an uncooperative native population and that, instead, all his problems can be reduced to a 'White Man's Quarrel' (22), he decides to put an end to his rival Case's hegemony. This masculine adventure narrative reaches its climax in a brutal shoot-out between Wilshire and Case in the darkness of the bush. While the homosocial sphere clearly fails, and Case is graphically stabbed, the domestic succeeds, as Uma braves all the dangers of the wild woods to save Wiltshire. Indeed, as soon as Wiltshire leaves the orderly domestic sphere for the all-male dystopia of the woods, he is quite helpless. He narrates:

> As long as I was in the open, and had the lamp in my house to steer by, I did well. But when I got to the path, it fell so dark I could make no headway, walking into trees and swearing there, like a man looking for the matches in his bedroom. (61)

In Uma, the protagonist has literally found his match; and soon after her arrival in the wilderness, the woods are lit up and Wiltshire survives. Stevenson thus substitutes romance and adventure for realism and domesticity. This shift of focus also manifests itself in the title, which he changed from 'The High Woods of Ulufanua' to 'The Beach of Falesá'.[31]

Since the bonds between white characters are mostly dysfunctional in 'The Beach of Falesá', Wiltshire needs to find new parameters in order to construct a sense of belonging. Given that Stevenson wrote at a time when belonging was largely constituted through landscape, and bearing in mind Wiltshire's, from the reader's point of view, satirical self-definition – 'I'm a white man, and a British subject, and no end of a big chief at home' (23) – it is hardly surprising that the narrator's way of imagining himself in the South Pacific setting is coloured through a distinctly European lens. The island turns into an object of Eurocentric vision, as Wiltshire describes it in terms of European discovery, applying familiar similes to deal with the unknown, such as when a sight of island men, women and children puts him 'in thought of the 1st of May at home' (23). However, after Wiltshire is increasingly forced to interact with the native community and realises that, in Uma's words, 'Victoreea' may be a 'big chief', but she is simply 'too far off' (48), he develops new points of reference in Falesá.

Most importantly, the protagonist creates a home in the South Pacific through marrying and settling down with Uma, the 'island-girl' who is transformed into 'Mrs Wiltshire' in the course of the narrative (32, 63). Their home is essentially characterised by hybridity: together the two characters create and inhabit a 'third space', as defined by Homi K. Bhabha,[32] similar to the third space of the beach, that is, a liminal place of neither coloniser nor colonised. Wiltshire and Uma are, moreover, peripheral characters in the sense that they are both island outsiders: the one is white European and the other from another island and tabooed. In addition, if one believes himself superior in 'race', the other is superior in 'class': '[Uma] was a kind of countess really, dressed to hear great singers at a concert, and no even mate for a poor trader like myself' (12), which makes them a perfectly hybrid couple on more than one level. Jolly concludes:

> The marriage between Wiltshire and Uma, defying the European taboo on miscegenation, initiates a series of transgressions, both generic and ideological, whereby the story calls into question the boundaries that separate romance and realism, adventure and domesticity, masculinity and femininity, white skin and brown.[33]

Yet, while Stevenson endorses miscegenation, he remains ambiguous about the ending and offers no resolution to the problem posed by Wiltshire's half-caste daughters. Their existence in a realist story that is 'extraordinarily *true*' in any case disrupts the conventional topography of Victorian fiction.[34]

If Wiltshire's crossing the beach and marrying Uma demonstrates the proximity of the traversed space to the transgressive space, the boundaries between allowed and disallowed spaces are shown to be completely fluid in the topography of 'Prelude'. Early in the story Kezia seems to trespass when she embarks on an exploratory tour of their recently vacated house. Stripped of its familiar reference points, notably its inhabitants, Kezia's former home suddenly appears uncanny – *unheimlich* as Freud would say – literally, 'unhomely'. Angela Smith writes that many of Mansfield's New Zealand stories differ from those with a similar theme set in Europe 'in that their characters suddenly feel themselves to be in danger where they thought they were safest, in the supposedly known world of home'.[35] As soon as Kezia and Lottie leave that world behind, they are unsettled – 'although they were still in the town they were quite lost' (83) – and highly alert to their own place amidst strange surroundings: '"Where are we now?" Every few minutes one of the children asked [the storeman] the question' (84). Beyond the novelty of the children's position in between their old, now unfamiliar home and their new home, which promises familiarity through the presence of their family, the night further blots out the habitual landscape, and the wild natural space seems to take dominance over the orderly domestic one: 'Everything looked different – the painted wooden houses far smaller than they did by day, the gardens far bigger and wilder' (83). This foreshadows not only the recurrent contrast between light and darkness in the story, but it also hints at the special space of the garden as both domesticated and unruly.

The first sign of habitation in the new house is 'now one and now another of the windows [leaping] into light', and soon afterwards the children are welcomed by their grandmother, Mrs Fairfield, who 'came out of the dark hall carrying a little lamp' (85). She lights up the unknown, literally and metaphorically, and makes the children feel at home. Later, when Kezia is in bed, she does not leave the candle Kezia asks for, but stays with her instead; her presence simply dispels any thought of the uncanny. Additionally, the strong relationship between the two is emphasised by the grandmother's entrusting her granddaughter with carrying the lamp, which recalls the significance of the lamp as a symbol of interpersonal connection, as well as of illumination through art, in Mansfield's story 'The Dolls' House'. Unsurprisingly, and in line with her involuntary maternity, Linda Burnell prefers darkness and closure to light and openness; for instance: 'She hated blinds pulled up to the top at any time, but in the morning it was intolerable' (92).

In Mansfield's short story, 'home' is primarily constituted by people and their relations with each other. The Burnell/Fairfield household seems to pivot on the character of Mrs Fairfield, Linda and Beryl's mother and the children's mother substitute. In next to no time, Mrs Fairfield creates her own space in the new place; at this point it is useful to remember Michel de Certeau's distinction between space (*espace*) and place (*lieu*), saying that 'place' transforms into 'space' through the practices of living.[36] It is Mrs Fairfield who performs numerous rituals of everyday life in the house, such as tucking in the children at night or presiding over the kitchen:

> It was hard to believe that she had not been in that kitchen for years; she was so much a part of it. She put the crocks away with a sure, precise touch, moving leisurely and ample from the stove to the dresser, looking into the pantry and the larder as though there were not an unfamiliar corner. When she had finished, everything in the kitchen had become part of a series of patterns. (94)

When Linda enters the kitchen for the first time, she also remarks, 'It says "mother" all over', and admires her mother's physical presence, on which she professes to depend in order to construct her sense of belonging (95–6).

Linda's sense of belonging is highly precarious and certainly not rooted in a place, as she keeps dreaming about birds, about 'driving away from them all in a little buggy, driving away from everybody and not even waving' or imagining herself in a ship, crying '"Faster! Faster!"

to those who [are] rowing' (91, 114). Not only does she lack interest in the 'fine house and boncer garden' (105), but her apathy points towards a deeper alienation from her husband and children, who constantly infringe on her space – her body. She refers to Stanley as her 'Newfoundland dog' that she is 'so fond of in the daytime' (115), but, by implication, cannot stand at night, when he turns into a sexual being and terrifies her with his physical ardour. Given Linda's enforced childbearing, her sympathetic identification with the aloe, though itself a symbol of foreign infiltration as a plant that is not native to New Zealand, probably derives from the alleged infertility of the 'fat swelling plant' (98).[37]

At one point Stanley silently remarks upon the empty place at the top of the nursery table: 'That's where my boy ought to sit' (101). In the context of the production of 'Prelude', a refined and pared-down version of 'The Aloe' which Mansfield revised in 1916 a few months after her brother's death, one is tempted to read the short story as an elegy to her absent brother.[38] But 'Prelude' was conceived as something more than that – it is also a eulogy to her mother-country, to which Mansfield owed, as she began to realise, a 'debt of love':

> Now – now I want to write recollections of my own country.
> Yes I want to write about my own country till I simply exhaust my store – not only because it is a 'sacred debt' that I pay to my country because my brother & I were born there, but also because in my thoughts I range with him over all the remembered places. I am never far away from them. I long to renew them in writing.[39]

In 'Prelude' Mansfield fulfils that desire, but, paradoxically, she also seems to have edited New Zealand out in comparison with 'The Aloe', which included, among other things, a great number of place descriptions and reference to a Māori war. In 'The Aloe', for example, the reader learns the following detail about Kezia's birth:

> Kezia had been born in that room. She had come forth squealing out of a reluctant mother in the teeth of a 'Southerly Buster.' The Grandmother, shaking her before the window, had seen the sea rise in green mountains and sweep the esplanade.[40]

Kezia is thus portrayed as firmly rooted in New Zealand soil from the very beginning of her life. In 'Prelude' one has to read between the lines to find out about her deep connection with place in the country of her birth. As it does with other characters, the window represents an important symbol; in Kezia's case one that suggests her dislike for boundaries, as for instance: 'She went over to the window and leaned against it, pressing her hands against the pane. Kezia liked to stand so before the window' (82). Once her sister Isabel asks her where she is going, to which Kezia replies, '"Oh, just away"' (92). This answer implies that Kezia, the explorer, may not be interested in a particular fixed place, but rather in extending the limits of her horizon and in the crossing of spaces. While Isabel, who is eager throughout the story to establish affiliative bonds with the adult world, enjoys 'playing ladies', Kezia rejects such a game of social rules and prefers probing into 'the spread tangled garden', wondering if 'she would ever not get lost' in it (106, 97). She drifts almost seamlessly between the carefully-tended part of the garden space and the uncultivated wild one, similar to the young woman in Mansfield's short story 'In the Botanical Gardens' (1907) suddenly passing from the formal, manicured landscape into the 'silent and splendid' bush.[41] From Kezia's point of view there is, on one side of the garden, the part with a box border, a large variety of different flowers and 'all kinds of little tufty plants she had never seen before', and then there is 'the frightening side, and no garden at all' with 'tall dark trees and strange bushes', probably native plants (97). Yet, however frightening and strange discovering the 'undiscovered country' may seem to her, in the end the garden always remains safely attached to the borders of her home.[42]

Conclusion

If every movement away from the centre is a transgression, then the South Pacific on the margins of the British Empire offers a perfect setting to explore traversed and transgressive spaces. Stevenson's short story 'The Beach of Falesá' shows that it is impossible to cross the beach unchanged, and as far as the two authors discussed in this study are concerned the argument could be extended to say that nobody crosses the Pacific unchanged. At the beginning of *In the South Seas* Stevenson acknowledges the necessity of appropriating a new voice when he writes, 'I must learn to address readers from the uttermost part of the sea.'[43] Yet, his displacement and concomitant sense of alienation make it no easy task. Boehmer seeks to explain his apparent frustration at mapping the strangeness of the South Pacific landscape: 'No matter how diligently colonizers translated unfamiliar landscapes, from their cultural and geographic standpoint the original script of that unfamiliarity was doomed to remain inaccessible.'[44] Stevenson's task of interpretation involved re-evaluating his assumptions as the protagonist of his short story is forced to do. But in contrast to Wiltshire, who was, like many of the English readers Stevenson wished to address, 'sunk over the ears in

Roman civilisation',[45] Stevenson kept his ears open to what the foreign landscape and people had to tell him. At the same time he kept his eyes wide open and learned to look at the Pacific world through a different lens. In stories like 'The Bottle Imp' or 'The Isle of Voices', for example, Stevenson portrays positive native protagonists who travel between cultures in a thoroughly hybrid Pacific world. To British readers, however, such a world was unfamiliar and partly unwelcome; they perceived Stevenson as a writer in exile, who had gone both native and realist.[46]

Although Stevenson's exile in the South Pacific contrasts with Mansfield's exile from it, they both subvert and redefine marginality in their individual ways. For each one the South Pacific is not merely 'a theatre for dreams',[47] but the place in or through which their mature work is consolidated. While Stevenson's aesthetic is perfected in the South Seas, where he embraces the islands in their particularities, their realities as well as fantasies, Mansfield's art develops out of the crux of a yearning for an original homeland in the Pacific, expressed through the modernist means of fragmentation, as she is 'always conscious of [a] secret disruption'.[48] Mark Williams elaborates:

> Mansfield did not make herself a modernist by abandoning provincial New Zealand in favour of cosmopolitan Europe. What she needed was a means of distancing herself from the limitations of the colonial world while retaining the sharp focus of the massive collisions it contained. She carried her New Zealand with her to Europe, both the bourgeois New Zealand of her own family who frustrated and supported her and the wild New Zealand which seemed to her of interest because it was unformed, unruly, unsophisticated.[49]

Williams's mention of 'wild New Zealand' draws attention to the importance of the natural environment as a primary stimulus to Mansfield as well as Stevenson. Antony Alpers speaks of the 'silent character' in stories like 'Prelude' or 'At the Bay', referring to 'the stillness of the bush, the disdain of the lofty islands for their huddled little pockets of colonial intruders, the silence of the vast sea-desert that encircled them'.[50] In Mansfield's as well as Stevenson's writing, the South Pacific thus moves to the foreground in late Victorian anti-imperialist and European modernist fiction.

'The Beach of Falesá' and 'Prelude' are narratives of displacement, in which the characters cross fluid, hybrid spaces in the South Pacific and are thereby themselves transformed. Like the authors, whose transpacific journeys made them acutely alert to otherness, both in themselves and the perceived Other, the protagonists find themselves in places where they need to redefine their conceptions of 'home' and contest the 'persistent yet mysterious belief in a self which is continuous and permanent'.[51] 'Home', as a dynamic category, can then be found both in the country or place of origin and abroad, virtually at the other end of the world, but also in the interstices of the strange and the familiar.

Notes

1. Friedrich Nietzsche, 'The Gay Science: Book V', in Keith Ansell-Pearson and Duncan Large, eds, *The Nietzsche Reader* (Oxford: Blackwell, 2006), pp. 362–84 (p. 377).
2. Quoted in Iain Chambers, *Migrancy, Culture, Identity* (London and New York: Routledge, 1994), p. 1.
3. Vincent O'Sullivan and Margaret Scott, eds, *The Collected Letters of Katherine Mansfield*, 5 vols (Oxford: Clarendon Press, 1984–2008), Vol. 5, p. 341. Hereafter referred to as *Letters*, followed by volume and page number.
4. See also Alex Thomson, 'Stevenson's Afterlives', in Penny Fielding, ed., *The Edinburgh Companion of Robert Louis Stevenson* (Edinburgh: Edinburgh University Press, 2010), pp. 147–59. Thomson writes that nowadays Stevenson's work tends to be seen 'as an anticipation of "modernist" or even "post-modernist" literary trends' (p. 152).
5. Quoted in Alan Sandison, *Robert Louis Stevenson and the Appearance of Modernism: A Future Feeling* (Basingstoke: Macmillan, 1996), p. 13.
6. Quoted in Elaine Showalter, *Sexual Anarchy: Gender and Culture at the Fin de Siècle* (London: Bloomsbury, 1991), p. 79.
7. Mansfield experiments in pauses, ellipses and other features of an aesthetics of fragmentation, whereas Stevenson works towards longer syntactic forms, and greater emphasis on plot – more realist than modernist in fact, and more 'masculinist' from a narrative point of view.
8. Elleke Boehmer, 'Mansfield as Colonial Modernist: Difference Within', in Gerri Kimber and Janet Wilson, eds, *Celebrating Katherine Mansfield* (Basingstoke: Palgrave, 2011), pp. 57–71 (pp. 57–9).
9. For a fuller discussion, see Saikat Majumdar, 'Katherine Mansfield and the Fragility of Pākehā Boredom', *Modern Fiction Studies*, 55.1 (2009), pp. 119–41 (pp. 119–22).
10. Quoted in Ian A. Gordon, *Undiscovered Country: The New Zealand Stories of Katherine Mansfield* (London: Longman, 1974), p. xi, and in Margaret Scott, ed., *The Katherine Mansfield Notebooks*, 2 vols (Canterbury, NZ: Lincoln University Press, 1997), Vol. 1, p. 108 (hereafter referred to as *Notebooks*, followed by volume and page number).
11. *Notebooks* 2, p. 166.
12. *Letters* 5, p. 115. On her changing attitudes towards London see Ana Belén López Pérez, '"A City of One's Own": Women, Social Class and London in Katherine Mansfield's Short Stories', in Janet Wilson, Gerri Kimber, Susan Reid, eds, *Katherine Mansfield and Literary Modernism* (London: Continuum, 2011), pp. 128–38 (pp. 129–30).
13. Caroline McCracken-Flesher, 'Travel Writing', in Penny Fielding, ed., *The Edinburgh Companion to Robert Louis Stevenson* (Edinburgh: Edinburgh University Press, 2010), pp. 86–101 (p. 90).
14. Robert Fraser, *Victorian Quest Romance: Stevenson, Haggard, Kipling, and Conan Doyle* (Plymouth: Northcote House, 1998), p. 1.
15. Quoted in Ann C. Colley, *Robert Louis Stevenson and the Colonial Imagination* (Aldershot: Ashgate, 2004), p. 5.
16. Bradford A. Booth and Ernest Mehew, eds, *The Letters of Robert Louis Stevenson*, 8 vols

(New Haven and London: Yale University Press, 1994–5), Vol. 8, p. 159.

17. In her illuminating book *Illness, Gender, and Writing: The Case of Katherine Mansfield* (1994), Mary Burgan analyses Mansfield's creativity as inflected by her bodily experience of illness.

18. In this study Mansfield's New Zealand is subsumed as part of the South Pacific to articulate the proximity to Stevenson's South Seas.

19. Colley offers an excellent account and analysis of Stevenson's clothing in the South Seas in her article 'Stevenson's Pyjamas', *Victorian Literature and Culture*, 30.1 (2002), pp. 129–55 (especially pp. 135–6, p. 138).

20. Angela Smith, 'Introduction', in Angela Smith, ed., *Katherine Mansfield: Selected Stories* (Oxford: Oxford University Press, 2008), pp. ix–xxxii, (p. xv).

21. Scholars have ascribed a Peter Pan complex to each author; see Julia Reid, 'Childhood and Psychology', in Fielding, pp. 41–52 (p. 41) and J. Lawrence Mitchell, 'Katherine Mansfield and the Aesthetic Object', *Journal of New Zealand Literature*, 22 (2004), pp. 31–54 (p. 48). Stevenson continued to delight in his toy soldiers as much as the adult Mansfield was attached to her Japanese dolls. See Rod Edmond, *Representing the South Pacific: Colonial Discourse from Cook to Gauguin* (Cambridge: Cambridge University Press, 1997), p. 171; Cherry Hankin, 'Katherine Mansfield and the Cult of Childhood', in Roger Robinson, ed., *Katherine Mansfield: In from the Margin* (Baton Rouge and London: Louisiana State University Press, 1994), pp. 25–35 (p. 32).

22. *Letters of Robert Louis Stevenson* 7, p. 161.

23. Judy Giles and Tim Middleton, *Studying Culture: A Practical Introduction*, 2nd edn (Malden: Blackwell, 2008), p. 127.

24. All subsequent references to 'Prelude' are from Smith, pp. 79–120; and 'The Beach of Falesá' to Roslyn Jolly, ed., *South Sea Tales* (Oxford: Oxford University Press, 2008), pp. 3–72. Page numbers are placed parenthetically in the text following each quotation.

25. Ann C. Colley, 'Robert Louis Stevenson's South Seas Crossings', *Studies in English Literature 1500–1900*, 48.4 (Autumn 2008), pp. 871–84 (p. 878).

26. These are the words Stevenson used to describe Samoa in 1875. When he finally went there to settle, he predicted, 'I go there only to grow old and die', telling his correspondent, 'when you come you will see it is a fair place for the purpose' (*Letters of Robert Louis Stevenson* 6, p. 421).

27. Mary Louise Pratt, 'Arts of the Contact Zone', *Profession*, 91 (New York: MLA, 1991), pp. 33–40 (p. 34).

28. See Roslyn Jolly, 'Notes', in *South Sea Tales*, pp. 259–89 (pp. 259, 279).

29. Quoted in Vanessa Smith, *Literary Culture and the Pacific: Nineteenth-Century Textual Encounters* (Cambridge: Cambridge University Press, 1998), pp. 166–7.

30. *Letters of Robert Louis Stevenson* 7, p. 282.

31. Roslyn Jolly, 'Stevenson's "Sterling Domestic Fiction": "The Beach of Falesá"', *The Review of English Studies*, 50.200 (1999), pp. 463–82 (p. 465).

32. See Homi K. Bhabha, *The Location of Culture* (London: Routledge, 1994), p. 37.

33. Jolly, 'Stevenson's "Sterling Domestic Fiction"', p. 482.

34. *Letters of Robert Louis Stevenson* 7, p. 155.

35. Smith, 'Introduction', p. xxxi.

36. Michel de Certeau, *The Practice of Everyday Life*, trans. Steven Rendall (Berkeley and London: University of California Press, 1988), p. 117.

37. See also Mitchell, 'Katherine Mansfield and the Aesthetic Object', p. 33.

38. See, for example, Mitchell, p. 36.

39. *Notebooks* 2, p. 32.
40. Katherine Mansfield, *The Aloe* (New York: Howard Fertig, 1974), p. 15.
41. Katherine Mansfield, *New Zealand Stories*, selected by Vincent O'Sullivan (Auckland: Oxford University Press, 1997), p. 19.
42. In the journal entry where Mansfield speaks about her 'debt of love' to New Zealand, she writes that she wants to 'make our undiscovered country leap into the eyes of the old world. It must be mysterious, as though floating – it must take the breath. It must be "one of those islands" . . .' (*Notebooks* 2, p. 32).
43. Robert Louis Stevenson, *In the South Seas*, ed. Neil Rennie (London: Penguin, 1998), p. 5.
44. Elleke Boehmer, *Colonial and Postcolonial Literature: Migrant Metaphors*, 2nd edn (Oxford: Oxford University Press, 2005), p. 88.
45. *Letters of Robert Louis Stevenson* 7, p. 187.
46. See Roslyn Jolly, *Robert Louis Stevenson in the Pacific: Travel, Empire, and the Author's Profession* (Farnham: Ashgate, 2009), pp. vii, 27; John Kucich, 'Melancholy Magic: Masochism, Stevenson, Anti-Imperialism', *Nineteenth-Century Literature*, 56.3 (2001), pp. 364–400 (p. 396).
47. Edmond, *Representing the South Pacific*, p. 18.
48. *Letters* 5, p. 304.
49. Mark Williams, 'Mansfield in Maoriland: Biculturalism, Agency and Misreading', in Howard J. Booth and Nigel Rigby, eds, *Modernism and Empire* (Manchester: Manchester University Press, 2000), pp. 249–74 (pp. 256–7).
50. Quoted in Peter Mathews, 'Myth and Unity in Mansfield's "At the Bay"', *Journal of New Zealand Literature*, 23.2 (2005), pp. 47–61 (p. 49).
51. *Notebooks* 2, p. 204.

Literatures of Expatriation and the Colonial Mansfield

Anne Brown-Berens

Mansfield's Literary Contexts

In a novel of 1891 the following observation is made:

> I should think that to a young lady so much isolation from society and the constant sameness and tameness of everyday life in a wilderness like this, must be very irksome in comparison to the pleasure and gaiety of living in the town.[1]

Initial scrutiny might suggest that this passage is from a British novel yet in fact it belongs to a version of the colonial genre. Among the clues is the misleading assertion that town and country, cultivated interiors, social manners and landscapes, are successfully recreated. However, the tone of the novel from which the quotation is taken, Dugald Ferguson's *Vicissitudes of Bush Life in Australia and New Zealand* (1891), suggests that we could indeed be far from 'home', that is, England. Looking at the novels of empire, particularly those of the nineteenth-century social diaspora, we might well question what are the assumptions in fictional representations of the new society when 'place' does not quite exist. What embryonic symbols will emerge, when, despite assurances of sameness, of a presumed close accord and continuity with Britain, a sense of the incomplete nonetheless continues to persist instead? If the condition of expatriation affects the nineteenth-century colonist, how will Mansfield, writing in the twentieth century as an expatriate author and modernist, be affected as she looks back to the same society as the country of her birth? In Mansfield's case expatriation was two-fold: not only the leaving behind of the homeland (in contrast to England, the metropolitan homeland) but, more significantly, an exploration of new ideas in literary form and aestheticism leading to the moment of

Mansfield's expressed wish as an expatriate and ambitious modernist writer – 'to lift [that] mist from my people and let them be seen and then to hide them again'.[2]

This essay explores how expatriation and displacement occur both in Mansfield's modernist short stories and in the New Zealand diasporic novels of her Victorian forefathers. According to Lydia Wevers, only a portion of Mansfield's writing relates to New Zealand settler themes, with 'close to half' of the stories located in New Zealand, and continental Europe 'the setting for the largest number'.[3] Nevertheless, opportunities exist for comparison with nineteenth-century New Zealand novels that might illustrate a common 'sense of exile'.[4] In both colonial and modernist texts representations of settler gentility posit a colonist's expatriation in two distinct ways: first, as a means of averting or occluding the condition of separation from the original homeland, and second, in obviating the primitive[5] in contrast to settler attempts at gentility. Ferguson's confrontation with a colonial primitive of the masculine outdoors in *Vicissitudes of Bush Life* seeks less to avert the colonist's gaze than do Clara Cheeseman's depictions of the settler primitive in *A Rolling Stone* (1886). For Cheeseman, the need to characterise the natural environment as a form of European arcadia prompts the voice of the displaced settler in the narrator, whose conscious ordering of nature in preference to its 'disorder' at the periphery of the settler landscape is illustrated by, for instance, the following:

> Let us suppose that you have made the pilgrimage. If you were bold, and forded the bridgeless creek, or if you wisely preferred the longer way, and threaded the mazes of the damp, dark bush, you came at last to an open, sunlit space, where the trees no longer crowded together, struggling for light and air, but stood apart in groves and avenues, all the more beautiful because they were of Nature's own planting.[6]

In *Vicissitudes of Bush Life,* the surroundings of the Rolleston house are described from the colonist's perspective of his own habitat with a mild disdain for the colonial primitive, while later entry into the domestic interior ameliorates Rolleston's pioneer sensibilities with an illusion of the refinements usually associated with the 'town':

> The appearance of the station buildings I will forego describing. Like the homesteads of most squatters in those days, they were chiefly constructed out of the primitive materials of split slabs or round logs and bark. There was the inevitable woolshed seen in the distance with its surrounding yards and fences. Even the house of the owner was of the most unpretending appearance, with about half a dozen rooms or so. [. . .]
> On entering the house, the interior of which I discovered to be much

more pretentiously furnished than the exterior gave promise of, I found myself in the presence of three ladies in a rather tasteful looking sitting-room, arranged with almost fashionable fastidiousness.[7]

Writing as an expatriate, particularly after 1915 and prior to the 1922 publication of 'The Garden Party', Mansfield had literary and artistic motivations that clearly included the wish to recreate the ambience of her childhood. As she ventured into modernist impressionism, she drew for her aesthetics of interiors and artefacts as well as the natural environment, upon a sentimental symbolism similar to that found in the New Zealand colonial novel, a literature still attached to conventional form, popular imitation and a 'recording' style of narrative.[8] Although these more conventional colonial novels were readily available to Mansfield in her early years they may well have remained largely unfamiliar to her. What distinguishes Mansfield's literary evocations of New Zealand society and the world of middle-class childhood more specifically from the colonial text is her use of symbolism through which pioneer vulnerability and inherited social and cultural norms are delicately balanced, yet also deliberately exposed. In 'Millie' this symbolism of an empire, dense with cultural artefacts, is represented in the language of the displaced, and in cultivation of the narrative moment.

> She flopped down on the side of the bed and stared at the coloured print on the wall opposite, 'Garden Party at Windsor Castle'. In the foreground emerald lawns planted with immense oak trees, and in their grateful shade a muddle of ladies and gentlemen and parasols and little tables. The background was filled with the towers of Windsor Castle, flying three Union Jacks, and in the middle of the picture the old Queen, like a tea cosy with a head on top of it.[9]

In 'The Woman at the Store' the brutal realism of settler-primitivist description jars with the most recent, yet still distinctly aged, periodical of Queen Victoria's Jubilee. The gulf widens between the accepted norms of the empire's 'civilised' domestic spaces and the actuality of frontier settler existence:

> It was a large room, the walls plastered with old pages of English periodicals. Queen Victoria's Jubilee appeared to be the most recent number – a table with an ironing board and wash tub on it – some wooden forms – a black horsehair sofa, and some broken cane chairs pushed against the walls. The mantelpiece above the stove was draped in pink paper, further ornamented with dried grasses and ferns and a coloured print of Richard Seddon. (30)

In order to view Mansfield in terms of her 'Victorian ancestors' or 'literary Victorians', it is worth noting that her short lifespan (1888–

1923) overlaps the period of New Zealand writing between 1874–1914 known as 'Maoriland'.[10] The early (1864–89) and late (1890–1934) periods of the colonial novel genre each belong to the era of trans-Tasman 'Maoriland' publishing. The latter, like Mansfield's own early attempts at publication, was composed of a variety of genres, including verse, popular fiction and literary journalism.[11] A principal function of 'Maoriland' was to register 'the first literary evidence of a national consciousness'.[12] Such novels as Cheeseman's *A Rolling Stone* and Ferguson's *Vicissitudes of Bush Life,* according to Jane Stafford and Mark Williams, often remained 'virtually unread' and were emblematic of 'a culture of embarrassment'.[13] They refer to the 'shaping influence' of the colonial context in Mansfield's stories, arguing that her emergence into modernism was not derivative of other twentieth-century writers, but a consequence of her own synthesis and imaginative reworking of late nineteenth-century techniques and themes. The degree to which Mansfield looked toward 'Maoriland' remains uncertain, according to evidence found in her own journals and letters.[14] Stafford and Williams nonetheless argue that 'The Woman at the Store' indicates an earlier susceptibility on Mansfield's part to 'Maoriland'.

> ['The Woman at the Store' was] written in London and published in Murry's journal, *Rhythm.* Its closeness to colonial writing, especially the stories in Barbara Baynton's *Bush Studies* which appeared first in the *Bulletin* in the 1890s, indicates literary self-consciousness.[15]

From 1910 until 1913 Mansfield, the expatriate writer, worked closely under A. R. Orage's patronage on the periodical *New Age* and with Middleton Murry on *Rhythm.* Meanwhile, by 1914, the 'Maoriland' novel genre had exhausted itself.[16] I suggest that among Mansfield's aims in stories like 'Millie' and 'The Woman at the Store', was to re-envision a nineteenth-century European settler society in crisis through the lens of modernist writing. Despite their orientation toward the imperial centre',[17] the 'Maoriland' novels with their range of 'colonial yarns, ghost stories and romances' paradoxically offered indications of 'unsettlement', or degrees of uncertainty that reflected the 'incompleteness and arbitrary nature' of colonial existence.[18] However, a predisposition in early New Zealand literature's expression of landscape primitivism and imagery of the colonial interior toward materiality and symbol, might, it could be argued, constitute a commonality of unsettled reference for both the 'Maoriland' novel and Mansfield's own more self-aware, modernist depictions of the same conditions of colonial life. In each, notions of place and identity occur within an aesthetic of cultural symbolism. To examine this further it may be useful to observe how, in the colonial novel, settler and landscape primitivism implies an incongruity and transitoriness, again replicated in Mansfield's own narrative.

In Cheeseman's *A Rolling Stone* and Mansfield's short story 'Prelude', for example, the central image of the settler home portrays symbols of migrant white culture as a refuge of identity. This refuge, complete with its symbolic displacement, becomes peculiarly 'colonial'. Cheeseman writes:

> There is something very poetic in the idea of a man choosing a place for himself in the heart of the wilderness, building his little house under the giant trees, and hewing his way farther amongst them year by year, fighting with the forest for every foot of ground.[19]

For Cheeseman here pioneering colonialism is a brave, lifelong, hard, and intrinsically active *occupation*, primarily one of clearing and ordering. Compare this with the following from Mansfield's 'Prelude', where the very image of colonial cultivation itself prompts a disconnectedness that is experienced through feelings and articulated in metaphor; in sighs, vertigo, and a sleeping beast, even in the midst of what has long been thoroughly cleared and made orderly.

> She gave a long sigh, and to stop her eyes from curling she shut them . . . When she opened them again they were clanking through a drive that cut through the garden like a whiplash, looping suddenly an island of green, and behind the island, but out of sight until you came upon it, was the house. It was long and low built, with a pillared veranda and balcony all the way round. The soft white bulk of it lay stretched upon the green garden like a sleeping beast. (84)

In her going forth to 'encounter the "reality" which will be transmuted into art',[20] Mansfield therefore defines a subjective relationship between character, place and object in the narrative. She disrupts the stasis of empire novel writing which is mainly intended for the entertainment and informing of a popular readership. Identifying Mansfield with her nineteenth-century precursors means first of all to acknowledge her clear difference from them as a modernist or artist who rejects and challenges literary conventions, and to allow at the same time that she still embraces the cultural norms of the late nineteenth-century colonial milieu. Both the nineteenth-century colonial novel and modernist short story exploit conditions of the settler emigrant which are embarrassing or inconvenient. Mansfield's evident delight in the momentary, in the absurdity and pathos of settler expectations as seen in the woman's sitting room in 'The Woman at the Store', illustrates how a settler realism, based on the perception of the 'incompleteness' of settler habitation and the harsh environment, may effectively be adapted to the new modernist literary genre.

Settler Landscape

Among colonial novels of the early pioneer period (1864–89),[21] Clara Cheeseman's *A Rolling Stone* (1886) and Charlotte Evans's *Over the Hills and Far Away* (1874) together evoke an impression of the disconnected or 'displaced' settler in the colonial landscape. This can also be found in Mansfield's earlier story, 'The Woman at the Store' (1912) and her later one, 'Prelude' (1917). Inside *A Rolling Stone*'s settler cottage nothing is 'large and well developed', there is 'too little of everything [. . .] too little space, too few windows, and too few panes in them'.[22] For a romantic novelist like Evans, who emigrated to New Zealand in 1864, the surrounding hills of Canterbury in New Zealand's South Island represented what could only be 'enchanting' and 'everything new and colonial'.[23] Yet rather than describe these enchantments faithfully, or even with only a sense of verisimilitude, Evans directs her narrative outward and toward an essentially escapist vision of land and people. Standing at the verandah of the Cunningham station home, Lucy sees 'a long wooden house, roofed with shingle [. . .] lying at the head of a wide valley'.[24] A somewhat contrived and picturesque landscape stretches ahead, a vista enclosed by a garden dividing it 'from the paddock beyond', while an English lawn belies a surrounding wilderness 'on all sides' of hills of 'pale tussock grass'.[25] Lucy's new enchantment is, nonetheless, soon qualified by her realisation of the neighbourhood's lack of brush foliage, and any sign of relief from the 'wildness and desolation of the scenery'.[26]

A similar vista of the bereft landscape, of nothing but 'wave after wave of tussock grass' appears in Mansfield's 'The Woman at the Store' (27). Evans's landscape of stylised English artifice at the edge of wilderness, exhibiting the settler's need for points of safety or cultural familiarity, is seen in the later story 'Prelude' in which the Burnell family leaves behind their home in the city to travel through a strange terrain of 'unknown country' where 'everything familiar was left behind'. After passing along new roads into 'bushy valleys' and 'through wide shallow rivers' (83), the two little girls, Lottie and Kezia, travelling separately from their mother, arrive at the house and are confronted with images suggestive of contrived civilisation, including a 'high box border' and paths with 'box edges' (95). Already, there is a suggestion of transient discomfort in the face of such wilderness followed by relief at this image of the familiar. If Mansfield's sentimentalising here of the cultivated is somewhat reminiscent of Evans, her sudden shift towards metaphor in the aloe's appearance as 'a ship' with 'the oars lifted' (110), sees her transform the symbolic-figurative into something quite unexpected as the 'thick, grey-green, thorny leaves' (96) of the aloe begin to appear dangerously ugly, monstrous, even sensual, deserting the cultivated to become 'other' to the artifice-seeking gaze of the colonist.

Novels of the frontier period set in the colonial goldrush, such as Dugald Ferguson's *Vicissitudes of Bush Life* (1891) and Alexander Bathgate's *Waitaruna* (1881), when read as foregrounding periods of cultural transition, may also provide contexts for reading two further Mansfield stories: 'Ole Underwood' (1913) and 'The Garden Party' (1921). In *Vicissitudes*, Ferguson presents a contrast to the artificial formalities of Cheeseman and Evans by exploring the world of the 'civilised settler' as a gendered frontier split between the masculine outdoors and feminine domestic interior. Ferguson's station residences, described as 'huts simple and rude, with woolshed conterminous'[27] (a Victorian term for 'common boundary') seem increasingly incongruous with the process of colonialising, at the same time as they remain symbols of refuge in an otherwise hostile landscape.

Alexander Bathgate's 1881 novel *Waitaruna* envisages human residence in terms of dislocation by observing 'not a tree is to be seen, while only one human habitation is visible and that so far off, as to be hardly distinguishable [. . .] looking from the house the view is desolate and barren'.[28] In 'Ole Underwood' Mansfield's colonial realism conveys something of Ferguson's makeshift imagery, this time as an exchange between frontier primitivism and an urban displacement of the 'hideous' in a twilight zone of 'ugly little houses leading into the town, built of wood' (40). Mansfield once again displaces middle-class gentility in 'The Garden Party' to unequivocally portray a suburban vista of 'little mean dwellings' (293) as the 'greatest possible eyesore'. Having 'no right' (293) at all to be in the neighbourhood, these cottages, symbols of working-class habitation, both displace and are in turn displaced within the closed orbit of the middle-class Sheridans. In a different way, but with similar consequences, in 'The Woman at the Store', Mansfield, through her choice of the 'hut' image as the dwelling place of the European creates a symbolic clash between the narrative meaning of the primitive and civilised. The single place of living is jarringly overloaded with nostalgic references to the empire of origin, settler sensibilities, needs and refuge, and primitive realities. Furthermore, in the hut's naming as a 'whare', reader sensibility is persuaded even more subversively into the discomforting idea of the colonist as almost completely removed from the European cultural norm. With a determined exploitation of 'exotic currency',[29] Mansfield perversely responds to the colonial reader's desire for civilisation through introducing stark frontier realism.

Interiorisations of displacement recur in imagery of the confined and isolated settler in both *A Rolling Stone* and 'Prelude'. By contrasting the primitive landscape to notions of colonial shelter, Cheeseman offers the morally ordering force of a personified and feminised presence that beneficently plants, plans and re-forms the indigenous natural world into a more desirable reality. Envisaging the settler home as an image of centrality similar to Mansfield's portrayal of the Sheridan's house in 'The Garden Party', Cheeseman writes: 'miry tracks that led to it could hardly be called roads, the creeks that almost made it an island were unbridged, and the bush had closed around, as if determined to hide it from the eyes of the world' (95). As though to allay fears of the unknown in this landscape, Cheeseman then coaxes the imagination of the reader into a more safely designed vista of visual certainty, in which nature makes 'this park herself', where none can 'vex or interfere with her designs'.[30] Conversely, Mansfield's primitivist leanings in 'Prelude' lead her to internalise images of the natural with intimations of sensuality that may emotionally disconcert, as, for example, in the prospect of 'flat velvet leaves and feathery cream flowers that buzz with flies when they are shaken' (95). In directing Linda's gaze toward the unknown and unfamiliar in order to evoke 'the frightening side' of domesticity, the side that has 'no garden at all' (95), Mansfield seems to point the way to another nature whose reality traverses the boundaries of consciousness and suggests that edges are unstable, precipitating uncertain grounds of feeling. As an image of refuge, the Burnell homestead nonetheless reinforces its narrative positioning as a protective symbol against the disordering effects of the surrounding bush-scape and its implicit threat to cultural self-containment. The homestead is a 'radical break with the old country'.[31]

The Interior Symbolic

Through cultural imitation, gentility associated with interiors alleviates colonial sensibilities whilst also producing a disjunctive sense of apprehension and uncertainty about cultural norms and origins. At stake throughout all of the preceding are the settlers' attempts toward an imitation of their own culture of origin. Creating these mimetic interior spaces to soothe their uncertain sense of place and belonging necessarily leads to a more marked disjunction in the settlers' mind from what is not artificially recreated. There is an accompanying sense of apprehension about their own cultural norms and origins when those spaces are viewed against and within the larger settler spaces of the new colony.

In *A Rolling Stone* Mr Wishart's discomfort at a pictorial representation of royalty and empire is obvious; after all, he says: 'It was a time when there would indeed be no fewer than nine representations of Our Sovereign Lady in the room, no two of which were alike.'[32] He remarks: 'It was curious to see these things on the walls, it was more so to look upwards, and behold them gazing down on you.'[33] A dizzying cluster of images is presented, all with the same referent, all juxtaposed, none the same, echoing Mansfield's own re-envisaging of empire symbolism in the picture on the wall in 'Millie' of 'Garden Party at Windsor Castle' (43). In *A Rolling Stone*, as everything from 'a cattleshow' to the 'leaders of the house of commons' parades before Wishart's eyes in a 'bygone age' of 'balloon-like crinolines, bonnets [. . .] bishop sleeves, flounces, puffs and paniers',[34] the same symbols simultaneously betray to the imagination a sense of the 'dying' empire as a bulwark against the colony's geographic and cultural distance from the centre.

Charlotte Evans's account of studied placement and intellectual and artistic pretension in the colonies begins, however, with complete confidence: 'On each side of the fireplace was a shelf of handsomely-bound volumes – Kingsley in blue, Macaulay in brown, Thackeray and Dickens in red, and a complete set of the "Cornhill Magazine" in handsome bindings.'[35] But, Evans then confides: 'although in the centre of the mantelpiece, under a glass shade' a 'Parisian copy of the lovely bust of Clytie' lends the room 'an air of refinement', it would 'but for that and the books and one other thing' be 'completely wanting to it'.[36] In forming a bold contrast to Evans's form of reserve, Mansfield's series of visual effects and vivid contrasts of arrangement in 'The Woman at the Store' – of 'dried grasses and ferns' and a portrait of parliamentarian Richard Seddon surrounded by 'walls plastered with old pages of English periodicals' (30) – create a disjuncture within the symbolic form that is more emotively critical than Evans, yet also, perhaps, ironically reminiscent of Wishart's tableau of empire symbolism.

The foregoing discussion of settler life and expatriation within the novel and short story establishes how closely nineteenth-century settler primitivism (see note 5), amplifies intertextual awareness alongside Mansfield's twentieth-century modernism, and in the process conveys parallel notions of displacement. I believe that in attempting to impose a settler consciousness or settler identity, the novel creates formative contexts for modernist subjectivities in Mansfield. Referring back to a place undefined in conscious knowledge, a social milieu 'hidden' from Europe, Mansfield the modernist expatriate exists momentarily between realities. From being 'contemptuous of the smug provincialism of late colonial New Zealand', yet, not able to 'wholly escape Maoriland' either,[37] Mansfield's exiled self discovers in modernist aesthetics a key toward transcendence from the traditional world; from the 'ordinariness and embarrassments'[38] of the 'little colonial' into that of genuine art.

Notes

1. Dugald Ferguson, *Vicissitudes of Bush Life in Australia and New Zealand* (London: Swan Sonnenschein & Co., 1891), p. 237.
2. Vincent O'Sullivan and Margaret Scott, eds, *The Collected Letters of Katherine Mansfield*, 5 vols (Oxford: Clarendon Press, 1984–2008), Vol. 1 (1984), p. 331.
3. Lydia Wevers, 'Colonial Short Fiction to Katherine Mansfield', in Terry Sturm, ed., *The Oxford History of New Zealand Literature in English*, 2nd edn (Auckland: Oxford University Press, 1998), p. 260.
4. Ibid. p. 260.
5. I use the term 'primitive' throughout to refer to the uncivilised, wild settings/landscapes and even the coarse in settler existence. For instance, the settler building or homestead, and the artifice of contrived settler landscapes symbolise the settler's prior expectations of the 'civilised' in contrast with the natural, untamed state of the bush that surrounds them.
6. Clara Cheeseman, *A Rolling Stone,* 2 vols (London: Richard Bentley and Son, 1886), Vol. 1, p. 2.
7. Ferguson, pp. 23, 29.
8. Joan Stevens, *The New Zealand Novel 1860–1965* (Wellington: A. H. & A. W. Reed, 1966), p. 21.
9. Vincent O'Sullivan, ed., *Katherine Mansfield's Selected Stories* (New York: Norton, 2006), p. 42. All subsequent references to Mansfield's stories will come from this edition, cited parenthetically by page number.
10. Lawrence Jones, 'The Pioneer Novel' in Terry Sturm, ed., *The Oxford History of New Zealand Literature in English*, 2nd edn (Auckland: Oxford University Press, 1998), p. 120.
11. Jane Stafford and Mark Williams, 'Colonialism and Embarrassment', in *Maoriland: New Zealand Literature 1872–1914* (Wellington: Victoria University Press, 2006), p. 10.
12. Ibid. p. 10.
13. Stafford and Williams, 'Introduction: A Land Mild and Bold, Diffident and Pertinent.' New Zealand Electronic Text Centre, http://nzetc.victoria.ac.nz/tm/scholarly/tei-StaIntr.html (accessed 18/03/13).
14. Stafford and Williams, 'Katherine Mansfield: A Modernist in Maoriland', in *Maoriland*, p. 142.
15. Ibid. p. 142
16. Stafford and Williams, 'Introduction: A Land Mild and Bold'.
17. Ibid.
18. Ibid.
19. Cheeseman, Vol. 1, p. 6.
20. Stafford and Williams, 'Katherine Mansfield: A Modernist in Maoriland', in *Maoriland*, p. 142.
21. Jones, p. 120.

22. Cheeseman, Vol. 1, p. 16.
23. Charlotte Evans, *Over the Hills and Far Away: A Story of New Zealand* (London: Sampson Low, Marston & Co., 1874), p. 88.
24. Ibid. p. 79.
25. Ibid. p. 79.
26. Ibid. p. 84.
27. Ferguson, p. 29.
28. Alexander Bathgate, *Waitaruna: A Story of New Zealand Life* (London: Sampson Low, Marston & Co., 1881), p. 101.
29. Stafford and Williams, *Maoriland*, p. 169.
30. Cheeseman, Vol. 1, p. 1.
31. Stephen Turner, 'Settlement as Forgetting', in Klaus Neumann, Nicholas Thomas and Hilary Ericksen, eds, *Quicksands: Foundational Histories in Australia and Aotearoa New Zealand* (Sydney: University of New South Wales Press, 1999), p. 20.
32. Cheeseman, Vol. 1, p. 40.
33. Ibid.
34. Ibid.
35. Evans, p. 79.
36. Ibid.
37. Ibid. p. 152.
38. Ibid. p. 169.

CREATIVE WRITING

POETRY

Names and Places Poem

Driven at night
from Krakow to Ružomberok
a student beside me
        Natalia Križalkovičová
murmuring in the accent of Slovakia
      about the poetry of place –
William Wordsworth and the Lakes
Jaroslav Sieffert and Prague
             soon sleeping
      her round face lighting up
in the passing traffic
reminding me of Margaret Bell
friend of my youth:
             woods and fields
               and villages,
fields and petrol stations
and woods –
      three hours on the road
and the professor
Janka Kaščáková
      waiting at half past midnight
to greet me barefoot
at the ski-lodge door
      so tall and slim and young
        I wanted to apologise
          for being eighty.
Sixty might have sufficed,
fifty would have been better,
forty near-perfect.
Margaret Bell could have told her

> how dashing I was
> when still in my twenties.
> In earshot of running water
> I stared up at stars
> through the dark shafts of firs
> where fireflies described
> their brilliant journeys
> to the sleeping bears.
>
> Next morning at nine
> when I delivered my wisdoms
> I was still eighty.
> A mysterious rain
> was drifting over the woods
> and haunted ramparts
> of Oravský Hrad
> and the fast clear streams
> running down from the mountains.

C. K. STEAD

Excavating the Bones

For Gerri
We are excavating the bones,
studying emotional geology,
reconstructing from nodes and fractures
an unfamiliar landscape we know
only from photographs, scraps of text,
torn pages from a life lived
beyond our knowledge. We
finger the calcified digits,
a fragment of cloth, a brooch;
grave goods. But they are only
themselves, animated by our need
to articulate the skeleton,
colour in the blanks, bridge absences,
construct a narrative out of shards.

KATHLEEN JONES
Katherine Mansfield Conference
Ružomberok, Slovakia, 2012

Nightmare

'It slowly dawned on me – the conviction that in that dream I died'
Katherine Mansfield, Ospedaletti, 1919

Out of the darkness and the silence
something is looming.

The dumb cherry tree is
torturing itself outside the window.

Bridal white under the moon
it can never bear fruit.

There is something in the room
I can't look at. It sits

in a corner and turns the page.
The paper is white. Bare

as the bones that nest inside
my flesh, waiting to rot out.

The darkness recognises me.
It waits. If I could only wake

it would be daylight and the sun opening
the morning gently. Everything clear.

KATHLEEN JONES

L'Incubo

Dal'buio e il silenzio
qualcosa sta sorgendo.

L'albero muto di cilegio si tortura
fuori della finestra. Bianca

sposa sotto la luna, ma
non puo mai produrre la frutta.

C'e qualcosa nella camera
che non posso guardare. Aspetta

nel'angolo e gira la pagina.
La carta e bianca e nuda

come le ossa che nidificano all'interno
della mia carne, aspettando di marcire.

Il buio mi riconosce. Aspetta.
Se solo potessi svegliarmi sarebbe l'alba

e il sole apre la mattina, piano,
piano. Tutto sarebbe chiaro.

KATHLEEN JONES
Italy 2012

THREE POEMS TO KATHERINE MANSFIELD

1. Katherine Mansfield's Mirror (Châlet des Sapins)
A chalet of the old type, cuckoo-clock roof,
ornate, the balcony creaking,
and the view she saw each day
across to the Weisshorn above Sierre –
these I saw too, as with her eyes:
the perpetual snows, the vines in neat plots;
it's hardly changed at all since she was there,
since her bid to cure her lungs in Alpine air.
'*Oui, c'est le même,*' the concierge nods,
key-laden, at the door, '*aussi les sapins*'.
Evergreens, omnipresent, guard the chalet –
'*the last romantic thing left in Montana*'
wryly the concierge smiles, takes me up
to Katherine's room, her balcony, her mirror.
The mirror in its wooden frame
on a wall between two windows:
I move forward eagerly, look – and look away,
and cannot stand in front, not wanting to imprint
my own reflection on this glass. It should be kept
unlooked in, any vestige of her glance preserved

like the high snows, unvisited and pure.
And then a deeper reason shows its face:
I am afraid; in this mirror, at her disease
she stared, seeking the trace of a Colonial girl
in the troughs of her dark eyes. My own lungs
weak, prey to the wheeze of allergy, I fear
her bleak reality in that mirror: in there
I might fall and sink, be swallowed
in her consuming truth.

2. 'This Nettle, Danger'
at Fontainebleau early light
filters the forest screen
cigarette smoke drifts
through crumbling shutters

December winds stir the lake
brushing the taut timpano
moving lethargic pines
to cough and rasp, dying
their long death, grey
tattered lines of ragged
shawls

in the darkest foliage
scarlet berries spilled
like blood beads –
here the nettles, black mass
thick as Gurdjieff's beard,
will multiply in spring
holding their secrets
within the latent sting

on sandy paths residual snow –
lake-edge blanched like the foamy
beach at Menton, sheets of washerwomen
white banners in cobbled yards:
a world ago that Mediterranean sun,
the orange groves, those purring afternoons,
aromatic evenings, art the anodyne

now winter boughs encircle the lake
where Lamartine once wept for his lady
with the burnt-out lungs

*'This nettle, danger' from the Shakespearian inscription on Katherine
Mansfield's gravestone at Fontainebleau, where she died 9 January
1923.*

3. Poem for Jeanne's Birthday
(Born 20 May 1892, sister of Katherine Mansfield)

At Wellington the southerly busters blow
from the straits, deepening the harbour's bite,
flattening grasses on the Tinakori hills –
these and the manuka trees
are as you remember, like the elements
unchanged. And other essentials:
the toi-toi, waving its head-dress
like a Maori chieftain; Alpine heights
and boiling springs; the surrounding surf,
its scarves of mist and spray;
yellow-fruited Karakas; and the ever-elusive
Kiwi. You tell me, as if to convince yourself,
that you've made your last return –
all is held in the mind. Memory's cargo
wrapped and bound. Yet at times you strive
to recall a family's laughter, Father's wit,
your sisters' competitive company, the smile
of a soldier brother, dead in France.

From your window now, you watch
a great wind agitating the beech trees
which stand at a polite distance
across these Gloucestershire lawns.
Katherine's writings are on your bookshelf –
and in your mind; the family gathers round
in photographs, with a few remnants
of your elegant home. Always positive,
you smile, describe the Home as a large liner
each voyager in a single cabin:
at night, all windows lit,
your ship slides into Wellington harbour.

GLADYS MARY COLES

SHORT STORY

Waiting for La Petite Anglaise

Witi Ihimaera

1.

June, 1922

All week the clouds have been lowering themselves into the valley.

Now a torrent of rain comes to darken the sky, lashing around the hotel.

'Quickly Berthe,' Madame Gay-Crosier, calls to me, 'we must make sure all the shutters are closed.' My mistress always relies on me to obey instructions promptly; she is somewhat heavy and, being middle-aged, not able to get around the hallways and corridors as nimbly as I can.

And after all, there are so many rooms.

One suite in particular I must check with urgency. It is on the second floor, the north wing, and the hotel has guests coming this afternoon, La Petite Anglaise and her husband; they will stay in the suite for their duration: two rooms which, although simple, smell of pinewood, and comprise a large bedroom, with a small reception area (why do the English always insist on calling such an area a 'living room'!) and a vestibule off to one side with a writing desk.

Ah, the writing desk. It is an arresting and handsome piece of furniture, antique, which Madame Gay-Crosier ordered the valet, Gabriel, to bring specially from her own rooms. 'My little bureau,' she addressed it fondly as it was put into place. 'Who knows what beautiful words the small Englishwoman will compose on you, no?'

La Petite Anglaise's husband was insistent that there must be a desk.

'For my wife,' he wrote when giving instructions, 'if possible having a view across the mountains.' Perhaps he was hoping that the Muse would be as beneficent to the famous writer as she was when La Petite Anglaise was in Montana last year. Although I have never read her books I have been told by others that the small Englishwoman wrote five stories there: among them two with titles that fascinate, La Garden-Party and La Maison de poupées. 'Whether she composes stories or not,' her husband continued, 'my wife will spend much of her time writing letters.'

Indeed, La Petite Anglaise writes as other people breathe, the words opening ecstatically onto the page in her swift hand.

Just as I expected, the windows of the suite are wide open. The curtains, although heavy and weighted at the hems, are being wrenched this way and that by the storm; they are like wild birds fighting and flapping their frightening wings at each other. And the wind has overturned one of the beautiful vases of wildflowers. The flowers lie scattered across the floor, as if by some careless bridegroom as he undressed and hastened to cover his bride's gleaming alabaster body with his.

The curtains are unruly and I need help to close them before I am able to secure the shutters. 'Mistress!' I call, as they wrap around me like a smothering shroud.

Instead of Madame Gay-Crosier it is Gabriel, the valet, who comes to my aid.

'What are you doing here?' I ask him, cross. I am fighting the curtains so much that he is able to steal a kiss, fondling me. He would go further were it not for being interrupted by Madame.

'Gabriel,' she reprimands, 'you should be at Bluche, waiting at the funicular for our guests. I will not have them standing in the rain! Why must I always keep an eye on you?'

Gabriel makes a hasty retreat; he knows his employment is on notice. As my mistress and I tame the wilful curtains, and just before I close the shutters, I see him in the trap, hastening the pony along the track. Although the sound of the spearing rain through the billowing mist is all pervasive I hear, as the pony steps proudly away from the hotel, the lovely tinkling bells on the harness.

'Oh, Berthe,' Madame Gay-Crosier says as she surveys the suite, which the wind and rain has made unruly. 'And this morning, we made it into complete perfection.'

'We have time to repair it,' I answer.

'Yes,' she answers as she checks that a set of small teacups has not been broken. 'We must make the best impression, you know that, don't you.'

La Petite Anglaise and her husband are the hotel's only guests; indeed, we have not had guests for some time. If they like it here, however, they will tell their many English friends when they eventually go back to Grande-Bretagne and perhaps those friends may come and do what the travelling Englishwomen and gentlemen always loved to do before the War: rest and relax in our beautiful Swiss Alps, and take splendid constitutional walks in the alpine heights.

'Le retour des Anglais,' that is Madame Gay-Crosier's dream.

And of course my mistress needs the money.

2.

Permit me to introduce myself more precisely.

I am Berthe Cuenod, and I am in the service of Madame Jeannette Gay-Crosier, and her sister Adeline Michellod. They own this hotel together with my mistress's son-in-law Simeon Robyr. The Robyr family has always taken an active and entrepreneurial interest in providing for the foreign travellers to the region; my pride in being in their employ, a simple village girl, is such that sometimes I feel overwhelmed at my good fortune.

The full name of our hotel is L'Hotel de Montana et d'Angleterre, but people near and far call it L'Hotel d'Angleterre; it was designed as a place of rest and relaxation, of tranquil convalescence, particularly with the English traveller in mind. Originally it was supposed to have been located in the valley below at the lovely town of Sierre. This was in 1910, but instead Monsieur Robyr had the bold idea to build it higher up at an altitude of 1,256 metres where it would have splendid views over the Alpes Valaisannes and the Rhone Valley. 'There,' he explained, 'it will be halfway between Sierre and the upper plateau and, being equidistant, with the funicular connecting, will enable the hotel to take advantage of clients from above as well as below.'

He was always persuasive was Monsieur Robyr, his confidence was disarming even if the idea was tinged with a delirious folly. With typical enthusiasm he acquired, at a price of 20 centimes per square metre, a piece of flat land known as Les Possessions and soon got a local architect and designer on the job.

Oh, there was so much competition among the village girls to work here! I remember that when Madame Gay-Crosier selected me, nobody could believe it, least of all myself! My mistress explained, 'You are not as pretty as the others, Berthe, but pretty girls can be a problem as working staff. As well, you are sturdy and could work outside as well as in, no?'

On 1 July 1914, with great anticipation of success, Madame Gay-Crosier opened the hotel's doors and from the beginning it attracted interest:

Open All Year
Modern Comforts

Pine Forests in Close Proximity
Tennis and Skating
Splendid Views

During the first week I wandered through the 55 bedrooms both downstairs and upstairs, bouncing on each bed for joy!

The hotel, of course, would not have worked if there had not been a funicular, stopping at Bluche. But even with the funicular, the proposal was doomed from the beginning.

3.

There, the suite is now tidy again.

I have refilled the washing bowl but how odd it looks, without an accompanying mirror so that you can look at yourself after your ablutions.

'There is to be no mirror at all,' La Petite Anglaise's husband had instructed.

His command was not to do with vanity. Apparently the small Englishwoman is not well and does not wish to look at herself. But I wonder why the instructions included no chairs or settees?

Madame Gay-Crosier sighs, 'What would I do without you, Berthe?'

My mistress is a stern looking woman with a severe parting in her hair. She is wearing a high-necked black dress which is now somewhat damp from the rain. Together we have gathered the flowers up from the floor and returned them to their vases, and I have mopped the floor dry. The only after-effect of the open windows and shutters is that the curtains are spotted with rain and there is a certain odour of dampness coming from them.

'You will let me know if Gabriel's attentions become too . . . insistent?' Madame asks.

'I can handle Gabriel,' I reply.

My mistress smiles hopefully to herself, 'I am sure you can.' She becomes aware that her dress has a crumpled look from our exertions and goes to change it, but I myself do not require repair. A quick look at my reflection in the window reassures me. 'There you are Berthe!' I laugh. I am in such high spirits because of my mistress's affection that I don't mind looking upon my plainness. Alas, the only attentions I ever attract are from men like Gabriel.

At that moment the windows shift a little, preventing me from indulging in self-pity, the changing light causing an alteration in the perspective. I catch my breath, close my eyes, trying to calm my heart.

Oh, but there was one young man I loved!

I open my eyes and smile sadly into the darkness reflected behind me. 'Vous êtes de nouveau là?' I ask. 'Are you there again?'

It is the Russian boy, Dimitrijj. As he emerges out of the gloom I see that he bears a bouquet.

The flowers have long browned and wilted.

It hurts to remember the circumstances under which I met him.

Indeed, the ultimate sadness of my love for Dimitrijj is almost too difficult to bear but let me try to explain.

Nobody expected the Great War to happen.

Three days before the opening of the hotel, the Archduke Ferdinand was assassinated, leading to the international crisis that became known as the Great War. News travelled slowly, however, and so Madame Gay-Crosier lived in blissful ignorance, preparing for guests who would never come. Meanwhile, I skipped from room to room, dusting and smoothing and, whenever I had spare moments, I loved to look out from the top floor at the ornamental garden, sloping gently into woodland. At the back was a big natural lawn, where black cows grazed in companionship with sheep in a happy pastoral idyll. Beyond was the vegetable garden, the stable and outbuildings where hay was stored.

Of course the bottom fell out of Monsieur Robyr's expectations. When it became clear that we were waiting in vain for English travellers, he had an urgent conversation with Madame Gay-Crosier. 'What are we to do?' he asked.

'What else can we do, cher Simeon,' she sighed. 'We must keep the hotel running. We have investors to pay.'

Fortunately there were other hotels which were also suffering, so the banks were generous and offered a moratorium on debts. And permit me to venture a personal opinion but our dilemma was as nothing to the lives of the soldiers fighting in France.

'I will have to let you go,' Madame Gay-Crosier said to me.

The Hotel d'Angleterre has become my home,' I answered.

'I cannot pay you, you foolish girl!'

Tears were brimming her eyes – and mine.

I set my lips with determination. 'I am staying.'

For two years Madame Gay-Crosier held on by a flimsy thread, while the apocalyptic conflagration played out in France. Switzerland maintained our political neutrality but every Sunday, at Mass, I would pray for the poor soldiers.

Then in 1916, Monsieur Robyr came running from the funicular with the news. 'The Swiss Federation has agreed with the Holy Roman See to an initiative in the name of humanity,' he cried. 'Soldiers ill or wounded in the war, no matter their country of origin, will be able to seek in Switzerland the physical and moral comfort to rebuild their wellbeing.'

'But what does that mean to the Hotel d'Angleterre?' my mistress asked worriedly.

We soon found out. The tourist industry was struck, as if by a whip and the slender thread became frayed by anxiety, because where were the soldiers to be interned? Why, what better place than in establishments like ours? Accordingly, hotels in the region bordering Austro-Hungary were assigned to welcome the German convalescents. Meanwhile French, Belgian and English soldiers were interned in Eastern Switzerland including Montana.

Here, our hotel became one of a number composing a Sanitorium of the Allies.

4.

'Berthe! Berthe, where are you?'

Madame Gay-Crosier comes hastening into the suite, disturbing my thoughts.

'The rooms are a bit chilly,' she says. 'Perhaps we should prepare the fireplace for La Petite Anglaise?'

I notice that she has not pinned her hair properly. I make her stop and re-pin it for her; although she is my mistress and I am a simple village girl we are almost like mother and daughter, thus permitting small acts like adjusting her coiffure. 'What is she like . . . the small Englishwoman?'

'Well,' Madame Gay-Crosier begins, 'I have seen photographs of her. When she was a young woman she was, how they say, somewhat modern. She is not really English at all but comes from Nouvelle Zélande, choosing to follow her career in literature by going to Grande-Bretagne. Writing must be in the family as she is cousin to Elizabeth von Arnim.'

'Our Madame Arnim?' I ask. 'Why, she is a famous English novelist who lives in Randogne, not far from here.'

'Yes,' my mistress answers, 'and she is far better known than La Petite Anglaise. However, the small Englishwoman has the higher reputation, particularly in certain English literary circles, and people there talk of her in the same way they do of Chekhov's fiction, as maintaining the short story at the highest level of excellence. Sadly, her vivacious sensibility has been tempered by illness. She is infected by tuberculosis.'

I begin to shiver, my fingers trembling in my mistress's hair.

'This is why she came to Montana last year,' my mistress continues, 'and I have had it reported to me that here she wrote some of her finest work. Perhaps it is a matter of less oil in the lamp makes the flame burn brighter?'

Madame Gay-Crosier gives an apologetic laugh.

'But I am waxing poetic! La Petite Anglaise has been travelling for some time in search of impossible restful places to be, for forgetfulness of her worries, for a compatible climate and for treatment which apparently she is beginning to believe in less and less. She comes again to Montana, directly by train from Paris where she has been having treatment.'

My mistress leaves. I go down to the cellar to fetch some small twigs to start a fire with and some dry logs. Back in the suite, I prepare the fireplace. I put a taper to the fire and it is soon burning merrily and filling the room with a rosy glow.

I remember again those days before my Russian boy came to me as if they were a prelude.

With great warmth our valley welcomed the first convalescents. They arrived at Sierre in February 1916 after receiving a warm welcome all along the Rhone Valley; the Mayor gave a rousing speech. People of the valley lined the ascent of the funicular to cheer the soldiers as they rose to Les Possessions and alighted here. The old men were so grand in their black suits, handkerchiefs in breast pockets; they saluted the interns. Women and children threw flowers.

Our hotel became La Clinique Militaire. By August, over 500 patients were stationed here and also at the Sanitorium Victoria and Mirabeau, Bella Vista, Rawyl, Pas de l'Ours and L'Hotel du Golf et du Sports. Of course the premises had to be satisfactorily renovated. Monsieur Robyr supervised the ground floor conversion into a large vestibule with parquet floors.

Nobody could deny the nobility of the Swiss-Vatican initiative but, 'Oh, our beautiful hotel,' my mistress exclaimed, wringing her hands in despair.

The dining room, la salle à manger, seated ten men at each table. In the medical wing, seven doctors prescribed treatment such as solar therapy, electro therapy and quartz lamp treatments and X-rays. Some of the rooms were converted into a salon for the men to relax in. To aid recuperation there were different kinds of workshops: basket weaving, vegetable growing, language training, lessons in accountancy, law, history, mathematics. There was also the gym, the men stripped to the waist, lifting weights and performing calisthenics. Recalcitrant patients required to be kept under lock and key in holding rooms in the cellar.

Madame Gay-Crosier had to submit to Captain Dr Theodore Stephani, who had overall responsibility for the patients but, 'Sir,' she advised him firmly, 'although the men are in your hands, management is my sole responsibility.' Oh, the battles of wits they had!

As for me, I was running everywhere, 'Berthe do this! Berthe do that!' I must admit, the proximity of so many young men made me flirtatious. Some of them even found me attractive! 'Come sit on my knee,' they would invite but, as all women know, that is the beginning of our undoing, isn't it!

'At least we are paid 4 to 6 francs a day,' Madame Gay-Crosier sighed to Monsieur Robyr, 'plus 50 centimes for service expenses. It is not enough . . .' she gave a small moue '. . . but it is better than nothing.'

And Dimitrijj?

The Great War may have ended in 1918, but the Russians went on fighting until last year, 1921. It was they who appealed most to our Swiss imagination.

I remember first catching a glimpse of Dimitrijj at Mass, where his fellow soldiers punctuated the ceremony with numerous signs of the cross. My admiration and adoration of him was spontaneous and immediate. Who would not have fallen in love with a boy, winsome, who looked as if he was only playing at being a soldier? Of course there were other girls of the village, prettier than I was, who made their intentions clear to him. Thus did I agree to myself to worship him from afar.

The reason why he was invalided to La Clinique Militaire?

During the War Dimitrijj had been in the trenches when they had been smothered by the lethal gas pumped across the Front by the Germans. Nobly offering his gas mask to an injured friend, his lungs had been invaded. The consequence was the immediate deterioration of his lungs and ongoing collapse of their oxygen bearing capacity beyond renewal and repair.

Indeed, tuberculosis was the most widespread of all respiratory ailments, so the Allies therefore added to their humanitarian efforts three wards in the forest which dominated the small mountain lake Grenon and Ycoor. There were discussions between Monsieur Robyr and the officials in Berne to provide care for the tubercular at the Hotel d'Angleterre too.

However, there was some hostility from the villagers to the idea.

One day, after Mass, Dimitrijj created great animation when, cajoled by the villagers he agreed to play his balalaika and sing for us. Oh, he should not have done so, given his condition, but he was courteous and wishing only to please:

'However, for this song,' he said in his hesitant French, 'I need a pretty girl to sing to.'

He pulled me out from the crowd. 'Please, choose one of the others,' I pleaded.

He wouldn't hear of it. Despite my protestations, he began to sing to me:

Ochi chornyye, ochi strastnyye
Dark and burning eyes
Dark as midnight skies . . .

I may have resisted the amorous advances of other soldiers but I could not resist Dimitrijj. From the moment he sang, I loved him all the more, only him.

'Don't lose your head,' Madame Gay-Crosier warned.

4.

Dimitrijj . . .

I have a small portrait of him. He had a small face, glowing eyes and hair curling down to his shoulders. Can you see his vivacious sensibility? He was among the younger Russian men at La Clinique Militaire and greatly loved by them.

All the Russian interns had been loyal to the Czar. They feared going back to their country, now that the Czar and the Royal family had been assassinated, and the Bolsheviks had come to power.

Gabriel was jealous of Dimitrijj but, poof, he meant nothing to me.

Oh, I must have known from the beginning that Dimitrijj was not long for the earth but that did not stop me from falling for him with a passion that belied my virgin heart. Indeed, while our love was never consummated, that did not prevent me from thinking the most intimate thoughts about him.

I loved to take him by wheelchair into the sunlight overlooking the valley below. After all, Nature was the one which had given Montana its fame, and to be with Dimitrijj in the rich pastures, among thousands of wildflowers – or sitting with him within the forest, in the shade of cool leaves – or looking up at the immaculate summits sparkling in the sun, the villages of the Haute-Plateau beneath – made me feel an ecstasy like unto none I had ever experienced.

I must make a confession.

Although I may have led you to believe I was unaware of La Petite Anglaise, I must put away my pretence. It was Dimitrijj himself who first told me of her and, indeed, my own curiosity about her is whetted because of his own interest in her. For instance, when he discovered that she was in Montana – last year, when she was staying at the Chalet des Sapins – his excitement knew no bounds.

I never saw him so animated. 'I must go to her,' he pleaded, his eyes wide with feverish excitement. 'I have read her work in Russian translation. Our hearts beat as one!'

He couldn't stop talking about her art, her intensity, the beauty of her observation . . . and its pitiless truth. But he was much too ill to make any visit to meet her – the military doctors forbade it – no matter how short it was.

Dimitrijj pleaded with me to get a letter from him to her. 'Perhaps she will come to visit me instead,' he said.

I sent the letter to my cousin, Ernestine Rey, who was working at the Chalet.

'Has La Petite Anglaise replied yet?' Dimitrijj would ask. 'Has she? I would move heaven and earth to meet her. To listen to her voice would ravish all my senses.'

La Petite Anglaise never did reply. Perhaps she was too ill herself or had already left the Chalet.

And then my sweet Dimitrijj had to face his own impending crisis.

Oh, I suppose I was in denial about it, no matter that he was coughing his life away. Even when he died, I held his hand long after all warmth had seeped from his body.

'Dimitrijj! Dimitrijj!' I mourned.

A priest came from Martigny to officiate at his burial. I could hardly bear the sight of the earth closing upon him.

They are long gone, the soldiers.

When the last of the Russian soldiers left us, some of them wanted to take Dimitrijj back to their home country with them. I am glad they didn't.

Soon afterward, Monsieur Robyr and Madame Gay-Crosier converted the Clinique Militaire into a hotel again. 'We return at last to our great dream,' my mistress exclaimed.

She found me one days putting wildflowers on Dimitrijj's grave.

'Dry your tears ma petite,' she reproved, 'I never thought you would have such a melodramatic strain in you. Your devotion to the dead boy

142

is unseemly, even the advances of Gabriel are to be preferred, surely, the dead to the dead the living to the living. There will be other young men.'

How wrong she has been! Not long after she spoke to me I saw a shimmer of dust, like gold raining through the sunlight. 'Est-ce que c'est toi?' I asked, scarcely daring to breathe.

Since then Dimitrijj has always attended me.

And now, seven months later, has come to the Hotel d'Angleterre the woman he had wanted to meet:

La Petite Anglaise.

5.

From afar off, I hear the blast of the horn which Gabriel always sounds to alert us that he is coming.

'They are approaching!' Madame Gay-Crosier says, smoothing her hair and dress.

We go to the front door, open it and peer through the driving rain.

'La Petite Anglaise will be soaked to the skin,' my mistress says.

At her bidding, I go down the steps in the driving rain with a large umbrella. The pony stops with a loud whinny; the bells on his reins are tinkling, silver chimes to delight the ear but . . .

The rain, the driving rain. The darkness, gathering in the sky. The mist, enveloping the trees.

'Ma femme,' her husband instructs me with a brusque tone. 'Take my wife into the hotel first. Quick! She is much fatigued.'

A flock of crows feather the air.

I obtain an impression of solidity in La Petite Anglaise's husband and a face shadowed with ferocity. She, however, has her head averted and all I have time to notice is the raindrops as they stain her thin, white neck and the dark hair bundled beneath her hat.

'Madame,' I say to her. I help her from the cart by offering her my hand to balance her. She is wearing gloves. Her grip is strong, despite the sense I obtain of the frail shell beneath.

'Thank you,' she answers, her voice low and tired.

While I am assisting her, I hear Madame Gay-Crosier ask Gabriel, 'Were you at Bluche when the funicular arrived?' Her voice is harsh, ready to reprimand him if he had not been on time.

'Yes, mistress,' he replies hastily. 'I saw the funicular rattling up through the rain from the misty valley below. I think our guests were relieved to dismount, the ascent being so frighteningly steep. The husband was gasping like a fish in an attempt to equalise the pressure in his ears.'

'He is in such a mood!' my mistress responds.

'A reason might be because when he and his wife left the train at

Sierre,' Gabriel whispers, as he hastens up the steps with the luggage, 'he mistakenly gave the porter 500 francs rather than fifty. But the rain . . . there was no time for further conversation. I seated them in the back, under the shelter of the cart, loaded their luggage and we set off, with the pony stepping sure and swift along the track. The conditions were terrible! The track from Bluche was like a muddy river with the cart sometimes up to its axles in the mud.'

'Are we the only guests in the hotel?' the husband of La Petite Anglaise asks as he signs the register. 'Why is everything so cold and bare? I was expecting something a little more . . . luxurious.'

'Perhaps Monsieur will feel more kindly disposed once he has seen the suite,' my mistress tells him, to placate him.

She signs to me to go ahead, to make sure the fire is at its highest and that the rooms are warm.

Quickly I hasten up the stairs.

And so I wait at the threshold of the suite to welcome La Petite Anglaise and her husband.

I am curious to catch my first close glimpse of her. A sudden shimmer of gold in the darkness, and I see that Dimitrijj has joined me again.

'You are curious too?' I ask him.

There comes the sound of three people ascending the stairs. Madame Gay-Crosier lingers back while the husband strides into the room. He is a hulking presence as he assists La Petite Anglaise through the door to the suite.

'Merci,' she says to Madame Gay-Crosier.

I never thought I would hear a voice so incisive and so thrilling.

She placates her husband. 'Perhaps it will be necessary to know the Hotel a little while before we have any opinion to offer. And after all, the air, the panorama . . .'

Her face! Luminous, the skin tight across the cheekbones, the dark deepset eyes! I gasp and turn to Dimitrijj. Has he noticed? Although La Petite Anglaise is already walking towards God, she is transfigured.

His expression is merciless. Dimitrijj does not need me to advise what he should and should not see. I am suddenly made desolate because . . . look! He bestows upon the small Englishwoman more intensity, desire and love – yes love – than he ever did upon my own foolish, expectant, heart.

Cruel knowledge! He has indeed moved heaven and earth . . .

I realise with humiliation that I am superfluous to him, perhaps I have always been . . . unimportant.

It is a revelation no woman should be required to admit.

144

The small Englishwoman turns and takes off her hat. Her husband helps her out of her wet coat.

Madame Gay-Crosier motions me forward.

I am reluctant. Why should I acknowledge La Petite Anglaise and curtsey to her?

'Berthe!' my mistress reprimands.

Bitterly I take a step forward to curtsey.

La Petite Anglaise is suddenly overtaken by a terrible fit of coughing and, when she puts a handkerchief to her lips it comes away bejewelled with specks of blood. Alarmed and frightened she looks around and then over my shoulder at the Russian boy.

Does she see him? Surely not. Dimitrijj shows himself only to me. *Me.*

I am very angry as I turn to him. He is acting like a bridegroom. 'I thought you had stayed here because of me,' I say to him. 'But that's not true, is it?'

His eyes glow in the darkness. He heeds me not.

'It was unfair of you to flirt with me and to keep visiting me,' I say to him, 'I know that now. You were toying with me as a cat with a mouse, a claw piercing my throat.'

The bitterness of cloves fills my mouth. All this time, why had I not seen it before, all he has been doing is waiting . . .

Waiting for La Petite Anglaise.

The small Englishwoman, however, is pitiless.

She is la belle dame sans merci, moving past Dimitrijj to the windows, ignoring him as he reaches for her. With a swift, purposeful gesture she opens the heavy curtains. They unfold, as if reluctantly, and the grey light seeps in.

I see her face reflected in the panes of the windows, the rain falling in wreaths through it. I wonder at her cruelty and the reason for it. In her is a triumphant flame, and Dimitrijj's poor heart is immolated in it, let it burn forever, I do not care.

La Petite Anglaise clenches her fists and opens the windows. Immediately I hear the wind whiplashing around the hotel. A sudden gust sweeps her dress around her like dark wings. Flowers fly into the air as if thrown by an unseen throng.

She cries out:

'To live! To breathe! To write!'

She turns to us all, her body doubled with pain, the words hissing out, insistent, demanding, as if we had the power to grant her command:

'Life! Life! I must have life!'

145

In the shocking silence which follows comes the faint sound of tiny harness bells as, below, Gabriel leads the pony towards the stable.

Then all there is, is the roaring silence of the mountains.

*   *   *

Thanks to Simone Oettli and her husband Max and family for hospitality and friendship. Simone invited me to attend a Symposium at Crans Montana to commemorate Katherine Mansfield's two sojourns in Switzerland in 1921 and 1922. Mansfield was staying at the Hotel Château de Belle Vue in Sierre when she saw the Chalet des Sapins in Montana advertised, which she would go on to rent in 1921 and early 1922; later in 1922 she stayed at the Hotel d'Angleterre.

I greatly appreciated the friendship of other attendees, particularly Gerri Kimber, Chair of the Katherine Mansfield Society, who invited me to write a story about Katherine Mansfield which, originally I had expected to set in the Chalet des Sapins. There, Mansfield had the sympathetic devotion of a servant companion Ernestine Rey; I was invited by Gerri and Simone to join them in a visit organised by Jennifer Walker to Ernestine's niece, Mme Rose Simon-Rey in her home, a memory I will always treasure. Perhaps I will re-visit my earlier proposal, which was more ambitious than time allowed – a counterpointing of a visit to Mme Simon-Rey in 2012 with the story of the affection between her aunt Ernestine Rey and Mansfield in 1921 – at some later time.

Fortunately, a visit to the abandoned Hotel d'Angleterre soon had my imagination running in the different, easier, direction traversed by Waiting for La Petite Anglaise. I wish I had known that Gerri, Janet Wilson, Angela Smith and others had risked arterial bleeding by climbing through the broken glass door of the hotel to explore inside; I would have joined them.

I must point out artistic licence on my part: according to a letter written by Mansfield to Ida Baker on 4 June 1922, there were no servants at the hotel, and Madame Jeannette Gay-Crosier and her sister Adeline Michellod did everything themselves. Personally, I could not imagine that such a large building would not have some other help, which is why I have interpolated the fictional character Berthe, in unpaid service to Madame Gay-Crosier, and the valet, Gabriel.

Some of the information contained in this story was obtained from L'Encoche: revue d'information de la commune de Montana, *December 2000 – No.4. Credit to Hugues Rey – 3963 Montana.*

Katherine Mansfield left the Hotel d'Angleterre because she had difficulty breathing at that high altitude. She stayed for another six weeks in the Hotel Château de Belle Vue in Sierre and then left for London and Paris in a final attempt at obtaining a cure for her tuberculosis. She entered the Gurdjieff Institute where she died soon after.

REPORTS

Figure 2. 'Ricordi' postcard. Alexander Turnbull Library, Manuscript Collection, MS-Papers-11326-002. Reproduced by permission of Pollinger Limited and the Estate of Frieda Lawrence Ravagli.

The Lawrences, Katherine Mansfield and the 'Ricordi' Postcard

Andrew Harrison

Scholars have known for some time about the postcard which D. H. Lawrence sent to Katherine Mansfield from her birthplace, Wellington, on Tuesday 15 August 1922, during his first (one-day) stop en route from Sydney to San Francisco with his wife Frieda on board *R. M. S. Tahiti*.[1] Mansfield mentions receiving it in a letter to John Middleton Murry written five weeks later and first published in 1951: 'I had a card from Lawrence today – just the one word 'Ricordi'. How like him. I was glad to get it though.'[2] In the absence of the postcard itself, these few comments led people to assume that it contained no more than that single Italian word, meaning 'Memories' or 'Remembrances'.[3] The poignancy of Lawrence's gesture in sending the card has naturally attracted attention from biographers, several of whom have noted the uncanny coincidence of Lawrence writing it on 15 August and Mansfield bequeathing Lawrence one of her books in her will the day before, on the other side of the world.[4]

Fortunately, the postcard has now come to light in the cache of papers belonging to the Murry family recently acquired by the Alexander Turnbull Library.[5] It is reproduced here for the first time. The new details it reveals shed a fascinating light on specific aspects of the complex and troubled friendship between Lawrence and Mansfield. We can now see for ourselves that Frieda Lawrence added her own greeting beneath her husband's (a fact that Mansfield did not report in her letter to Murry); we can also recognise the significance of the Lawrences' choice of image for the card, which underscores the warmth of the feeling conveyed.

149

The postcard reads:

> Mrs Katharine Murry,
> c/o The Lady Ottoline Morrell
> Garsington Manor
> Nr. <u>Oxford</u>
> <u>England</u>

Ricordi   DHL
We thought so hard of you here!   FL

The handwriting in the first line of the address suggests that the Lawrences may have deliberated over whether to send the card to 'Katharine Murry' or 'Katharine Mansfield'.[6] They must have chosen to send it care of Lady Ottoline Morrell because they were unsure of Mansfield's whereabouts that summer.[7] Reading the greetings *in situ* we can see how the two messages subtly interact and modify each other's meaning in the manner of a shared gesture. Lawrence's 'Ricordi' evidently refers *not* primarily to Mansfield's memories of her birthplace, but to their memories of each other. Such mutuality is wholly fitting, since Lawrence's friendship with Mansfield had originally developed not in isolation but through the affection between the two couples (Lawrence and Frieda, Murry and Mansfield).

The Lawrences clearly enjoyed discovering together suitable picture postcards to send home to family and close friends during their day in Wellington:[8] different images from the same card series were sent to Mansfield, to Frieda's elder sister Else Jaffe, to Lawrence's younger sister Ada, and to Catherine Carswell. While photographs of Māori guides in front of the carved wooden archways of a Māori fortress in Whakarewarewa were chosen for Else and Catherine, and a landscape image of Mitre Peake, Milford Sound, for Ada, Mansfield was sent a more personalised card.[9] The choice of an intimate moment in the life of a Māori family combines a suitable invocation of a native homeland with an affectionate focus on the '"Hongi" or Maori Greeting' (the traditional pressing together of nose and forehead).

Their arrival in Mansfield's birthplace caused Lawrence and Frieda to think 'so hard' of her, and of their early friendship, but it would also inevitably have reminded them of their conflicts and differences, and especially of Lawrence's bitter quarrel with Mansfield and Murry two and a half years before, in late January and early February 1920. The severity of this quarrel forms one of the unspoken contexts to the sending of the postcard, since the Lawrences had lost contact with Mansfield and Murry in the intervening period.

The other unspoken context is the precarious state of Mansfield's health. Back in January 1920, Lawrence knew that the worsening symptoms of her consumption had caused Mansfield to move from Ospedaletti (near San Remo, on the Italian Riviera) to a private nursing home in Menton, south-eastern France.[10] At that time, outraged by what he believed to be their callous conspiracy in rejecting articles he had submitted to the *Athenaeum* in early December, Lawrence had sent separate, angry letters to Murry and Mansfield, calling Murry 'a dirty little worm' and telling Mansfield: 'I loathe you. You revolt me stewing in your consumption.'[11] Mark Kinkead-Weekes has argued that Lawrence's rage was exacerbated by an Italian postal strike, which meant that the rejection letter which Murry sent on from Ospedaletti (at the end of a visit to Mansfield) arrived with Lawrence in Capri at the same time as a personal letter from Mansfield, containing details of her condition along with her new Menton address.[12] The idea of Mansfield scheming to reject his work at the same time that she sought to arouse his sympathy for her situation proved too much for Lawrence; it helps us to account for the virulence of his outburst, though it hardly excuses his cruel jibes about her illness. In August 1922, with the passage of time, the anger had been defused; the Lawrences would have understood that she might not have long to live. The restrained manner of Lawrence's greeting from Wellington seems to tacitly acknowledge the significance of their earlier quarrel; the single Italian word tellingly harks back to the time immediately before, when they were both living in Italy and on good terms with one another. It is left to Frieda to express their feelings in a more effusive fashion.

We can interpret the writing of the postcard either as a memorial to their former friendship, as an understated attempt at reconciliation on Lawrence's part, or as a rather offhand expression of contrition. Mansfield, in any case, was grateful to receive it. She saw the terseness of Lawrence's greeting as characteristic; her positive reaction arguably reveals her enduring fondness for him, and her appreciation for what he tactfully leaves unsaid. Her failure to mention Frieda's note in the letter to Murry reflects the fact that it was Lawrence alone who had engineered the break with them all those months ago; it was Lawrence's decision to write to her again that would interest Murry, who had, in any case, a rather low opinion of Frieda at this juncture.

The postcard had a salutary effect in bringing about a partial reconciliation, at a distance, between the two couples. Murry and Lawrence exchanged letters in December 1922, by which time Lawrence had settled in New Mexico. When Murry sent word (via their mutual friend S. S. Koteliansky) of Mansfield's death the following month,[13] Lawrence responded by writing him a sensitive and sympathetic letter:

Yes, it is something gone out of our lives. We thought of her, I can tell you, at Wellington. Did Ottoline ever send on the card to Katharine I posted from there for her? Yes, I always knew a bond in my heart. Feel a fear where the bond is broken now. Feel as if old moorings were breaking all.[14]

This offers conclusive proof that Frieda's scribbled note on the post-card, hidden from us until now, was written with Lawrence's blessing and carried the full force of his own feelings for Katherine Mansfield.

Notes

1. The Lawrences left Sydney on 11 August 1922. They stopped at Wellington (15 August), Rarotonga (20 August) and Tahiti (22–3 August), arriving in San Francisco on 4 September.

2. *Katherine Mansfield's Letters to John Middleton Murry, 1913–1922*, ed. John Middleton Murry (London: Constable, 1951), p. 663. The letter is reproduced in Vincent O'Sullivan and Margaret Scott, eds, *The Collected Letters of Katherine Mansfield*, 5 vols (Oxford: Clarendon Press, 1984–2008), Vol. 5, p. 268. Murry dates the letter Wednesday 20 September 1922, while O'Sullivan and Scott suggest 19 September 1922.

3. See, for example, *The Letters of D. H. Lawrence*, Vol. IV, ed. Warren Roberts, James T. Boulton and Elizabeth Mansfield (Cambridge: Cambridge University Press, 1987), p. 283, fn. 1.

4. See Harry T. Moore, *The Intelligent Heart: The Story of D. H. Lawrence* (London: William Heinemann, 1955), p. 295; Antony Alpers, *The Life of Katherine Mansfield* (London: Jonathan Cape, 1980), p. 366; Mark Kinkead-Weekes, *D. H. Lawrence: Triumph to Exile, 1912–1922* (Cambridge: Cambridge University Press, 1996), pp. 563–4; and John Worthen, *D. H. Lawrence: The Life of an Outsider* (London: Allen Lane, 2005), pp. 465–6, fn. 38.

5. Alexander Turnbull Library MS-Papers-11326-002.

6. Lawrence tends to use 'Katharine Murry' in the extant correspondence. However, the copy of *Amores* which he gave to her as a personal gift is inscribed 'To Katharine Mansfield from D. H. Lawrence' (See the *Christie's Catalogue* for the Twentieth-Century Books and Manuscripts auction of Friday 16 November 2001, p. 14). The postcard was sent as a personal greeting to Katherine.

7. Mansfield received the postcard at 6 Pond Street, Hampstead NW3. She had moved back to England from Sierre, Switzerland, in mid-August 1922.

8. For a discussion of Lawrence's interest in picture postcards, see Oliver Taylor, '"The Day of my Letters is Over": D. H. Lawrence's Picture Postcards from the Americas', *Journal of D. H. Lawrence Studies*, Vol. 2, No. 3 (2011), pp. 131–59.

9. The photographs were taken by Liverpool-born New Zealander Frederick George Radcliffe (1863–1923). The card to Else Jaffe was 3648 FGR; to Catherine Carswell 4636 FGR; and to Ada Clarke 192 FGR. Mansfield was sent 422 FGR. The 'Real Photo Post Card' series was produced by Frank Duncan & Co., Auckland.

10. Mansfield moved to L'Hermitage, the private nursing home in Menton, on 21 January 1920.

11. See *The Letters of D. H. Lawrence*, Vol. III, ed. James T. Boulton and Andrew Robertson (Cambridge: Cambridge University Press, 1984), pp. 467–8 and p. 470.

12. See Mark Kinkead-Weekes, *D. H. Lawrence: Triumph to Exile, 1912–1922*, pp. 559–64,

and his essay 'Rage against the Murrys: "Inexplicable" or "Psychopathic"?', in *D. H. Lawrence in Italy and England*, ed. George Donaldson and Mara Kalnins (Basingstoke: Macmillan, 1999), pp. 116–34.

13. Mansfield died on 9 January 1923.

14. *The Letters of D. H. Lawrence*, Vol. IV, p. 375.

'A Little Episode': The Forgotten Typescripts of Katherine Mansfield, 1908–11

Chris Mourant

In the summer of 1908, not yet twenty years old but determined to become a successful writer, Katherine Mansfield left New Zealand and sailed for England. It was the second time she had made such a journey. The daughter of Harold Beauchamp, the wealthy Wellington banker, Mansfield was sent to Queen's College School in London between 1903 and 1906 to complete her education. In this time she learnt French and German, bought fashionable clothes and styled her hair, devoted herself to playing the cello, wrote stories for the school magazine, and developed an obsession for the works of Oscar Wilde. Compared to the provincial tedium of life in New Zealand, London represented a space of self-development for Mansfield and was indelibly connected in her mind with the fiercely protected independence she considered necessary for becoming a writer. Despite her early optimism, however, the immediate years following Mansfield's return to London in 1908 proved to be one of the most painful periods in her life.

As a teenager, Mansfield had fallen in love with a young cellist named Arnold Trowell. Arnold's virtuosity overshadowed the talent of his twin brother Garnet, a less attractive and more retiring violinist. The twins left New Zealand together in 1903 to study in Germany and at the Brussels Conservatoire before moving to London to join their family, who had since relocated there. Mansfield regularly wrote to her 'Caesar' – the nickname she gave to Arnold – and nurtured fantasies of their future life together. Returning to London in 1908, Mansfield promptly reconnected with the Trowell family, and just as quickly transferred her feelings for Arnold to Garnet; it seems that she was less in love with either boy than with the entire family, who represented an alternative to the commercial values and middle-class priorities of the Beauchamp family. In December 1908, Mansfield moved into the Trowell family home in St. John's Wood. It was at this time that she became pregnant by Garnet. While Garnet was away with a touring opera company, his parents discovered the true nature of his relationship with Mansfield and forced her to leave the family home. In March 1909, seeking legitimacy for her unborn child, Mansfield married a singing teaching in his early thirties, George Bowden. She wore a black suit and hat to the ceremony and not only refused to consummate the marriage but left Bowden that same night. Hearing of her recent behaviour, Mansfield's mother made the journey from New Zealand and took her daughter to Germany, abandoning her soon afterwards. It was here that Mansfield suffered a miscarriage.

Mansfield's experience at the Pension Müller in June 1909 was channelled into the dark, satirical stories which comprised her first book, *In a German Pension* (1911). Yet, biographical material from this time is scant: Mansfield burnt all her notebooks and ordered her schoolfriend Ida Baker – who would become Katherine's lifelong companion and devoted servant throughout her later illness – to destroy all her letters. Without the letters lovingly kept by Garnet from the autumn and winter of 1908 and the later testimonies of Baker and Bowden, we would have little record of Mansfield's life during this formative time.

It was whilst working in the King's College London Archives that I came across a file of typescripts within one of five boxes simply marked 'Mansfield'. These boxes are part of the archive of *ADAM International Review*, a literary magazine edited by Miron Grindea until 1995. The archive has been consulted very rarely and the significance of these documents has remained obscure until now. Two of the typescripts are particularly noteworthy: the short story 'A Little Episode' (1909) and a collection of fifty aphorisms entitled 'Bites from the Apple' (1911). Neither work has been published. The University of Texas research library holds fragments of 'A Little Episode' and a three-page typescript of 'Bites from the Apple' but the discovery of these two works in the KCL archives gives us access to the full texts for the first time. In particular, 'A Little Episode' is important for Mansfield scholarship because it sheds new light on Mansfield's own feelings regarding the events of 1908–9. Of course, literary critics should always be careful about reading too much biographical detail into works of fiction. Yet, characters and plot lines in Mansfield's work were very often drawn from real people and events. Mansfield's sister Jeanne Renshaw once described 'At the Bay', for example, as 'the most perfectly planned story' and 'vivid' representation of their own family outings to the beach, saying: 'that really is biography'.[1]

'A Little Episode' opens with a description of a young woman, Yvonne, who moves slowly up a 'long, brilliantly lighted Concert Hall',[2] bowing slightly to acquaintances as she goes. The reader learns about Yvonne through the dialogue of two society ladies, their voices 'full of withering contempt': her father 'went to Paris and took to Art' before marrying 'some little obscure weed' who died in childbirth; she was raised 'helter-skelter in a dreadful way' before her father died when she was seventeen; left without a penny, she was then 'rescued' by her aunt and uncle, 'nice, quiet, thoughtful Church of England people in Bellevue Avenue'; finally, her 'reformation' complete, she married Geoffrey, Lord Mandeville, 'a very good, practical fellow' (539). The public dialogue of these women, the cynical arbiters of English morality, is juxtaposed with the internal thoughts and impulsive movements of Yvonne, who sits in her seat anxiously waiting for the concert to begin. When the music starts it triggers 'a motley, mad, fascinating troupe' (540) of recollections in her mind of Paris days: the pianist, Jacques Saint Pierre, is Yvonne's former lover. Going to see Jacques in the Artists' Room after the performance, Yvonne tells him how she has been 'caged' first by poverty and then by marriage: 'I was friendless – homeless – helpless' (541).

Like the protagonist in Mansfield's unfinished novel *Juliet*, Yvonne in 'A Little Episode' is clearly a self-portrait of Mansfield, with Jacques Saint Pierre representing Garnet Trowell and Geoffrey Mandeville standing in for George Bowden. When she left for England in 1908, Mansfield was given an allowance of £100 a year but she was notoriously bad at managing money: having grown up in a wealthy family, she was accustomed to regularly buying flowers, clothes, books and presents. Her limited means, coupled with the luxuriousness of her tastes, meant that Mansfield quickly found herself fighting against impending poverty. Indeed, Mansfield's argument with Garnet's parents seems to have been instigated by Mrs Trowell asking Mansfield to pay for her own washing; Mansfield refused, most likely because she couldn't pay. Yvonne's poverty therefore has clear parallels with Mansfield's own situation. When Yvonne is 'rescued' from her poverty by her aunt and uncle, she is brought 'to Mexchester'. This detail in the original typescript is echoed at the end of the story, when we see Jacques Saint Pierre 'in his rooms at the Hotel Mexchester' (544). Believing this to be a typing error, the editors of *The Edinburgh Edition of the Collected Works of Katherine Mansfield: Volume One* have changed 'Mexchester' to 'Manchester', a detail which is supported by Mansfield's biography. When Mrs Beauchamp arrived in 1909, she took Mansfield to the hotel in Manchester Street, London. With these two references to her own life, Mansfield connects her mother with the relatives of Yvonne, and Yvonne's words become her own: 'They crushed all my ideals – all my hopes' (541).

Leaving the concert, Yvonne and Jacques walk to a little gardener's cottage where she keeps 'all her Paris treasures' (542) hidden from her husband; here, they reignite their love affair. The dichotomy that has been established in the story between art and society, between the life of impulse and the sterility of convention, is reiterated at the critical moment:

> Primitive woman she felt – with primitive impulses – primitive needs – all conventions – all scruples were thrown to the four winds. (543)

Yet, this is a moment also overshadowed by death, with Yvonne moaning 'O, you are killing me' (543). Indeed, pain is a recurring theme throughout the story: the 'thunderous, deafening burst of applause' following the first piece of music at the concert is a 'sharp, hard sound' like many 'brutal blows' that 'hurt her physically' (540); and when Jacques holds Yvonne's hand, 'it was as though she held her life in her hand – and he crushed it' (542). In the story, love has the potential to inflict not only emotional but real, bodily pain. Furthermore, Yvonne moves 'convulsively' and is repeatedly 'placed' by Jacques or lies 'passive in his arms' (542–3). The recurrence of pain coupled with Yvonne's inability to command the body and lack of physical volition, I suggest, reflect Mansfield's own feelings about being unable to control her body and reveal her anxieties surrounding her pregnancy. We know that 'A Little Episode' was written in 1909, but the references to the hotel in Manchester Street might provide a clue as to when exactly the story was composed: the late spring of 1909 was a time in Mansfield's life in which she was desperately trying to conceal her advanced pregnancy from her mother.

'A Little Episode' ends with two scenes which happen 'about the same time'. In the first, we see Yvonne entering the hall of her home, 'dishevelled – flushed'. Slowly mounting the stairs to the bedroom, she deflects the questions of husband. Then, looking at herself in the mirror, she cries 'O, I have lived – I lived' (543) and talks excitedly about seeing her lover the next day. In the second scene, Jacques is sitting in his hotel room writing a letter:

> 'To-night – think of it – I saw Yvonne – she is quite a little Society lady – and I assure you – no longer one of us – But she bores me – she has the inevitable feminine passion for trying to relight fires that have long since been ashes – Take care, little one, that you do not – like wise. I hear her husband is very wealthy – and – what they call here – a "howling bore."
>
> Adieu – cherie – I shall be with you in two days – if I manage to avoid the charming Yvonne – There is the penalty, you see, for being so fascinating.
>
> Jacques Saint Pierre.' (544)

Figure 3. Katherine Mansfield and John Middleton Murry at the Villa Isola Bella, Menton. Private collection.

Figure 4. Katherine Mansfield in the garden at the Villa Isola Bella. Image courtesy of King's College London Archives, *Adam International Review* Collection.

This shattering ending emphasises Mansfield's perception of the discontinuity between the male and female experience of love. When Yvonne looks at 'the wide, empty bed' and hears the sound of bolts being drawn downstairs, she experiences a 'feeling of intolerable disgust' and flings herself on the bed, covering her face 'as though to hide something hideous and dreadful' (543–4). This sense of isolation, entrapment and revulsion, expressed through a gesture of concealment, is perhaps reflective of Mansfield's own feelings during this time.

'A Little Episode' is prefaced with an epigram from Wilde's *The Picture of Dorian Gray*, which expresses a sentiment that is then echoed in Jacques Saint Pierre's letter:

> The one charm of the past is that it is past. But women never know when the curtain has fallen. (538)

Mansfield became fascinated by Wilde and his ideas around 1904. By 1906, she was filling her notebooks with Wilde's aphorisms, such as 'The only way to get rid of temptation is to yield to it.'[3] Mansfield would then supplement these aphorisms with her own. The influence of Wilde is seen throughout 'A Little Episode': in the social arbitration of morality and marriage, for example, and in the flippancy of Jacques Saint Pierre's letter. In 1911, though, Mansfield directly emulated Wilde by composing a collection of fifty aphorisms. As the title suggests, the thematic focus of 'Bites from the Apple' is carnal knowledge. Medical evidence later given by Mansfield suggests that she contracted venereal disease late in 1909, when she began a love affair at the Pension Müller in Germany with the Polish translator Floryan Sobieniowski. Disease and infection are recurring themes throughout 'Bites from the Apple':

> I keep the God of my childhood hanging round my neck by a string, like a little camphor bag – an old-fashioned remedy for warding off infectious and dangerous complaints. Of course there is one disadvantage . . . when I wear evening dress . . . it is impossible. Most women do the same – that is why men find my sex so far more vulnerable when they are décolleté.

> Love is the germ – passion the disease.[4]

Passion as a disease, as something which grips the body, is represented in 'A Little Episode': the piece which Jacques Saint Pierre plays at the concert is Beethoven's 'Appassionata' (Piano Sonata No. 23 in F minor, Op. 57), music of passionate violence which causes Yvonne to be 'seized by an ungovernable impulse' as she rises and 'swiftly' passes out of the hall. In this story, Mansfield links movement and motion with impulse and emotion, an equivalence which helps us to situate her aesthetic as an affective response to the changing spatial relations of the early

Figure 5. John Middleton Murry, Dorothy Brett and Katherine Mansfield in Hampstead, 1920. Private collection.

Figure 6. Ida Baker visiting the offices of *ADAM International Review* in South Kensington. Image courtesy of King's College London Archives, *Adam International Review* Collection.

twentieth century. In 'Bites from the Apple', Mansfield demonstrates her awareness of this when she writes: 'The sooner Eve meets the serpent the better – then she leaves the Garden of Eden and has the whole world before her.'[5] Mansfield links the experience of having 'the whole world before her' to gender politics: with clear parallels to her own biography, global travel becomes an act of defiance. Nevertheless, the tone of Mansfield's collection of aphorisms is overwhelmingly pessimistic and cynical. For instance, other aphorisms from 'Bites from the Apple' include:

> Love is the Wine of Life – Marriage the non-alcoholic beverage.

> In these days of social depravity we do not look <u>under</u> the bed before retiring, but <u>in</u> it.

> Love feeds upon itself – that is why it is so soon starved to Death.[6]

Among the typescripts found within the King's College London Archives were also four of the five stories Mansfield wrote for the Queen's College magazine and four stories grouped under the collective title of 'The Thoughtful Child'. When Mansfield left Queen's College and returned to New Zealand, she made plans to produce a book for children with her friend Edith Bendall, a gifted artist: Mansfield was to write the stories and Bendall was to provide illustrations. However, the book came to nothing and many of Mansfield's stories from the proposed collection were subsequently considered lost. We can now read three more of the stories which were to comprise the collection, all written in 1908: 'The Thoughtful Child and the Lilac Tree', 'The Thoughtful Child: In Autumn' and 'Hand-in-Hand with the Thoughtful Child'. The literary value of these stories is negligible, however: they are sickly-sweet meditations on the innocence of childhood and nature. The following passage is representative:

> In this Spring weather a bird in the lilac tree on the lawn sings each day – a little brown bird – its song is about a fairy stream running through a dream forest. (529)

The stories are significant, though, in highlighting the profound changes that events produced in the development of Mansfield's writing. Compared to 'The Thoughtful Child' stories, 'A Little Episode' (written only months later) and 'Bites from the Apple' emerge as accomplished, mature and rather dark works, the fruits of bitter experience. Mansfield would become renowned for her portrayal of young and vulnerable central characters, her thematic focus on fragile emotions and half-understood feelings, and the economy of her narrative

Figure 7. Ida Baker at her New Forest home with Miron Grindea and his wife Carola. Private collection.

Figure 8. Miron Grindea in the 1960s. Private collection.

style: 'A Little Episode' can be considered as an early and highly successful experiment in the development of these qualities. Likewise, the brevity, wit and sharp impersonality of the aphorisms would become defining traits of Mansfield's later writing. The discovery of these two works therefore provides a new lens through which to assess Mansfield, a pioneer of both the short story form and of literary modernism.

* * *

These typescripts came to be part of the King's College London Archives after they were given to the editor of the literary magazine *ADAM International Review* in the mid 1960s by Ida Baker. Edited by Miron Grindea, a Romanian Jew who sought refuge in London at the outbreak of World War Two, *ADAM* was one of the first magazines in Britain genuinely to promote the idea of 'comparative' or 'world literature'. *ADAM*, its title an acronym for 'Arts, Drama, Architecture and Music', was wide-ranging and eclectic in focus. Special issues were dedicated to individual authors and composers as well as to different national and continental literary and artistic traditions. Unlike most little magazines, *ADAM* was also long-running; established in Bucharest in 1929, it continued until Grindea's death in 1995. The sheer scope of *ADAM*, both in focus and chronology, yielded an extensive archive of close to 500 boxes. The five boxes relating to Mansfield contain, as well as the typescripts, copies of letters and a cache of photographs taken by Ida Baker, some of which are reproduced here.

Grindea was a man driven by personal obsessions, and each of his subjects received a level of bio-bibliographical attention rarely seen in other magazines: Proust, for instance, was the focus of eight special issues of *ADAM*. In the early 1960s, Grindea turned his attention to Katherine Mansfield, publishing a lavish celebratory issue of *ADAM* in 1965 (No. 300), which contained forty-six previously unpublished letters by Mansfield to Anne Estelle Rice and to Sydney and Violet Schiff. This was followed by another special issue devoted to Mansfield, published in 1973, to mark fifty years since her death. For Grindea, Katherine Mansfield was the subject of a decade-long obsession.

Grindea first wrote to Ida Baker in September 1964, on the pretext of collecting material for a biography of Mansfield in French by his friend Anne-Marie Monnet. At this time Baker was an old woman, living in a remote cottage in the New Forest. Still haunted by the memory of her intense friendship with Mansfield, she had nevertheless grown tired of being pursued by biographers for details. In October 1964, however, Grindea visited Baker. Afterwards, he wrote to her saying:

> With the risk of exasperating you I must say it all over again – and at the
> top of my voice – that you are more than a charming lady and hostess, you
> are a person of immense dignity and kindness, a real human being and, to
> cap it all (!), an intellectual . . . a term you no doubt don't approve of. Yes,
> you express yourself with perfect searching insight, with an intense and
> original power of characterisation, and especially with a lucid grasp of so
> many human frailties and vanities.[7]

It appears that Baker responded well to being described in such flattering terms and she began a regular correspondence with Grindea, who
assured her that he was not intent on 'hounding' her for details but
was instead looking to 'clear up a number of things which have been
cheapened by hasty or ill-meaning "students" of literature'.[8] Indeed,
in highlighting the distortions made by others to her own picture of
Mansfield, Grindea was instrumental in encouraging Baker to write her
own memoirs, offering to type and proof-read her early drafts. Grindea
also drew Baker's attention to the fact that Antony Alpers, in his biography of Mansfield (1954), had published private letters without her con-
sent. On discovering this, a 'horrified' Baker wrote to Grindea: 'He has
taken my inmost private life and cut it up'; and, 'I feel so very <u>exposed</u>,
for my past and for K. M. – angry – why should small personal details of
clothes and laundry be given to the common curiosity of the world?'[9]

It seems to have been at this point, in late 1964 or early 1965, that
Baker gave Grindea the letters, photographs and typescripts, as well
as some Mansfield memorabilia that she asked him to sell in London.
She wrote to him in 1965: 'The only really valuable part – the letters – are, of course, only for your eyes. How are you wishing to use
the rest?'[10] By 'the rest' she almost certainly meant the typescripts,
which were valuable only in a literary rather than commercial sense.
Signed 'K. Mansfield' in Baker's handwriting and initialled 'I. C. B.'
(Ida Constance Baker), the typescripts were probably produced as part
of the work Baker did for John Middleton Murry in the years after
Mansfield's death, typing up her work for posthumous publication. In
all likelihood, Baker entrusted these documents to Grindea because of
assurances that he was interested in their literary rather than financial
value. In 1967, however, Grindea writes: 'I should be very disappointed
indeed if money matters were to spoil our friendship. All I am hoping
for is that my suggestion (and offer) will get fair consideration before
you part with the material which you've shown me.'[11] This material
included some of Koteliansky's letters to Mansfield as well as letters from
Mansfield's cousin Elizabeth (Countess Russell, formerly Elizabeth von
Arnim). In June 1968, Grindea was informed by a friend of Baker's that
this material would be auctioned at Sotheby's. Grindea wrote to Baker

expressing his disappointment and failure 'to understand why, after all, you distrusted this friend so much as to resort to other channels'.[12] After this, Grindea and Baker continued to correspond, but the relationship had evidently soured. When carrying out research for the 1973 special issue, Grindea contacted Baker again, but he met with a short reply: 'I have already written and said all I wish to on the subject of Katherine Mansfield – so have nothing at all more to say.'[13]

Grindea's diary for 1973 makes several references to meetings with Peter Day, Baker's adopted grandson and literary executor. In his book *Privileged Moments* (2001), Jeffrey Meyers rather cruelly describes 'the intensely mannered and affected Peter Day (Doris to his chums)' who had

> tried to prevent me from seeing the elderly Ida Baker when I was writing the biography of her sometime lover, Katherine Mansfield, and raised a great fuss when he found out I'd disobeyed his wishes and simply rung the doorbell of her cottage in the New Forest.[14]

In the 1960s, Day worked as a reader for the publisher Michael Joseph, and was instrumental in seeing that Baker's memoirs found publication. As the quotation from Meyers' book reveals, Day also considered himself to be the protector of Baker's interests: Baker was incredibly naïve about both literary and financial matters, and it is likely that Day coordinated the sale of her Mansfield memorabilia at Sotheby's. Grindea's familiarity with Peter Day might provide a clue as to why he never published the stories and aphorisms by Mansfield. *ADAM* was practically synonymous with the *inédit*, renowned for publishing previously unseen work and ephemera. Among his most significant editorial coups, Grindea published an unseen cadenza by Mozart, letters from Dickens to the Count D'Orsay, drawings by Proust, and a play by Jean-Paul Sartre. It therefore seems inconceivable that Grindea would not publish documents of significance that were in his possession. One possible explanation is that he intended to publish the stories and aphorisms in a third special number of *ADAM* dedicated to Mansfield, which never came to fruition. Another more likely explanation is that Grindea honoured an agreement with Ida Baker – mediated by Peter Day – not to publish the material.

The stories 'A Little Episode' and 'The Thoughtful Child', as discovered in the King's College London archives, are published for the first time within an appendix to the first volume of the new collected edition of Mansfield's work edited by Gerri Kimber and Vincent O'Sullivan and published by Edinburgh University Press. 'Bites from the Apple' will be published in 2014 in the third volume of the edition, which brings together Mansfield's poetry and critical writings. Mansfield once described her work as 'little stories like birds bred in cages'[15] (a tendency towards self-deprecation also evident in the title 'A Little Episode'). Together with the typescript for this story in the KCL archives was a long list of other works by Mansfield given to Grindea by Baker. Among the many references to published stories are a number of unrecorded texts, such as 'Whiskey or Mirabelle' and 'The Brandons'. Perhaps yet more works by Mansfield are waiting to be found within archive collections, like birds locked away in cages.

Notes

An earlier version of this article was first published in the *Times Literary Supplement*, No. 5714 (5 October 2012).

1. Moira Taylor, *Her Bright Image: Impressions of Katherine Mansfield* (1973–4), CD.
2. Gerri Kimber and Vincent O'Sullivan, eds, *The Edinburgh Edition of the Collected Works of Katherine Mansfield*, Vol. 1, *The Collected Fiction of Katherine Mansfield, 1898–1915* (Edinburgh: Edinburgh University Press, 2012), p. 538. All further references to this story are to this edition and page numbers placed parenthetically after each quotation.
3. Ida Baker, *Katherine Mansfield: The Memories of L. M.* (London: Taplinger, 1972), p. 25.
4. In King's College London Archive (KC/ADAM/MS/18).
5. Ibid.
6. Ibid.
7. In King's College London Archive (KC/ADAM/FIL/50).
8. Ibid.
9. Ibid.
10. Ibid.
11. Ibid.
12. Ibid.
13. Ibid.
14. Jeffrey Meyers, *Privileged Moments: Encounters with Writers* (Madison: University of Wisconsin Press, 2001), p. 106.
15. Vincent O'Sullivan and Margaret Scott, eds, *The Collected Letters of Katherine Mansfield: 1922–1923*, Vol. 5 (Oxford: Oxford University Press, 2008), p. 346.

The 2012 Alexander Turnbull Library Mansfield/Murry Acquisition

Fiona Oliver

The Ghost in the Library

Katherine Mansfield's writing came to be a defiant gesture against illness; for years she knew how precariously she lived: the medical report among her papers in the new acquisition makes the situation quite clear. Her final pleas were a delirious, optimistic bargaining: give me more time; I am ready to write authentically. She sketched out a plot to A. R. Orage a few weeks before she died: 'Two people fall in love and marry. One, or perhaps both of them, has had previous affairs, the remains of which still linger like ghosts in the new home [. . .] the ghosts still walk.'[1] In a sense, that unwritten story played itself out after her death. There was Murry's disquieting marriage to her likeness, Violet le Maistre, and Mansfield walked through her husband's next two relationships too, as he obsessively lionised her life and work, her stories gained a wider audience and her biographies were written. Decades later, long after Murry's death in 1957, Mary Gamble, Murry's fourth wife, was an active participant in maintaining Mansfield's legacy. The papers brought into the Turnbull in 2012 show that Gamble continued to field correspondence relating to Mansfield, all the while nursing her own aspirations to be a writer. More than that, each new acquisition of Mansfield's papers into the library resuscitates her spirit, bringing her back into sharper focus and allowing us to see her from new angles, cast in new lights.

Mansfield-Collecting at the Turnbull

In the years following Mansfield's death the Turnbull was slow to begin acquiring her papers – at that time it did not focus its collecting activity on modern literature. In any case, Murry had said he was unwilling to relinquish the letters and journals during his lifetime. However, when he was approached in 1948, he admitted he had already sold some of her manuscript stories to the US, in 1938. Finally, in need of cash and determined to get a good price, Murry offered to sell the Turnbull just two notebooks, for £320 – the cost of a new tractor for his farm. In those days that was a very high price. The Chief Librarian was not impressed, reporting to his Department Head that 'the ethics of this gentleman ... were not flattering'. It didn't help that Murry mislaid one of the notebooks. He ended up selling the library a manuscript notebook containing part of 'Prelude'/ 'The Aloe' for £250 (about £15,000 today).

The Turnbull lobbied for a bequest, but Murry was more interested in selling the papers to the British Library. In his will he offered them the letters for £1,000, with the manuscripts and notebooks to be auctioned; but the British Library declined it all. So the Turnbull bought the lot – almost 500 letters and 50 notebooks – for almost £3,600 (£150,000 today). It was by far the largest purchase made by a New Zealand collecting institution.

It was assumed that this was the entirety of Mansfield's papers. But more came from estate sales in the 1970s, and further purchases followed into the early 2000s. In 2012 the papers relating to Mansfield, and the subject of this report, were purchased from Marie Carty, a granddaughter of Murry, after some years of investigation and negotiation. Gerri Kimber was the first to view some of these papers in 2005, and immediately recognised their literary worth. Further access was denied her, but subsequently afforded to Kathleen Jones, who was researching her biography of Mansfield and Murry. In the meantime, Dr Kimber alerted Professor Vincent O'Sullivan to the material, who approached the Turnbull and asked if negotiations could be made with the family to acquire it.

Arrangement and Description

The material came into the Manuscripts Collection in August 2012, after almost two years of negotiations. Papers relating to Mansfield make up only about one-sixth of the total, although the entirety had clearly been organised around them. We do not know who organised the papers in this way. They were accompanied by a provisional inventory prepared by Kathleen Jones and her notes were in the folders.

The sorting was roughly into four groups: papers by and about Mansfield; Murry's personal papers; Murry's literary and professional papers; and papers by and about D. H. and Frieda Lawrence. Most were a mix belonging to Murry and Mary Gamble. Some consideration was given to separating their papers into two distinct collections, but since Mary's and other contributors' papers had been so thoroughly integrated, it was treated as a whole. This determined the provenance and title of the collection ('Murry family literary and personal papers').

The Turnbull Library has maintained the arrangement of the papers as we received them, following the archival principal to respect the original order of a collection, however it came to be that way.

The four original groupings of manuscript material have been broken down into seven series:

> Series 1: Papers relating to Katherine Mansfield
> Series 2: John Middleton Murry – diaries and journals
> Series 3: John Middleton Murry – correspondence and personal papers
> Series 4: John Middleton Murry – literary works and interests
> Series 5: Literary drafts sent to John Middleton Murry
> Series 6: Mary Middleton Murry (née Gamble) – papers
> Series 7/1: Correspondence of D. H. and Frieda Lawrence
> Series 7/2: Other papers relating to D. H. and Frieda Lawrence

There is not the space in this report to provide a detailed description of the entire acquisition. What follows is a brief overview of its scope and contents, with particular detail given to the papers relating to Mansfield. A full catalogue listing of manuscript items can be viewed at www.tapuhi.natlib.govt.nz (search for reference: MS-Group-2101 in the Manuscripts and Archives Collection).

Series 1: Papers Relating to Katherine Mansfield

The Mansfield papers are for the most part fragmentary and piecemeal, but are immensely rich in their diversity and content, and span a wide date range, possibly dating from as early as 1898.

Correspondence makes up the greater part of the Mansfield series, and includes that written by Mansfield, others written to her by friends and relations, others about her:

- A postcard from Wellington, addressed to Mansfield, from the Lawrences. It reads: 'Ricordi' signed D. H. L. and 'We thought so hard of you here' signed F. L.
- Telegrams from Murry to Mansfield.

- Letters to Chaddie Perkins from Murry and the Bank of NZ, and one to the Foreign Office, relating to Mansfield being stranded in Paris in 1918.
- Postcard from Mansfield to 'Dear little brother', Richard Murry, beginning 'This is the end of an imperfect day . . .'
- Two letters to Princess Bibesco, 1921: in the first, Mansfield scolds her for flirting with her husband; the second, unfinished, is a response to Princess Bibesco's reply.
- Letter addressed to 'Dearest' (probably Garnet Trowell) in which Mansfield gives lyrical impressions of places and people seen from trains travelling through Holland and Germany. Written on Hotel Marquardt, Stuttgart, letterhead and dated 'Whit Monday'. Murry's pencil note dates it '? about 1909'.
- Letter written at Isola Bella to Hugh Walpole, beginning, 'Please do not praise me'.
- Unsigned letter to Lady Rothermere written from Le Prieuré, expressing regret that Lady Rothermere is not coming to Fontainebleau until January.
- Letter written from Victoria Palace Hotel, Paris, to Elizabeth von Arnim: 'It seems so much more real now than when I last wrote to you. Then I felt that at any moment I would be whisked back into my cage.'
- Unfinished letter to Lady Ottoline Morrell describing daily life in the Victoria Palace Hotel, Paris, where Mansfield and Murry had adjacent rooms: 'I am 134 and Murry is 135.' Describes her reaction to reading Joyce's *Ulysses*.
- Letter from Ida Baker to Murry written from Ospedaletti on 11 January and 2 February, describing her concerns about 'Katie's' health – 'Her depression and weakness have frightened me terribly [. . .] many times I have found her just quietly crying & crying.' Another written from Paris before Ida left France for England, about a picture of Murry's which Ida wishes to return to him.
- Letter from James Young, perhaps c. 1922–3, written from the Gurdjieff Institute in Fontainebleau, describing life in the community and the teaching of Gurdjieff.
- Letters from Harold Beauchamp to his daughter, 1916 and 1919.
- Two undated letters (possibly c. 1918) to Mansfield from Violet, the housekeeper at Hampstead, discussing domestic matters, kittens, and the anticipated return to the house of Mansfield and Ida Baker.
- Unfinished letter from Mansfield, 1922, relating to 'The Garden Party': 'It was like you two not to have mentioned the big holes in

The Garden Party. But I know they are there and I'll try and mend them next time . . .'

- Unfinished letter, 1921, on paper from the Grand Hotel Chateau Bellevue, Sierre, addressed to Murry and relating to Mansfield's failure to find a doctor in Montreux, and her journey to meet a Doctor Stephani in Sierre.
- Two letters from Frieda Lawrence: one to Mansfield, c. 1917, describes a winter in Cornwall, discussing visitors, clothes, her health and her husband's writing; the other is written to Murry at Mansfield's death, from Del Monte Ranch, Ouesta, and describes her fond memories of Mansfield and offers condolences.
- A letter addressed to 'My dear Kathleen', written two days before her death by Tom L. Mills, editor of *The Feilding Star* (NZ).

Literary papers include drafts of stories, poems and vignettes, and papers relating to her work as a critic and editor:

- Mansfield's handwritten notes on Lawrence's novel, *The Lost Girl*. The tone is critical: 'The whole is false – ashes'; 'Earth closets too!'
- Poems, dated and undated, including 'Evening' (c. 1898–1903), 'Escapade Undertaken by a Green Raspberry and a Kidney Bean' (1903), 'A Common Ballad (1906), 'The Spring Wind in London', (c. 1908–9), 'To Pan' (1908), 'A Version from Heine' (1917), 'Verses Writ in a Foreign Bed' (c. 1918), 'Sunset' (1919), 'Men and Women' (1919), 'Et Après' (1919), 'When I was Little', 'Winter Bird', 'One Day', 'Tragedy', 'The Ring', 'A Song for Over Real Children', 'You Won't Understand This – 'Cause you're a Boy', 'The Butterfly', 'Caution', 'Friendship', 'The Clock', 'The Bath Baby', The Last Thing'.
- A number of untitled poems.
- Several vignettes.
- Complete and unfinished stories, some with manuscript corrections and annotations, including the following undated stories: 'Aunt Emily', 'Aunt Fan', 'At the Club', 'There is no Answer', 'The Thoughtful Child', 'Along the Gray's Inn Road', 'The Clinic Garden', 'Life is not Gay', 'Dark Love', 'The Pessimist', 'Autumns', 'A Family Dance', 'Two Little Girls', 'Festival of the Coronation', 'Hat with a Feather', 'The Lily', 'Lucien', 'Mrs Sheridan', 'One Day', 'That Woman'.
- Short stories, among them are 'Last Words to Youth' (c. 1898–1903), 'Three 20th Century girls. Chapter one. The great examination' (1901), 'The Pine Tree, the Sparrows, and You and I' (1903), 'Die

Einsame' (1904), 'Your Birthday' (1904), 'A Fairy Story' (c. 1910), 'Sumurun: An Impression of Leopoldine Konstantin' (1911), 'New Dresses' (1912), 'A Marriage of Passion' (1912), 'Virginia's Journal' (1913), 'The Beautiful Miss Richardson' (1916), 'The Boy with the Jackdaw' (1918).

- Translations of Chekhov: 'To his Brother Alexander Tchekhov, April 1883, Moscow'.
- Fragments of writing, including the title sheet of 'Dry Land' (1913), pages 2–4 of 'In a Café', written in Wellington (c. 1909), single page 'The beginning of a story by Katherine Mansfield', portion of a review, 'The pages suffer from overloading', and the draft section of a story: 'At precisely the right moment, neither too early nor too late, their large blue car turned in at the iron gates . . .'
- Mansfield's list of some of her stories.
- A poem called 'Nuts', based on a party game.

Personal papers include:

- Shopping lists, such as the one under the heading 'Villa Pauline' for cooking ingredients, soap, matches and paper.
- Prescription for menthol, methylsalicylates, bismuthe oxychlor and vaseline on notepaper from the Grand Hotel Beau Rivage, Bandol.
- Two envelopes containing dried flowers taken from letters, Bandol.
- Mansfield's passport, issued in 1918 and still valid at her death.
- Chequebooks with stubs made out to various people and institutions including Drs Bouchage and Le Blanc, Ida Baker, Jack, 'self' and Institute.
- Receipt detailing the exchange of a dressing gown for a navy coat.
- Pen-and-ink drawings. One, made c. 1915–16, is of a hilly landscape with a house and trees, and the sea, with Mansfield's message below it: 'This is the kind of place that would be so nice, Bogey. You observe we are driving from the sea; and I am sitting with my back to you & the horse to watch the waves. Tig.' The other is a design formed by writing addressed to 'Honourable Parentchik' from 'Your sonchik RIB'.
- Five bills from the Headland House Hotel for 'board residence' and items including milk and cream. Each has a one-penny stamp attached, over which is written the receipt note and date.
- Beginning of a journal entry dated 28 November 1918 [or 1916], beginning 'L. M. and I are really the bitterest enemies imaginable.'
- Words of a song, beginning, 'I walked all day, for forty cents pay.'
- Russian vocabulary, written in Roman script.

- Mansfield's recipes for orange soufflé and cold-water scones.
- Medical report by Dr Bouchage of Menton, outlining her visits between 1920 and 1921, her symptoms, medical history, treatment, pathology and the progress of her diseases. Refers to a 1919 diagnosis by Dr Victor Sorapure in London.
- Handwritten history of Mansfield's mother's family, the Dyer family, by Winifred Parsons (1934).

There are several newspaper cuttings, including obituaries.

Papers relating to Murry's work on Mansfield after her death include some (selectively indexed) correspondence, which relates mainly to his publications of Mansfield's writing:

- Notes by Murry for talks given in the United States after Katherine's death.
- Letters to Murry from Bowden, Violet Schiff and others relating to the publication of Mansfield's letters.

Series 2–7: Murry, Mary Gamble, D. H. and Frieda Lawrence

Papers relating to Murry are contained in Series 2 to 5. There are original journals written by Murry, extracts from his journals and diaries edited by his son, Colin, unedited photocopies of extracts from his diaries, and a draft of an unpublished sequel to his autobiography, *Between Two Worlds*. There is inward correspondence and copies of some outward correspondence, with correspondents including T. S. Eliot, Richard Murry and Max Plowman. Murry's many books, essays, reviews and lectures on literature, social issues, politics and religion, his poetry and autobiographical writings are represented in draft form. His research into the life and works of John Keats features prominently.

There are papers, mainly literary drafts, submitted to Murry as editor of the *Adelphi*. Many of them were subsequently published. Writers represented include H. G. Wells, George Santayana, Arnold Bennett and Dorothy Richardson.

Mary Gamble's papers, in Series 6, include letters sent from Murry in the early years of their relationship, correspondence relating to the writing of Murry's biography by F. A. Lea, and correspondence from literary researchers. There are papers relating to Gamble's own literary endeavours, including poetry, her autobiographical *To Keep Faith* (1959), and drafts of her other publications. There are a number of her journals and notebooks.

The Lawrence papers have received much academic interest, and scholars have already confirmed a number of hitherto unpublished pieces. Series 7/1 covers personal and literary correspondence between Frieda and Murry, and personal letters from Lawrence to Frieda. It also includes letters to Frieda from Aldous Huxley. Other papers (Series 7/2) include drafts of literary works by Lawrence sent to Murry as editor of the *Adelphi*. The remainder of the papers in this series mainly relate to Murry's writings on Lawrence, including essays, lectures, book reviews and his biography (and attendant drafts, correspondence, reviews), *Son of Man* (1931). The series also contains correspondence between Murry and researchers interested in the Lawrences.

Transfers

The following items were transferred from the Manuscripts Collection to other Turnbull collections:

- A photograph album and folder of photographs (PA-Group-00820) went to the Photographic Archive.
- Four Hogarth Press first editions went into the Rare Books and Special Printed Collections. They are Virginia and L. S. Woolf, *Two Stories*, Virginia Woolf, *Kew Gardens*, Katherine Mansfield, *Prelude* and T. S. Eliot, 'Two Poems'. Issues I, II and VII of *The Wanderers* and issue X (November 1912) of *Rhythm* went into this collection, as did three copies of the 1919 Heron Press edition of Mansfield's *Je ne Parle pas Français*, and an announcement of publication of *Prelude* by Heron Press.
- A painted wooden box owned by Mansfield was transferred to the Curios Collection (Curios-045-001).

Contributions of the New Acquisition

The 1212 acquisition is the largest body of Mansfield papers to come into the Alexander Turnbull Library since the 1950s. It adds to what is the world's foremost Mansfield collection. The Turnbull has a large corpus of published material by and about Mansfield, including foreign-language and rare editions, and some pocketbooks that once belonged to the writer herself. It holds hundreds of manuscripts, photographs, and an intriguing group of personal items such as locks of her hair, a Māori head carved from kauri gum, her cloak and typewriter. In the broader view, the varied range of the new acquisition as a whole contextualises Mansfield within British literary modernism. There is much to be explored in this regard.

Within the Mansfield papers themselves, new material has already been recognised. During her February 2013 visit to the Turnbull, Gerri Kimber identified a hitherto unknown vignette or fictionalised review, 'Sumurun: An Impression of Leopoldine Konstantin' (1911), as well as more than a dozen unpublished poems, many story fragments, diary entries, miscellaneous jottings and photographs. The wealth of new material in the acquisition promises to reinvigorate Mansfield studies and keep scholars engaged for years, analysing the papers and positioning the new information alongside what is already known of Mansfield's life and work. The papers offer possibilities for a new and exciting reassessment of the writer's development and the themes of her work, and will breathe richer detail into what we already know of her life.

Notes

I would like to acknowledge the contribution of colleagues at the Alexander Turnbull Library, especially David Colquhoun, Marion Townend and Kevin Stewart, in the preparation of this report.

1. A. R. Orage, *On Love with some Aphorisms and Other Essays* (London: Janus, 1966), p. 45.

Two French Books Belonging to Katherine Mansfield

Gerri Kimber

Two French novels owned by Katherine Mansfield have recently come to light (now in a private collection): *La Femme de Trente Ans* (*A Woman of Thirty*) by Honoré de Balzac (Paris: Calmann-Lévy, c. 1900), and *La Jeune Fille Bien Élevée* (*The Well-Bred Young Girl*) by René Boylesve (Paris: Calmann-Lévy, c. 1919).

Both spines are backed with brown paper with autograph titles inscribed in ink by Mansfield and John Middleton Murry respectively; given the publication date of the Boylesve volume, the repairs must have been carried out post-1919. The Balzac novel has Mansfield's signature on the first inside blank page, dated and located 'at Marseilles, March 1916'. The Boylesve volume has her signature on the front wrapper. Murry has also written 'Q7' and 'P3' in pencil on the first inside blank page of each volume, as a shelf mark for his own library.

During the winter of 1915–16, Mansfield and Murry were to be found in Bandol on the French Riviera, initially at the Hotel Beau Rivage and sub-sequently from January 1916 at the Villa Pauline, where Mansfield started revising her story 'The Aloe', which would eventually be transformed into 'Prelude'. Her sister Chaddie had written to her there, announcing she would be passing through Marseilles in late March; thus on 20 March, Mansfield travelled to Marseilles, taking a room at the Hotel Oasis where she and Murry had briefly stayed the previous November, on their way to Bandol. From there she wrote to Murry on 21 March: 'Cooks [. . .] referred me to the P and O people Rue Colbert (opposite the Post office). And I found out that the Sardinia is *definitely* expected at 8.30 AM. on Thursday morning.'[1] Mansfield met Chaddie, who had sailed in from Bombay on the *Sardinia* en route to England, on 23 March. She then rejoined Murry at Bandol. They returned to England together on 27 March, following a request by the Lawrences to move to Cornwall with them.

Figure 9. Two French books owned by Katherine Mansfield – front view.
Private collection.

Figure 10. Two French books owned by Katherine Mansfield – side view.
Private collection.

Conceivably, the Balzac novel might have been purchased to while away the time whilst waiting for her sister's ship to dock in Marseilles. In *A Woman of Thirty* (1842), Balzac provides a fascinating commentary on the position of women in marriage in the early 1800s. With Mansfield's own thirtieth birthday less than a year and a half away, the book's title might also have resonated with her.

In an early notebook from 1909, Mansfield had written:

> [Balzac] makes his characters so demean themselves that their slightest gesture shall be the expression of their souls. So there is more colour. It is a portrait, but the flesh covers the bones. He was trained under the severe eye of Flaubert.[2]

She had read a good deal of French literature, including Balzac, as a young woman in New Zealand during 1907–8, borrowing books from the library at Parliament House in Wellington as a special concession, obtained through contacts of her father Harold Beauchamp (a Governor of the Bank of New Zealand and friend of R. J. Seddon, the then New Zealand Prime Minister). Records from this time show that she was reading Maupassant, Balzac, Mérimée and Flaubert – all in French.[3]

There is evidence that in 1919 Mansfield started translating a French novel into English:

> I am idiotic from translating. I am turning into English La Jeune Fille Bien Elevée [sic] for an American publisher, and every moment one wants to say: but it's so much better in French – do let me leave this little bit in French.[4]

Unfortunately, there is no record of this translation of René Boylesve's novel of 1909 (a *Bildungsroman* depicting the education and subsequent marriage of a young girl called Madeleine), ever being published, or any evidence of the actual translation in her papers. Her work on the project was almost certainly abandoned, given that after page 69 the pages are mostly uncut. By late May 1919, Mansfield was living in Hampstead with Murry in the tall, thin, grey house, which they nicknamed 'The Elephant'. It is possible that her translations of Chekhov's letters, in collaboration with S. S. Koteliansky, also being worked on at this time and serialised in the *Athenaeum* from April–October 1919, coupled with her worsening health, forced her to abandon the French translation. By mid-September 1919, she would be back on the Riviera, initially in Italy and then in France, once more in search of a healthy climate to assuage the symptoms of her tuberculosis.

Ultimately she would turn away from France and the French as

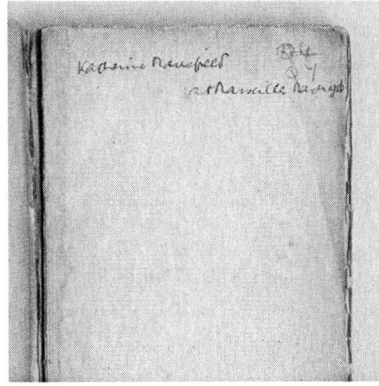

Figure 11. *La Femme de Trente Ans* – inside cover signature. Private collection.

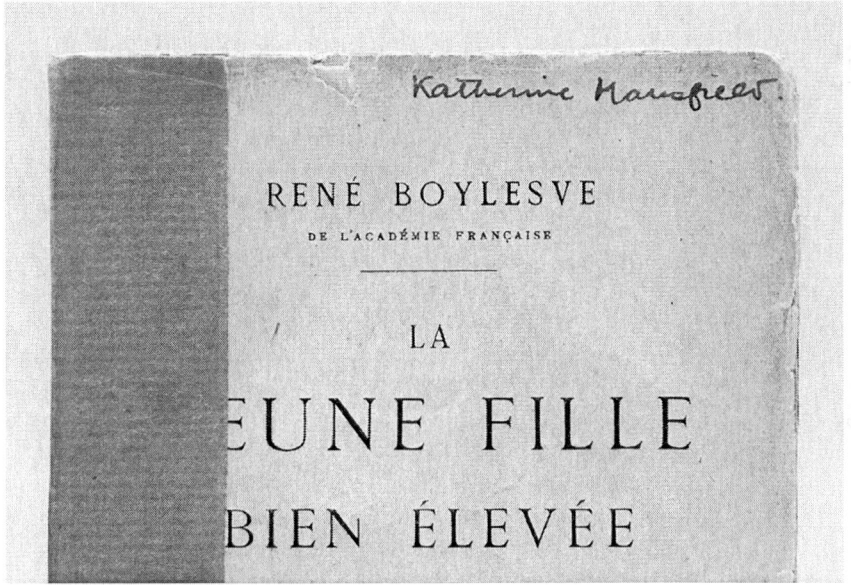

Figure 12. *La Jeune Fille Bien Élevée* – signature. Private collection.

evidenced by a letter she wrote to Ottoline Morrell on 2 February 1921:

> But I mean to leave the Riviera as soon as possible. I've turned *frightfully* against it and the French. Life seems to me ignoble here. It all turns on money. Everything is money. When I read Balzac I always feel a peculiar odious exasperation because according to him the whole of Life is founded on the question of money. But he is right. It is – for the French. I wish the horrid old Riviera would fall into the sea. It's just like an exhibition where every single side show costs another sixpence. But I paid goodness knows what to *come in*.[5]

This quotation epitomises Mansfield's love/hate relationship with France and the French and her own vacillating response to the country which, nevertheless, enriched both her life and her aesthetic response in so many ways.

Notes

1. Vincent O'Sullivan and Margaret Scott, eds, *The Collected Letters of Katherine Mansfield*, 5 vols (Oxford: Clarendon, 1984–2008), Vol. 1, p. 253, 21 March 1919. Hereafter referred to as *Letters*, followed by volume and page number.
2. Margaret Scott, ed., *The Katherine Mansfield Notebooks*, 2 vols (Minneapolis: University of Minnesota Press, 2002), Vol. 1, pp. 165–6, April 1909.
3. The enduring importance of French literature to Mansfield is well documented. See in particular my book, *Katherine Mansfield: The View from France* (Bern: Peter Lang, 2008).
4. *Letters* 2, p. 321, late May 1919.
5. *Letters* 4, p. 171, 2 February 1921.

Editing the New *Collected Fiction of Katherine Mansfield,* 2 vols (Edinburgh: Edinburgh University Press, 2012), Gerri Kimber and Vincent O'Sullivan, eds

Vincent O'Sullivan

There's always that discreet warning ringing in an editor's ear: Mansfield pretty much telling Murry not to hang on too eagerly to every scrap that survives her, and that she wants to leave as little evidence of her camping ground as possible. To stretch that metaphor, the editors' job (Gerri Kimber and myself), in this edition at any rate, has been to get as big a pile of soup cans, half full bottles, and scarcely opened packets as possible. In one sense – if you're tempted to be cynical about it – the untidier Mansfield's camp site remains, the better we've done our job. Which, happily, a good reviewer understands. As a long review in the *London Review of Books* by Kirsty Gunn puts it:

> By giving us every draft and fragment in the order of their production – including schoolgirl jottings, drafts that never made it into print, and the four recently discovered short stories that were the subject of press interest last year – the editors of the Edinburgh edition are able to show us, on the page, the craftswoman learning what she needs to learn in order to be published and become well known, and then learning from those lessons in order to forget them.[1]

It is also an essay that brilliantly homes in on the point of how:

> Her notebooks and reviews return again and again to the split between fiction as art and 'entertainment', the glory of the perhaps failed attempt as against the safe complacencies of technique. [. . .] So there are the stories here that she wrote specifically – for causes, for magazines, for money. And there are the others that slowly, piece by piece, in version after version, arrive at the full expression of her ambition, when Mansfield can be seen for what she is: one of our great Modernists, the creator of a narrative form so familiar to us that we barely think of it as one at all.[2]

The reviewer's point is not so far from what Frank O'Connor wrote so brutally in one of the most appreciative pieces written on her – an essay that loathes her as a person, misinterprets her biography, misses numerous points that should be grasped, yet gets to his conclusion, which is one of wonder to him, of taking in 'the true and moving story of the brassy little shop girl of literature who made herself into a great writer', arriving at 'masterpieces' that 'can be linked with Joyce and Proust [. . .] They set out to do something that had never been done before, and do it in a manner that had never been used before.'[3]

Until now, most readers of Mansfield have based their response to her on the two slender collections she put together in the last years of her life, the fourteen stories in *Bliss* and the fourteen in *The Garden Party*. How she arranged those stories was an aesthetic choice, not a chronological one. Very few commentators have thought it important to consider when and where and why each story was written, although naturally enough, that is something her three important biographers have attended to. Alpers, especially, remains both scholar and editor we have been most indebted to, the great Mansfieldian whom generations of academics and commentators have plundered, at times with such discretion we might scarcely have known he is the source. The debt of this present edition to Alpers is enormous, even when, occasionally, we may have disagreed with him. We were indebted too, and massively so, to Margaret Scott's permission to draw transcriptions from her two-volume edition of the *The Katherine Mansfield Notebooks*. Although I expect both Antony and Margaret would have had what one might call temperamental reservations at being jointly praised, I hope our acknowledgment of them in the text is generous enough to be just, and just enough to make clear that even generous thanks is still inadequate.

Well, as the *LRB* review lays down, the importance of this edition is that those who care to, can now read Mansfield in a way that was not possible before – that is, to read her as she wrote, month by month, at times even day by day: to make connections, to trace filaments of style and emphasis and thematic obsession, to align and realign patterns of emotional force. As the Introduction points out, although there is a span of twenty-four years between her first story as a nine year old, and her last, six months before her death, 'that final story, written in the Swiss Alps, is set in the same Wellington street she lived in when she wrote the first, imagining she was in England'. That fact alone is biography in miniature. What Edinburgh University Press permits us to do, for the first time, is closely to follow a writer always in transition, before the full clarity of biography, or the weight of posthumous success, can be assumed. We can follow her writing in fact as the contours of that biography emerge, as she alters tack, puts aside, works to break old habits, to drive through to new forms – the messiness of the workshop that surrounds the established works.[4]

I'll mention just a few examples of how this new edition allows us more conveniently, and in a more nuanced way, to read Mansfield. One obvious aspect is the extent to which fairy-stories, the traditions of Grimm and Victorian children's stories, the rhythms and imagery of Wilde's stories, are far more pervasive, far more varied and psychologically deployed, than anyone so far has attended to. And how much more might be said about Mansfied and Māori than so far has been the case. There have been useful and interesting observations, of course, on Pearl Button, on the haunting figures of the Botanical Gardens, the perspectives of the Urewera notebook, the relationship with Maata Mahupuku. But we can add to that the straightforward, unsentimental depiction of the friendship between a pakeha girl and a Māori who are neighbours in Tinakori Road, and how one can extend Mansfield's curious ploy of what you might call transposed naming, in a story like 'Summer Idyll' in 1907, where a Māori woman called Marina is the sophisticate, in a European sense, and a younger pakeha woman, with the name Hinemoa, the ingénue.

There is so much else that might now, much more easily, be looked at more attentively – quite how an almost diary-like record of siblings, moves more freely into fiction; how to record is also to punish; that thread of sadism and masochism that is so much more evident than has yet been traced out, freedom even defined in terms of self-maiming; the early obsession with fainting, and with premature death, in so many stories. And one is not yet even up to page one hundred.

What the editors of this edition aimed for, along with completeness, was temporal accuracy. Almost always it's been possible to assign a story to its particular year, and for the most part, to when it was written in that year, so we have the correct order of composition. Usually, the accuracy of the text we were able to confirm by using the last version in print, or the manuscript or typescript Mansfield last attended to. But occasionally there were problems that couldn't easily be resolved. Take *Juliet* for example, the novel she hoped to write, and began in London in 1906, and continued back in Wellington the following year. She wrote it in the one notebook, but not in sequence. Scott's transcription reproduced Notebook One in page order, that is, with its sense of dislocated and confusing fragments. There can be no certainty about the order Mansfield finally intended, but clearly some attempt had to be made to present the text not as an exact transcript, but as a story. There are enough hints to hints to establish a rough sequential line, but 'rough' is the insistent word. There are, for example, two quite separate and distinct beginnings, the earlier, written in London, a realistic depiction of family and social life in Wellington, the other, a feverish dreamlike episode, expanding a motif of losing consciousness, and falling. As for the rest, there are missing episodes, name confusions, uncertain timelines, obscurely referred to events. The version we present is accurate textually, but its overall structure is necessarily tentative. But all this is made very clear in the annotations. Similarly with *Maata,* written in 1913, again intended as a novel, but left in random episodes. Yet again she was returning to the details of her broken love-affair with Garnet Trowell, and her friendship with his family when she first returned to England in 1908. There is no certainty about how the sections relate, although Mansfield did complete, for the one and only time, a full synopsis of the novel, which is a scaffolding one can draw on. Although she herself at once departs from it. So again, our arrangement can't help but be tentative. But we're not claiming to be more than that.

There isn't time to do more than glancingly remark on similar if lesser problems with later stories. That splendid incomplete story, 'Six Years After', with parents on board ship remembering the death of their son in the war six years earlier. Murry took his text in *The Dove's Nest* from a manuscript that does not survive, although there is part of an earlier draft dated October 1921. Alpers inserts this section into the story as he prints it in his Oxford edition. But as Mansfield did not include it in the longer version Murry used, we do not insert it into that version, but print it as a fragment of a surviving earlier draft. I can see you can make a case for both, but it seems ours leaves a little more choice for the reader, and a lesser assumption on ours.

Finally, a remark on rather a tricky area. The notes always begin with the source of the text, details of where it was published. If it was unpublished in Mansfield's lifetime, details are given of what later printed source, or surviving manuscript, was used. With many of the incomplete and abandoned stories and fragments Murry included in either the *Scrapbook* or his editions of the *Journal,* he gave titles that were his, not Mansfield's. So we have dropped these, as having nothing to do with her text, and given as title the first words or phrase which begins the manuscript. For example, there is a short piece in the *Scrapbook* called 'Baby Jean', which Murry chose as a title because of the child in the story. Mansfield left the story after a few paragraphs, and we have simply given it the title of 'There are certain human beings', which is the opening phrase. But she did not leave it there entirely. She had another shot at writing it, and so another version of those few paragraphs is also included. As for the unfinished stories, or the unpublished stories, that Murry included in the posthumous volumes, *The Dove's Nest* and *Something Childish,* we have returned to the manuscripts or typescripts, when they're available, and restored Mansfield's original punctuation, and attempted at times to give the stories the shape they had when she left them, rather than as Murry later and more tidily presented them. This means a fascinating story like 'Daphne', about a rather louche visiting painter to Wellington, now reads differently from what you will find in the version that has been around for almost ninety years. The story Murry called 'Second Violin', from 1921, now appears with sections he had placed elsewhere in the *Scrapbook,* and again looks very different. There can sometimes be something rather untidy about accuracy. But that's what the campsite looks like.

Notes

This is a version of the talk delivered by Vincent O'Sullivan in February 2013 at the Wellington launch of the new *Collected Fiction of Katherine Mansfield,* co-edited with Gerri Kimber.

1. Kirsty Gunn, 'How the Laundry Basket Squeaked' (Review of Gerri Kimber and Vincent O'Sullivan, eds, *The Collected Fiction of Katherine Mansfield,* 2 vols (Edinburgh: Edinburgh University Press, 2012)), *London Review of Books,* 35: 7, 11 April 2013, pp. 25–6, p. 25.
2. Ibid.
3. Frank O'Connor, 'An Author in Search of a Subject', in *The Lonely Voice* [1963] (Melville House: Brooklyn and London, 2004), pp. 132–3, p. 137.
4. Vincent O'Sullivan with Gerri Kimber, Introduction to Gerri Kimber and Vincent O'Sullivan, eds, *The Collected Fiction of Katherine Mansfield,* 2 vols (Edinburgh: Edinburgh University Press, 2012), Vol. 1, p. xx.

Names Painting – Katherine Mansfield

Penelope Jackson

It is just over a century since Katherine Mansfield sailed out of Wellington harbour in 1908, never to return. It is 125 years since she was born Kathleen Beauchamp in Thorndon, Wellington, in 1888. Mansfield's reputation as an innovative modernist writer continues to grow and she has inspired numerous artistic endeavours. Indeed, this *Journal* reaffirms Mansfield's artistic legacy with every volume. As a writer, Mansfield has fascinated academics and readers globally. As an art curator my own interest lies in the many images of Mansfield, made both during her lifetime and in the near century following her death. Adorning the covers of many publications over the years is the now familiar Anne Estelle Rice portrait,[1] held in the Museum of New Zealand's collection, but Mansfield's image has continued to provide inspiration for artists, especially in the last two decades, when there appears to have been something of a renaissance in portraits of her.

In 2004 I visited a Wellington dealer at the Tinakori Gallery, to view well-known New Zealand artist Nigel Brown's latest work.[2] However, not on display, but kept in the stockroom of the gallery, was a much earlier work by Brown entitled *Names Paintings – Katherine Mansfield*.[3] It caught my eye instantly and I purchased the large portrait. What I did not know at that time was that the acquisition of this work would begin an interesting journey for me as both a private collector and curator of a public art gallery. Not only would I find and research other images of Mansfield, together with illustrations of her stories, but it would also begin an ongoing conversation with the artist.

Nigel Brown (b. 1949) grew up in Tauranga, New Zealand, and only left when he relocated to Auckland to attend art school. As a budding young artist, he held his first exhibition at the Tauranga Public Library in 1963 – no mean feat for a schoolboy. His childhood was challenging at times with his mother confined to a wheelchair through illness. Brown's father, R. F. Brown, an orchardist, found solace in writing poetry and reading his work aloud to the family. Brown was therefore brought up with his father's fascination and passion for words and text.[4]

Brown attended the University of Auckland's School of Art from 1968 to 1971. At that time New Zealand's most influential artist to date, Colin McCahon (1919–87), was a member of staff and Brown was significantly influenced by him. The inclusion of text in paintings was McCahon's trademark and it subsequently became an element of Brown's oeuvre. In the mid-1980s Brown painted a series – *The Names Series* – of which Mansfield is just one. All together Brown selected ten cultural icons: Rita Angus, Colin McCahon, Edvard Munch, D. H. Lawrence, Paul Gauguin, Janet Frame, Amedeo Modigliani, James K. Baxter and Vincent van Gogh. A combination of national and international writers and artists, this selection represented, for Brown, artists and writers whom he admired and who had some influence on him as a creative individual. On completion of the series in 1986, the suite of portraits was exhibited at the New Vision Gallery, Auckland. The Mansfield portrait was not sold at that time and was later re-worked, hence its date, 1985–93, in the bottom left hand corner.

Brown's portrait of Mansfield offers various pictorial clues about the sitter and her context. Positioned in the centre of the composition, Brown has placed her under a heavy dominating archway. The strong use of dark thick lines gives the image, and the others in the series, the appearance of a stained glass window found in a place of worship. In a sense, the portrait can be likened to a memorial. The arch shape echoes the curvature of Mansfield's head and shoulders, framing her in an almost Madonna-like pose.

The background contains pictorial elements associated with Mansfield's life story. The two-storied colonial house is reminiscent of the Wellington neighbourhood of Thorndon where Mansfield grew up, a place central to many of her New Zealand-based stories such as 'Prelude' (1917). There is no doubting the New Zealand origins of the house – its weatherboard exterior is classic to New Zealand's architectural history. On the right-hand side, the tiny figure in comparison with the other elements that make up the painting is John Middleton Murry. By making Murry small in stature, Brown intentionally highlights Mansfield's strength of character, which he likens to his mother's.[5] The deciduous tree, having lost its leaves in autumn, symbolises the autumn of Mansfield's life. Brown's appropriation of a 1920 photograph for his portrait of Mansfield signposts the writer's troubled final years, living and working under the duress of incurable tuberculosis.

Brown's palette is one of rich and intense colours. On close inspection of the subject's face, multiple colours can be seen, the overall effect being a bluish pallor, reinforcing the intimation of Mansfield's illness. This is a similar treatment to Anne Estelle Rice's portrait in which Mansfield's skin is ghostlike in its pallor, pre-empting her early death. Brown has captured despondency in Mansfield's facial expression – the sharp short application of paint in this area assists in achieving this look of melancholy.

The text in the portrait reads:

> If you speak for your generation; speak,[6] but don't say, 'I speak for my generation.' For the force is then gone from your cry. When you know you are a voice crying in the wilderness, cry, but don't say, 'I am a voice crying in the wilderness.'[7]

The text originates from Matthew 3: 3, when John the Baptist complains that no one is listening to his pronouncement about the coming of the Lord. Keen to know about his choice of text, I asked Brown if he could explain further. His response, from one who is usually very articulate, was somewhat ambiguous. Brown had lost trace of his reference for the text. He did say, however, it was from a letter. Mansfield was a prolific letter writer and her published letters stretch to five volumes. Eventually I located the text in one of three letters she wrote on 5 December 1919 to Murry.

It is the final sentences of her letter to Murry that feature in Brown's painting. This was a period in her relationship with Murry characterised by misunderstanding and doubt. Mansfield felt abandoned in Menton as Murry had deposited her there with Ida Baker, and then returned to England. As Vincent O'Sullivan suggests, 'By early December, there was the most bitter understanding yet between herself and Murry.'[8]

In addition, Mansfield had financial worries at this time. Her medical bills were unpaid and, as Claire Tomalin notes, she and Murry had had another acrimonious exchange about money. Murry apologised for his meanness, explaining that there was 'a certain amount of real insensibility in me', and followed this up by telling her he had taken out a large life insurance policy, and sent her elaborate accounts as a way to offer some comfort.[9]

Unlike the artist Anne Estelle Rice, Brown did not have the luxury of studying his sitter in person and thus working from life. Brown relied on a photograph of Mansfield taken in 1920 by Ida Baker at the Villa Isola Bella, Menton. The distinctively striped collar of Mansfield's attire, and her iconic hairstyle, is the visual referencing clue to Brown's source.

The personalities that Brown selected for this suite of works, including

Mansfield, have had varying degrees of influence on him. He explains: 'I would not say Katherine Mansfield was of huge significance to me. In fact the reality of her gets confused with my mother. [. . .] My mother was small, had a similar haircut, was plagued with illness most of her life.'[10] Brown's mother Veronica was wheelchair-bound, and living on an orchard whilst bringing up three boys was arduous for her. Perhaps Mansfield's carefully crafted words had resonance too with Veronica Brown, who suffered but did not say she was a voice crying in the wilderness. More recently Brown commented,

> I think what struck me with KM most keenly was that bit about not expecting pity which possibly relates to New Zealand attitudes of practical, 'don't be a moaner', sort that Katherine Mansfield was escaping but also wanting deeper layers of thinking than in a colony.[11]

Brown's image of Mansfield has an international perspective about it; a New Zealand-born writer based in the South of France, flanked by her English husband and colonial roots.

Brown is very much a global artist and refers to himself most ardently as an artist of the Pacific. He has, however, painted further afield than this Pacific nomenclature might imply, including Russia and Antarctica. Mansfield herself cannot be described simply as a New Zealander. She was one of that first generation of New Zealanders who having grown up in New Zealand left to further their careers. Engaging with international audiences and writers was necessary in a time when the cultural context of New Zealand was somewhat limited and claustrophobic. In 1908 Mansfield noted in her journal that she left New Zealand in search of 'power, wealth and freedom'.[12] Brown's dark portrait of Mansfield conveys his sense that she did not realise her dream completely.

Notes

1. Anne Estelle Rice, *Portrait of Katherine Mansfield* (1918), Museum of New Zealand Te Papa Tongarewa, 1940-0009-1.
2. Tinakori Gallery has traded as the Page Blackie Gallery since 2007.
3. Nigel Brown, *Names Painting – Katherine Mansfield* (1985–93), oil on hardboard, 1018 x 753 mm, collection of Penelope Jackson, Tauranga, New Zealand. Cover image taken by Grant Thompson.
4. In 2009 a retrospective of Nigel Brown's Tauranga years, *The Brown Years*, was exhibited at the Tauranga Art Gallery Toi Tauranga, New Zealand. See Penelope Jackson, *The Brown Years* (Tauranga, NZ: Tauranga Art Gallery, 2009).
5. Nigel Brown in email conversation with Penelope Jackson, 2013.
6. 'speak' is italicised in the original letter.
7. Vincent O'Sullivan and Margaret Scott, eds, *The Collected Letters of Katherine Mansfield*, 5 vols (Oxford: Clarendon Press, 1984–2008), Vol. 3, p. 141. Letter written to John Middleton Murry whilst staying at the Casetta Deerhom, Ospedaletti, 5 December 1919.

8. O'Sullivan and Scott, p. 141.

9. Claire Tomalin, *Katherine Mansfield: A Secret Life* (London: Viking, 1987), p. 195.

10. Nigel Brown in email conversation with Penelope Jackson, 2008.

11. Nigel Brown in email conversation with Penelope Jackson, 2013.

12. Margaret Scott, ed., *The Katherine Mansfield Notebooks*, 2 vols (Canterbury, New Zealand and Wellington: Lincoln University Press and Daphne Brasell Associates, 1997), Vol. 1, p. 88.

REVIEWS

Frank O'Connor, *The Lonely Voice,* [Introduction by Russell Banks] (New York: Melville House Publishing, 2011), 224 pp., US$17.95, ISBN 9781935554424

Of the more than 120 books Mansfield reviewed for the *Athenaeum* between April 1919 and the end of 1920, there were fewer than a dozen collections of short stories. Most of what Murry chose to assign to her were inferior novels. Occasionally her reviews were too easily dismissive, as with a reprint of George Moore's *Esther Waters,* or when she failed to engage with E. M. Forster or Gertrude Stein as seriously as she might have done. Almost always though her writing is alert, focused, stylish, witty, and at times impressively generous. Yet there is little we can take from her *Athenaeum* columns that tell us much about what she demanded or hoped for in the short story. Only infrequently does a sentence bear on her own writing, or on the form she is famous for, as in her praise for writing that echoes Chekhov's melding of symbolism and naturalism to intensify our awareness 'of the rain pattering on the roof all night long, of the languid, feverish wind, of the moonlit orchard and the first snow, passionately realized, not indeed as analogies for a state of mind, but as linking that mind to the larger whole.'[1] Or when, writing admiringly of the Belgian Louis Couperus, she draws a distinction between those who merely depict life, and those who 'by accepting life [. . .] question it profoundly'.[2]

As she reads Dorothy Richardson, Mansfield comes close to putting her finger on what some would think a weakness in her own writing, that quick glancing at life as it plays out, the sense of passing spectacle she claimed so fascinated her. What she chastises in Richardson, this 'Darting through life, quivering, hovering, exulting in the familiarity and the strangeness of all that comes within her tiny circle' is what, in another review, she labels 'the writer's "literary" longing to register the moment, the glimpse, the scene'.[3] Only the finest writers raise such moments to rare coherence, a 'vision' so much larger, of the kind she praises in Virginia Woolf's *Kew Gardens,* with its movement from 'the tiny rich minute life of a snail', to a flowerbed 'filling a whole world'.[4] This is the sense of completeness, timing, conviction, that Frank O'Connor thought must be there in any first-rate story.

It is sixty years since the Irish writer delivered at Stanford University the lectures that have become the most enduring account of the modern short story. (A pity, one notes in brackets, that this welcome reprint of O'Connor's 1963 text is so marred with misprints.) His eleven chapters are too well written ever to be mistaken for an academic argument. They seem rather more like a civilised conversation than a set of instructions, as a great practising writer lets us in on what he thinks about the craft he is good at, about what strikes him as he reads others in his guild. O'Connor limits himself to a handful of writers who, for one reason or another, he deeply admires, even if at times they do things he deeply deplores. His assessment of Mansfield will possibly provoke as much as delight. It is the strongest case mounted against her in a hundred years and is riddled with prejudices. At its core is a profound antipathy to the kind of woman he takes Mansfield to be, and her meretricious personality. One feels he would like to be able to dislike her even more, this 'clever, spoiled, malicious woman', this 'woman with a homosexual streak who envies men and attributes their imaginary superiority to the greater freedom with which they are supposed to be able to satisfy their sexual appetite' (127). He finds much of her writing sentimental, which is another way of dismissing it as insincere. She is 'girlishly overdramatic' and at the end of her life she is taken in by 'the dreary charlatanism of Fontainebleau' (131, 132). He loathes the kind of people she presumably admires in such a story as 'The Garden Party' – 'Nothing, one feels, can be expected of the Sheridans' (135). Murry's account of his wife is judged fraudulent, because it 'gave no indication of the false personality' she so obviously was (132). It is difficult to think of what else O'Connor might line up to charge her with. It becomes an astringent but necessary exercise for any admirer of Mansfield to confront what he says.

You could begin perhaps by countering that although he had Antony Alpers' first and sketchy biography to hand, O'Connor wrote without the benefit of the later, monumental *Life,* without full access to her letters, with only the dismembered versions of her notebooks. I don't believe they would have made much difference to his steely misogyny. You could critically dispute, story by story, that swathe of her work that he is happy to discard. You could do all that, but there is really no great need to, should you want to salvage Mansfield for higher praise. Even the depth of O'Connor's dislike for her seems not so important after all, if we attend rather to what he himself calls 'the miracle' of 'the true and moving story of the brassy little shopgirl of literature who made herself into a great writer' (132–3). The charm and the paradox of O'Connor's vitriolic attack is that it sharpens, not so much his case against Mansfield, but his astonishing admiration for what he takes to be her best work, those 'masterpieces' that 'set out to do something that had never been done before and to do it in a manner that had never been used before' (137). Her big Wellington stories in fact are 'deliberate acts of magic' (137), putting her up there with Joyce and Proust.

Among the few prescriptive views O'Connor imposes on the short story is his belief that unlike the novel, which so assumes an extended sense of community, this more modern narrative form explores 'a submerged population group' – prostitutes with Maupassant, the 'tragedy of human loneliness' in Chekhov, 'secret societies' in Kipling (81, 105). You might think Mansfield's 'submerged group' would take in those mostly female characters whose expectations are cut down, whose hoped-for epiphanies curdle, who mistake hysteria for 'life'. But no. O'Connor reads those familiar Mansfieldian figures as unconvincing, as back-lit, so to speak, by sentimentality, rather than Chekhovian compassion. What is it then, one wonders, that O'Connor so judges her to have 'done splendidly' (131), in spite of all? The source of her greatness, he asserts, is as much religious as literary. It is that pledge she made to her brother as she brooded on his death, her sense of 'a duty to perform to that lovely time when we were both alive' (131). Instead of willing herself to write, as she usually did, from her muddled, complex social personality, she now settled for 'pure contemplation' (133). His contention is that the New Zealand stories she wrote because of that vow to Leslie succeed because New Zealand does not in fact exist in them. Nowhere does. As O'Connor puts it, 'to introduce a real country into "At the Bay" would be to introduce history, and with history would come judgement, will and criticism. The real world of these stories is not New Zealand but childhood, and they are written in 'a complete, hypnotic suspension of the critical faculties' (135). He considers the scene in 'Prelude' when Pat decapitates a duck. He writes:

> For me this is one of the most remarkable scenes in modern literature. [. . .] This is the Garden of Eden before shame or guilt came into the world. [. . .] These extraordinary stories are Katherine Mansfield's masterpieces and in their own way comparable with Proust's breakthrough into the subconscious world. [. . .] They set out to do something that had never been done before. (136–7)

One can hear the rage of postcolonial critics beating at the gates and of so many of those who have commented sensibly, or fashionably, on Mansfield over the past thirty or so years. He seems to snub so much of what they thought was central to her work – her background, her experience, and seemingly her thinking on *anything*. Yet his judgement is as admiring as any made by a comparably great writer, as astute as any in his reading of her work as enchanted tales where no sense of evil intrudes, where animals talk, where the world is not *divided,* as that of adults always is. What is, is right. His point, ironically enough, is one that Mansfield herself had touched on, in discussing an Irish novel in a review called 'The Magic Door'. 'How', she asks, 'shall a child express what is for us the essence of childhood, its recognition of the validity of the dream? It is implicit in the belief of the child that the dream exists side by side with reality; there are no barriers between.' But for the writer who looks back, 'to return is not to be a child again. What the exile, the wanderer, desires is to be given the freedom of his two worlds again – that he may accept reality and live by the dream'.[5] Which is pretty much what O'Connor insists she does.

I sometimes imagine a selection from the now thousands of essays, articles, reviews and dissertations that have been written on Mansfield's stories, ranked in order of importance. In the final sifting, I suspect there would be few more essential than this bitchy, inadequately informed, celebratory, brilliantly perceptive chapter from *The Lonely Voice*.

Vincent O'Sullivan
Victoria University of Wellington

Notes

1. 'A Novel of Suspense', review of William Hay, *The Escape of Sir William Heans, Athenaeum*, 18 July 1919, in *Novels and Novelists*, ed. J. Middleton Murry (London: Constable, 1930), p. 51,

2. 'A Foreign Novel', review of Louis Couperus, *Old People and the Things that Pass, Athenaeum*, 12 December 1919, in *Novels and Novelists*, p. 126.

3. 'Dragonflies', review of Dorothy Richardson, *Interim, Athenaeum*, 9 January 1920; 'Portrait of a Little Lady', review of S. McNaughton, *My War Experiences in Two Continents, Athenaeum*, 25 April 1919, in *Novels and Novelists*, p. 140, p. 12.

4. 'A Short Story', review of Virginia Woolf, *Kew Gardens, Athenaeum*, 13 June 1919, 37–8.

5. 'The Magic Door', review of Conal O'Riordan, *Adam in Dublin, Athenaeum*, 11 December 1920, in *Novels and Novelists*, p. 288.

꧁꧂

The Collected Fiction of Katherine Mansfield, 1898–1915 (Volume 1) and *The Collected Fiction of Katherine Mansfield 1916–1922* (Volume 2), ed. Gerri Kimber and Vincent O'Sullivan (Edinburgh University Press, 2012), 528 pp., and 528 pp., ISBN 9780748642748 and 9780748642755, £85.00 and £85.00

'"Oh, mother, it is still raining, and you say I can't go out." It was a girl who spoke; she looked about ten' (1: 3). The schoolgirl who wrote this was nine years old. Her name was Kathleen Beauchamp, whom the world would come to admire as Katherine Mansfield, an undisputed master of the short story. The sentence is the opening of her first published short story. Titled 'Enna Blake', it appeared in the *High School Reporter* – the periodical of Wellington Girls' High School, which

Mansfield attended from May 1898 until May 1899 – in the second term of 1898. An editorial comment recorded that the story showed 'promise of great merit' (1: 4), an accurate prediction indeed, even though that talented girl would not live beyond the age of thirty-four. Yet in spite of her short life – burned out by the unforgiving fire of tuberculosis – Mansfield produced a monumental body of work. Over 200 stories and fragments have been collected for the first time in this two-volume edition. Her collected poetry, non-fiction and diaries are to be published soon in a similar, two-volume edition.

Edinburgh University Press are to be applauded for undertaking a task that was both necessary and daunting. This edition of Mansfield's fiction is impeccably edited by two eminent scholars, Mansfield veteran Vincent O'Sullivan, and Gerri Kimber, who has established herself as a knowledgeable and acute reader of Mansfield. This edition provides readers and scholars with the opportunity to appreciate all the short stories penned by Mansfield. The 220 fiction pieces – arranged chronologically from that first story in 1898 to her last, unpublished in her lifetime, completed in 1922 – include not only Mansfield's best-known stories but also 'uncollected, rarely seen stories and prose fragments'. It is these fragments that have led, and will continue to lead, to what the editors have defined as a 'complete remapping' of the author's fiction (1: xix).

Much has been written about Mansfield's life and work and their intersections. The latest attempt at a fictionalised biography – Nadia Fusini's esoteric reading of Mansfield's life, particularly of the last years, in the novel *La figlia del sole. Vita ardente di Katherine Mansfield*[1] – is a reminder that there is still much to be speculated upon. Indeed, an unyielding passion for writing and an aspiration to achieve, painstakingly, absolute perfection of content and form consumed Mansfield physically and mentally as much as the disease that killed her, or any other metaphysical inquiry that might have overshadowed the final stage of her far too short life. These two volumes shed further light on the process of Mansfield's writing, rewriting, editing and discarding, revealing a writer 'always in transition' through the process of tracking the 'uneven, sometimes blurred trajectory of work as it evolves' and 'the messiness of the workshop that surrounds the now-established works' (1: xx). Simultaneously, it opens up scope for more philological and critical analyses to be developed, such as that on which Davide Manenti at Victoria University of Wellington is currently working.

Placing Mansfield's work in context clarifies the main motives that drove her writing: to write something new and, even more importantly perhaps, to find the form – apart, of course, from the need to make money from writing, a necessity that became more pressing as her health deteriorated. Here her main stories sit alongside scraps, lesser pieces, backtrackings and abandoned proposals, thus offering an authentic picture of Mansfield's artistic development. 'For the first time', as the editors point out, 'a reader can follow Mansfield the writer, often month by month, as she alters tack, puts aside, mines an untried vein, works to break old habits, to drive through to new forms' (1: xx). In his Nobel lecture, *Crediting Poetry*, Seamus Heaney argues that (poetic) form 'is both the ship and the anchor' and 'is at once a buoyancy and a holding, allowing for the simultaneous gratification of whatever is centrifugal and centripetal in mind and body'.[2] I think Katherine Mansfield would have approved of this as her epitaph.

Mansfield's last completed story titled 'The Canary', dated 7 July 1922 – a manuscript now housed at the Newberry Library in Chicago – was written for her friend Dorothy Brett. The editors tell us that Mansfield 'was fascinated by the caged birds she watched from her window in the Victoria Palace Hotel, rue Blaise Desgoffe, near the Luxembourg Gardens' (2: 514). In her last poems she compared herself to 'a wounded bird resting on a pool' and the canaries 'came finally to serve as an image for what she considered the limitations of her own writing' (2: 514–5). In one of her last letters, written to her cousin Elizabeth von Arnim on the last day of 1922, Mansfield laments: 'I want much more material; I am tired of my little stories like birds bred in cages' (2: 515). Wondering 'how can one possibly express in words the beauty of their quick little song rising, as it were, out of the very stones', Mansfield then makes her own the feeling of sadness inspiring the canary's song, and asks herself this simple yet profound question: 'But isn't it extraordinary that under his sweet, joyful little singing it was just this – sadness? – Ah, what is it? – that I heard' (2: 514).What we can hear in page after page of these first two volumes of *The Edinburgh Edition of the Collected Works of Katherine Mansfield*, is the writer's unmistakable voice – sweet, joyful and sad.

Marco Sonzogni
Victoria University of Wellington, New Zealand

Notes

1. Nadia Fusini, *La figlia del sole. Vita ardente di Katherine Mansfield* (Milan: Mondadori, 2012).
2 Seamus Heaney, 'Crediting Poetry', in *Opened Ground* (London: Faber & Faber, 1998), p. 466.

Martin Hipsky, *Modernism and the Women's Popular Romance in Britain, 1885–1925* (Athens, OH: Ohio University Press, 2011), 324 pp., US$59.95, ISBN 9780821419700

Modernism and the Women's Popular Romance in Britain, 1885–1925 is an important and masterful analysis of the romance novel set in the wider context of emerging modernism and the notable shift in the literary hierarchies that accompanied it. The express intention of the book is to redress the 'romance gap in our literary-historical record' by focusing on a small group of romances that best exemplify 'the meteoric rise of once best-selling texts' (xii) by authors such as Mary Ward and Marie Corelli.

This sounds as though it could be an analysis that attaches importance to the notion of limited literary classification, especially because the Introduction and first chapter alert us to hierarchies of artistic and cultural 'brows' into which we might slip thoughtlessly the romances under discussion. This is not Hipsky's aim, however. Rather, he offers a challenge to twenty-first century scholars of modernism and illuminates the 'continuities and frictions' (xiii) between those texts considered popular and those deemed to be modernist in what he calls a 'zone of convergence' (xv). Instead of focusing on narrative and stylistic differences, his argument centres on commonality and 'complementarity of affect' (219). He suggests, for instance, that the best-selling romances of 1885–1925 offer representations of interiority that parallel the 'more self-conscious forms of psychic intensity' (xv) explored by, amongst others, Mansfield, Woolf and Lawrence. He is persuasive in connecting the quest for moments of modernist transcendence with the climatic, 'escapist' scenes of several romance novels, which also, like Mansfield's 'blazing moments' in particular, foreground the ultimate impossibility of achieving such a goal.

Hipsky's book first relies on unpacking definitions and drawing fine distinctions. To this end, in Chapter 1 he explores the evolution and shifting definitions of romance through seven centuries and suggests that a revisionist understanding of the term leads to the notion of the 'popular sublime' as a 'key element of the modern' (8). This, he argues, is discernable in popular romance and modernist writing alike, a point of continuity between the two that has frequently been overlooked in modernist scholarship. In Chapter 2, Hipsky engages with Bourdieu's later theories of literary production and critical reception, especially in relation to Mrs Humphry Ward's best-selling novel, *Robert Elsmere* (1888). Chapter 3 offers a fascinating reading of Marie Corelli's work, which turns on the notion that her novels are *'about* the romance mode' (xviii), a mode she regards as an antidote to encroaching, and dispiriting, modernity. Chapter 4 deals with the writings of Baroness Orczy, Florence Barclay and Elinor Glyn, and considers women's religious and secular romance as complementary rather than directly oppositional. Chapter 5 switches to the writing of Victoria Cross, Ethel Dell and E. M. Hull in a significant development of existing research into the 'orientalist or primitivist versions of the non-European Other' (xix), already associated with the work of Haggard and Kipling.

And so to Mansfield, whose writing – including her juvenilia – appears periodically throughout the book, before it receives more concentrated treatment in Chapter 6. Taking her early story 'The Tiredness of Rosabel' (1908) as a point of departure, Hipsky focuses on Mansfield's use of 'romantic moments' (219). His contention is that 'modernist and romance narratives served parallel functions for their early-twentieth century readers' (220), especially in their 'quest for transcendence' (xx). In addition, he argues deftly that romance and modernist texts – here exemplified by Mansfield's early forays into narrative experimentation – shared qualities that were directly set against the demands of 'high realism' (xx). In contrast to the social diagnoses of literary realism – the desire to educate and provide solutions for societal ills – Hipsky suggests that 'the metaphors and symbols of both modernist and popular-romance narratives may have acted therapeutically upon the anxieties and longings that readers' quotidian social experience . . . did little to allay or satisfy' (xxi).

That Hipsky chooses a story by Mansfield that includes an intertexual reference to a well-known romance novel allows for secure literary comparison between the genres that are investigated in this book. Furthermore, Mansfield becomes a test case for his central preoccupation with cross-genre interconnections. The significance of his inclusion of Mansfield extends beyond nuanced comparative reading, however, and places the focus firmly on 'the eve of modernist experimentation in British fiction' (xx) – before the classification 'modernist' was conceived and before it became increasingly codified by later scholarship. This releases the popular romance and Mansfield from the constraints of narrow literary classification. Hipsky's analysis of 'The Tiredness of Rosabel' is, of course, only one example of Mansfield's embryonic modernism and only one instance in which her writing reveals the antecedents from which it emerged and developed. Nevertheless, his argument adds welcome complication to our understanding of modernist literature and to its wider relationship with other kinds of writing in the period 1885–1925. In addition, the book as a whole establishes once again that, to rejig George Eliot's famous formulation, the women writers of popular romance were really not so silly.

Isobel Maddison
Lucy Cavendish College, University of Cambridge

❧

Alex Calder, *The Settler's Plot: How Stories Take Place in New Zealand* (Auckland: Auckland University Press, 2011), 299 pp., NZ$45, ISBN 9781869404888

Doreen D'Cruz and John C. Ross, *The Lonely and the Alone: The Poetics of Isolation in New Zealand Fiction* (Amsterdam: Rodopi, 2011), 407 pp., €85, ISBN 9789042034747

It's fair to say that the figure of the 'man alone' is a central trope in New Zealand literary studies. These two books consider the man alone theme, albeit in radically different ways. Doreen D'Cruz and John C. Ross propose that John Mulgan's seminal novel *Man Alone* (1939) belongs to a subcategory of the 'man alone' topos, one based on the isolation of fugitives and escapees who cannot be assimilated into social networks (50). This is a fairly standard view compared with Alex Calder's playful re-reading of the novel within the frame of the Western genre. Although *Man Alone* lacks the trappings of the Western genre, Calder argues, it is plotted along an identical trail, with multiple escapes from the city and from women who threaten the hero's freedom (232). Within New Zealand studies, Calder observes, the cultural history of the 1930s is often viewed in terms of a narrowly-focused nationalism instead of considering the possibilities of American cultural productions, such as the Western and the music associated with it.

The Lonely and the Alone offers a traditional study of New Zealand fiction, while *The Settler's Plot* deliberately breaks from the convention of writing about New Zealand fiction from the twentieth century exclusively, and casts the net wider to consider non-fiction works and lesser-known writing from the nineteenth century such as F. E. Maning's *Old New Zealand* (1863). Calder recognises that four writers – Katherine Mansfield, Frank Sargeson, Janet Frame and Allen Curnow – are 'irreplaceable' (ix) in any book-length consideration of New Zealand literature, yet he also wishes to consider writers from a larger group who are accomplished but often under-recognised. Although Calder confesses that his ambition is to 'change the canon', by exploring the work of lesser-known figures, his primary purpose is 'cartographic'. The book aims to connect the way stories take shape in various settings to the actual history of Pākehā settlement (vii). Calder uses the term '*Pakeha turangawaewae*' – indicating a place for Pākehā to stand – because the relationship with place is central to Pākehā New Zealander's sense of belonging: 'We feel we have a place to stand, and we have that place because we value nature' (4). He argues that it is difficult for Pākehā to talk about belonging without also talking about nature largely because Pākehā do not have access to another degree of belonging that is available to Māori. Therefore nature – and natural settings – have become central to considerations of belonging in New Zealand fiction.

By contrast, *The Lonely and the Alone* is organised around themes of loneliness and alienation from the New Zealand landscape. Along with a discussion of the recurrent 'man alone' theme, the authors extend their critical range to include the less fully explored representations of the 'woman alone', particularly in the work of Mansfield, George Chamier and G. B. Lancaster. D'Cruz and Ross perform close readings of two Mansfield stories, 'The Woman at the Store' (1912) and 'Millie' (1913), arguing that 'the sense of the uncanny, while palpably present to the awareness of the character of the narrator, makes its manifest impact through a grotesque or deviant alterity' (4). Comparing Mansfield's stories with the work of Chamier and Lancaster, they observe that 'the alienating power of the back-country invades the subject' (5) and that the eponymous woman in 'The Woman at the Store', isolated and sexually degraded as she is, expresses an 'embryonic subjectivity' that 'belies her otherwise objectified status' (29). The authors note that the child's drawing of her father's murder, revealed at the end of the story, suggests a 'horrifying possibility that lies outside narrative assimilation' (29). In 'Millie', the female narrator finds in isolation 'a dimension of self that is supplementary, or antithetical, to her dominant construction by men' (31). For D'Cruz and Ross, the significance of female isolation in the two texts is its ability to release repressed facets of the self that have been denied articulacy. In the authors' estimation, there is something simultaneously pitiful and powerful about the isolated female figures featured in these stories.

Following his interest in 'settings', Calder reads Mansfield in terms of suburbia rather than the back-country, observing that the Beauchamps were pioneers of suburban life in Wellington, enabling her to become 'one of the first writers in the world to put a very new kind of place on the map' (157). Although a great many writers have written about the suburbs, Mansfield was one of the first, allowing her to explore previously untapped subject matter. Calder notes that the possibilities of the

suburban setting are fully anticipated in some of Mansfield's best stories, such as 'The Garden Party' and 'Prelude'. For Calder, Mansfield is
not interested in suburbs per se; instead her focus is firmly fixed on 'the
gender and intergenerational patterns with which these settings will
become associated' (161). He observes that the proverbial 'great place
to bring up children' was also a kind of 'Sargasso Sea' for the women of
the house, as embodied by characters such as Beryl and Linda Burnell
(162).

In his idiosyncratic study, Calder explores some familiar – and lesser
known – territory from unexpected angles, interspersing personal musings with more 'objective' commentary, whereas D'Cruz and Ross tend
to stick to a fairly well-trodden path through their chosen literary terrain. Nonetheless, both volumes offer new and fascinating insights into
a range of New Zealand fiction.

Brigid Magner
RMIT University, Australia

Galya Diment, *A Russian Jew of Bloomsbury: The Life and Times of Samuel
Koteliansky* (Montreal and Kingston: McGill-Queen's University Press,
2011), 409 pp., £40, ISBN 9780773538993

This book is the first biography of Samuel Solomonovich Koteliansky
(1880–1955), a prominent translator of Ukrainian Jewish origin, who
was closely involved with many important British cultural figures in the
1910s–1940s, including Katherine Mansfield, John Middleton Murry,
Virginia and Leonard Woolf, H. G. Wells, Mark Gertler and Dilys
Powell. Although Koteliansky's collaborations with several Bloomsbury
writers and critics have been discussed before, the present study sheds
new light on Koteliansky's personality and his personal relationships
with many artists and writers in London. Diment points out that '[h]is
English friends would invariably call him a "rabbi" or "an Old Testament
prophet"', and '[f]or a secular Jew, Koteliansky was indeed interestingly
rabbinical in the way he conducted his life in England' (9). She defines
him as bookish and authoritative, especially because he spent most of
his life worshipping books written by Russian canonical writers, including Tolstoy, Dostoevsky and Chekhov.

Undoubtedly, Koteliansky's friendship and professional interaction
with British writers and critics had a significant impact on their reception of Russian realist and modernist writers. His correspondence with

Mansfield and Lawrence also provides a fascinating insight into the dialogue between the two cultural traditions. Although Koteliansky appears to have been in love with Mansfield and his feelings were not reciprocated, their friendship proved to be very special. Clearly, Mansfield saw him as a soulmate since she admitted to him that he was one of her kind of people. Diment does not explore their feelings of displacement in the context of postcolonial writing and gender studies, but it might not be far-fetched to suggest that Mansfield's own identity as a New Zealander and a female writer shared many common features with a provincial Jewish translator and critic from the south of Russia.

Diment's biography of Koteliansky consists of two parts as well as appendices: the first part is titled 'From Shmilik to Kot: 1880–1930' and the second is boldly related to Lawrence – 'After Lawrence: 1931– 1955'. The book provides many useful references to, and insightful observations on, the lives and aesthetic ideas of British and Russian modernists of the 1910s–1940s. It also highlights the existence of many idiosyncratic interpretations of Russian classical literary texts produced by British modernists. Thus, Lawrence's analysis of Dostoevsky's novel *The Brothers Karamazov* appears to be highly subjective; as Diment puts it, Lawrence's introductory chapter to Koteliansky's translation of the Grand Inquisitor section tells us more about Lawrence than it does about Dostoevsky (184).

Acknowledging the limitations on scope and length, it seems a pity that no comparisons with D. S. Mirsky's professional life in Britain are made. He is a Russian émigré and distinguished professor at the University of London and it would have been interesting to compare the tastes and outlooks of these two influential intellectuals from Russia who interacted with the same group of Bloomsbury writers and critics. Similarly, although Diment writes about Koteliansky's desire to promote Lev Shestov's writings and extensively discusses some problems with the copyright related to his translations of Shestov's works, she does not offer any comparative analysis between Koteliansky and Shestov's philosophical outlooks and this would have been interesting terrain to explore.

Undoubtedly, this book will be of interest to specialists in English literature, cultural studies, social history and comparative literature. Due to the lively and engaging reconstruction of life in Britain in the 1910s–1940s, Diment's well-researched and thoughtful account of Koteliansky's life in London will be of immense interest to the general reader as well. It testifies to the fact that modern aesthetic ideas and cosmopolitan life in London in the 1910s–1940s gave rise to the forma- tion of new hybrid identities and modes of writing that continue to shape contemporary views of translation as an important tool of cultural communication, as well as a specific literary practice that highlights hybridity and exile as the quintessentially modern tropes of creative production.

Alexandra Smith
University of Edinburgh

Notes on Contributors

Emmanouil Aretoulakis teaches English Literature and Literary Criticism at the Faculty of English Language and Literature at the National and Kapodistrian University of Athens, Greece. He has a PhD in English Renaissance Literature and his publications range from sixteenth-century British poetry and prose to twentieth-century Aesthetics. His latest article, 'Avoiding the Speed of Science: The Non-Quest for the New in Literary Studies', was published in the journal *Philosophy and Literature* (April 2012).

Ann Brown-Berens completed her MA in New Zealand literature at Victoria University of Wellington in 2010 and is currently a postgraduate at the University of Auckland. She has presented several conference papers on early period New Zealand literature and the stories of Katherine Mansfield.

Gladys Mary Coles lectures at the University of Liverpool. She has won many awards and prizes for her writing, and has ten published collections of poetry, three with Flambard Press who also published her acclaimed debut novel *CLAY* (2010). Widely anthologised by Faber, HarperCollins, Virago and other notable presses, she was selected to represent Britain in the Euro-Literature Project. She has published essays on Katherine Mansfield in *Contemporary Review* and *Stand Magazine*, and lectures on Mansfield's work. Her research for a biographical-critical study included weeks spent with Mansfield's sister, Jeanne Renshaw. Her poem 'Katherine Mansfield's Mirror' won the Michael Johnson Memorial Prize.

Delia da Sousa Correa is Senior Lecturer in English at the Open University and is co-editor of *Katherine Mansfield Studies*. She was educated in New Zealand, London and Oxford. Her published research centres on connections between literature and music in the nineteenth-century and modernist periods.

Louise Edensor is Lecturer on the International Foundation Programme at Middlesex University in Dubai and is the Editorial Assistant for

Katherine Mansfield Studies. She is currently a doctoral candidate at the University of Northampton, working on her thesis 'Katherine Mansfield and the Construction of the Self'.

Aimee Gasston, originally from Jersey, is a PhD candidate at Birkbeck, University of London, researching the modernist short story. She is a member of the Katherine Mansfield Society and New Zealand Studies Network and co-convenes the Modernist Magazines Research Seminar with Chris Mourant and Natasha Periyan.

Andrew Harrison is a lecturer in English Literature and Director of the D. H. Lawrence Research Centre in the School of English at the University of Nottingham. He is editor of the *Journal of D. H. Lawrence Studies* and a member of the International Advisory Board for *Katherine Mansfield Studies*; he is currently writing the volume on D. H. Lawrence for the Blackwell Critical Biographies series.

Witi Ihimaera is the author of thirteen novels and seven collections of short stories. His most recent publications are *The Parihaka Woman* (novel, 2011) and *The Thrill of Falling* (short stories, 2012). The latest, third, feature film based on his work, *The Medicine Woman,* will be released internationally in 2013. He is Emeritus Professor of English and Creative Writing, University of Auckland, and lives in Auckland, New Zealand.

Penelope Jackson is the Director of the Tauranga Art Gallery Toi Tauranga, New Zealand. She holds an MPhil (University of Queensland) in Art History and an MA in Art History (University of Auckland). The author of *Edward Bullmore: A Surrealist Odyssey* (2008) and *The Brown Years: Nigel Brown* (2009), she has contributed to *The Dictionary of New Zealand Biography* and several journals including *Art New Zealand, Art Monthly Australia, Studies in Travel Writing* and *Katherine Mansfield Studies.* More recently she has contributed to the *Journal for the Association for Research into Crimes Against Art* (2012) and a chapter 'Artists in Wonderland' in *Seven Artists Explore the South Pacific* (2011).

Kathleen Jones is a poet, biographer and fiction writer, author of seven biographies including *A Passionate Sisterhood* (1997), a group biography of the sisters, wives and daughters of the Lake Poets. Her most recent biography is *Katherine Mansfield: The Story-Teller* (2010). A collection of poetry, *Not Saying Goodbye at Gate 21*, and a novel, *The Sun's Companion*, were published in 2012. Kathleen has taught creative writing in a number of universities and is currently a Royal Literary Fund Fellow. www.kathleenjones.co.uk

Gerri Kimber, Senior Lecturer at the University of Northampton, is co-editor of *Katherine Mansfield Studies*, and Chair of the Katherine Mansfield Society. With Vincent O'Sullivan, she co-edited volumes 1 and 2 of the annotated *Edinburgh Edition of the Collected Works of Katherine Mansfield* (2012). She is the author of *Katherine Mansfield: The View from France* (2008), and *A Literary Modernist: Katherine Mansfield and the Art of the Short Story* (2008). In addition, she is co-editor of two essay collections on Mansfield published in 2011.

Isobel Maddison is Fellow, College Lecturer and Director of Studies in English at Lucy Cavendish College, University of Cambridge. She works on female modernism, especially the writings of Katherine Mansfield and Dorothy Richardson. She is also interested in the connections between popular and modernist literature. Her book, *Elizabeth von Arnim: Beyond the German Garden* (Ashgate, June 2013) is the first full-length critical study of von Arnim's writing.

Brigid Magner is a lecturer at RMIT University, Melbourne. Her PhD research was on trans-Tasman literary culture. She is currently planning a book on literary tourism in Australia.

Lorenzo Mari is a PhD candidate in comparative and postcolonial literature at the University of Bologna. His current research focuses on narrations and representations of the family in Somali postcolonial and diasporic literature. His publications include: 'Plural Ghetto. Phaswane Mpe's *Welcome to Our Hillbrow* (2001), Neill Bloemkamp's *District 9* (2009) and the crisis in the representation of spaces in post-apartheid South Africa' (2012).

W. Todd Martin is Professor of English at Huntington University, USA. His research focuses on twentieth-century British and American literature. He has published on a variety of authors including John Barth, e. e. cummings, Clyde Edgerton, Julia Alvarez, Edwidge Danticat and Katherine Mansfield. He is the Membership Secretary for the Katherine Mansfield Society and Assistant Editor of *Katherine Mansfield Studies*.

Chris Mourant is a PhD candidate at King's College London. His doctoral thesis explores Katherine Mansfield's relationship to periodical culture. Chris is a co-founder of the Modernist Magazines Research

Seminar at the Institute of English Studies and is a postgraduate representative of the British Association of Modernist Studies (BAMS).

Fiona Oliver is Curator, New Zealand and Pacific Publications at the Alexander Turnbull Library in Wellington, New Zealand. Her PhD took a phenomenological approach to the representation of the city, real and imagined, in Scottish literature.

Vincent O'Sullivan, Professor Emeritus, Victoria University of Wellington, has edited, with Margaret Scott, the five-volume edition of Katherine Mansfield's *Collected Letters*, published by Oxford University Press. He is also widely published as a poet, fiction writer, playwright and biographer. His most recent work is the poetry collection, *The Movie may be Slightly Different*, 2010. With Gerri Kimber, he has also co-edited volumes 1 and 2 of the annotated *Edinburgh Edition of the Collected Works of Katherine Mansfield* (2012).

Emily Ridge completed a PhD on luggage imagery in modernist literature at Durham University in 2012. She has published in *Kaleidescope* and *Textual Practice* and has further articles forthcoming in *Modernism/ Modernity* and *Journeys: The International Journal of Travel and Travel Writing*. She is currently working on a new research project on the subject of late modernist representations of hospitality.

Stefanie Rudig studied English and American Studies and Romance Studies (French) at the University of Innsbruck, the University of Wales, Bangor, and the University of Notre Dame. She also worked as a lecturer in the English Department at the University of Innsbruck and completed a master's degree in English 1800–1914 at the University of Oxford. She is currently working on her doctoral thesis at the University of Innsbruck (Austria) on Victorian New Zealand literature.

Alexandra Smith is Reader in Russian Studies at the University of Edinburgh where she teaches courses on Russian and comparative literature. She has authored two books and numerous articles on Russian and European literature and culture.

Marco Sonzogni is a Senior Lecturer in Italian in the School of Languages and Cultures at Victoria University of Wellington, where he is also the current Director of the New Zealand Centre for Literary Translation. A widely published academic and an award-winning editor, poet and literary translator, he edited *Second Violins. New Stories Inspired* *by Katherine Mansfield* (2008) and translated into Italian her stories *A Happy Christmas Eve* (*Una felice vigilia di Natale*, 2008) and *Brave Love* (*Coraggioso amore*, 2009).

C. K. Stead, Professor Emeritus, University of Auckland, is known as a critic of twentieth-century modernism, and of New Zealand literature, including Mansfield. He is the author of a dozen novels, and as many volumes of poems recently gathered in *Collected Poems, 1951–2006*. He was awarded a CBE in 1985, and in 2007 his country's highest award, the ONZ.

Janet Wilson is Professor of English and Postcolonial Studies at the University of Northampton. Her research focuses on postcolonial and diaspora cinema and writing, with special reference to New Zealand and Australian culture. She has co-edited *Rerouting the Postcolonial: New Directions for the New Millennium* (2010), *Katherine Mansfield and Literary Modernism* (2011), and *Celebrating Katherine Mansfield: A Centenary Volume of Essays* (2011). She is the editor of the *Journal of Postcolonial Writing*, and currently vice-chair of the Katherine Mansfield Society and the New Zealand Studies Network.

Join the Katherine Mansfield Society!

Membership benefits include:
- Subscription to the Society's peer-reviewed annual publication, *Katherine Mansfield Studies*, published by Edinburgh University Press
- Discounted rates for all KMS publications and events, including conferences, the annual Birthday Lecture, and items in our gift shop
- Three newsletters each year (average size – 20 pages) full of fascinating updates about the world of Mansfield studies
- Regular email bulletins to keep you in touch with all the latest Mansfield news

Standard membership: NZ$66 /£30 / €34 / US$50
Student/unwaged membership: NZ$44 / £20 / €23 / US$33
Visit www.katherinemansfieldsociety.org/join-the-kms
and pay via PayPal (preferred)
or post a cheque (payable to 'Katherine Mansfield Society') to:
NZ dollar cheques: KMS, P.O. Box 22-011, Khandallah, Wellington, NEW ZEALAND
Eurozone cheques: Professor Josiane Paccaud-Huguet, Faculté des Langues, Université Lumière-Lyon 2, 74 rue Pasteur, 69365 Lyon Cedex, FRANCE
UK Sterling cheques: Dr Gerri Kimber, School of The Arts, The University of Northampton, Avenue Campus, St George's Avenue, Northampton, NN2 6JD, ENGLAND

Join the Katherine Mansfield Society, a registered New Zealand Charity (CC46669), show your support, and help us to promote worldwide awareness of Mansfield's work. Remember, if you are a NZ resident, your membership donation is tax deductible.